Vivekananda
The Warrior Saint

Vivekananda

The Warrior Saint

A New Study and Analysis
for the 21st Century

•

India's first saint who revolutionised a decavent country in
few years, but could not complete his
mission owning to a very early death

by
the well known leftist thinker as well as activist and writer
of over a dozen significant books
—— Hansraj Rahbar ——

•

1ˢᵗ Edition 1999
10ᵗʰ Edition 2009

VIJAY GOEL
English-Hindi Publisher

S-16, Naveen Shahdara, Delhi-110032, India
E mail: farsight_p_d@rediffmail.com

ISBN : 81-86265-12-0

First Edition	:	1999
10th Revised Edition	:	2009
Publisher	:	Vijay Goel S-16, Naveen Shahdara Delhi-110032 ● Phone : 22324833 e-mail : goelbooks@rediffmail.com
Laser Typesetting	:	Computek System Naveen Shahdara, Delhi-110032
Printed	:	B.K. Offset Naveen Shahdara, Delhi-110032

CONTENTS

Why did I Write this Book?

I had long been thinking of conveying to Indian public my thoughts on the unique personality of Vivekananda as I saw or understood him among the leaders of men. When I revealed my desire to some of my friends, I found that they reacted differently, most of them feeling that I was going to add another book to my 'unmasked' series which I had earlier authored to expose national leaders like Gandhi, Nehru etc. One group of friends, belonging to the privileged intellectual class, had always criticised me, accusing me of one-sided propaganda against teh revered leaders even though they had not been able to point out a single instance of my so called prejudice against them. The other group of friends and leaders, all curious well-wishers, was keen to know why a staunch marxist like me should write on Vivekananda. After-all communists had always dismissed religion, specially Hindu religion, as reactionary.

To the latter, I gave an explanation, which answered their question, and gave the purpose of my writing this book. **In my opinion our country has not produced a thinker of Vivekananda's stature after him. Vivekananda has played the role which Hegel did in Germany.** Hegel drove the ideology of German idealism to the verge of historical materialism by proving it through the theory of mutual contradiction. He believed that the society was only the mirror of the prevailing ideology. Since ideology was an evolutionary process, society and institutions, too, were a growing phenomenon. They will keep on growing till they reach their zenith. Since to him, the then Prussian state in Germany had reached the acme of progress, there was no scope for further evolution.

The German leftists branded his theory as the official propaganda of the feudal Prussian government and rejected him outright. Marx came in to correct the error. Marx pleaded not to throw away the grain with the chaff. Hegel's theory was one of standing upside down it was necessary to put it back on its feet. It meant that the society was not a representation of thought, but that it was the thought that was a reflection of the society. In his struggle against nature, as has man advanced in the realm of economic and material world, so has the society and its various institutions developed and, with them has developed the element of thought. Marx replaced Hegelian dialectic by Marxist dialectic, and in this way he made it stand straight on its feet.

At the Parliament of Religions, held in Chicago, Vivekananda had declared; "Science is nothing, but the exploration of unity. As soon as science reaches perfect unity, it ceases to progress further, because otherwise it would reach its goal." Thus, we find, that chemistry could not progress further, unless it discovered one element, out of which all others could be formed. So, too, physics would stop, when it is able to fulfil its services in discovering one source of energy, of which all the others are its manifestations and; thus, the science of religion would become perfect after having discovered Him who is the one life in this mortal world; Him who is called the constant basis of this ever-changing world; that One who is the only Soul, of which all other souls are but delusive manifestations. Thus, it is through multiplicity and duality, that the ultimate unity is reached. Religion can go no further. This is the goal of all science.

For the first time; Vivekananda applied the theory of evolution on Indian philosophy and declared non-dualism as the ultimate stage of religion.

But it did not happen by chance. There were material

and economic reasons behind it—a special kind of necessity. To comprehend this, we have to look back at the social and political scenario of the time.

In the latter part of the nineteenth century, the capitalist class had just emerged and naturally wanted to expand. But the foreign imperialists had effectively checked its expansion. The British were militarily powerful. Their industrial civilization was decidedly superior to our feudal civilization. They commanded monopoly on trade and economy. Besides, to break the bone of our self-confidence and our feeling of nationalism, they resorted to cultural invastion. They gave the solgan that we were idol-worshippers, so uncivilized, and that theirs was a civilizing mission.

Our emerging capitalist class had to defend itself against the foreign onslaught, because the evolution of nationalism and political confrontation were dependent on it. As a reaction to foreign cultural onslaught, the age of renaissance set in at the very beginning of the 19th century, of which Raja Ram Mohan Roy was the first and Vivekananda, the last spokesman. In allegorical language, it can be said that **Vivekananda was a fully-blossomed lotus of renaissance—beautiful, as well as fragrant.**

Under the circumstances the bourgeois fought the political battle with the help of religion. Vivekananda took an aggressive stance at the Praliament of Religions and refuted that Christianity was the only true and, hence, the world religion. Of the three evolutionary stages—Dvaita, Vishisht-advaita and Advajta—Christianity was still struggling at the lowest rung of the ladder. **The Hindu religion had reached the apex thousands of years ago. We needed no religion, but means of living, food and clothes, which they were depriving us of.**

History bears testimony to the fact that the religion-based battle being fought till the end of the nineteenth century, turned into a political battle—with the struggle for Swadeshi in 1905. The British had to retreat and withdraw the proposal of dividing Bengal. Swadeshi, Boycott, National Education and Swaraj were the four means and objectives of the fight for freedom.

It is significant to note that, the underground revolutionary movements of those times were directly inspired, in 1908, by the teachings of Vivekananda. Whenever the police raided the houses of the revolutionaries, they invariably found and seized some Vivekananda literature. **We leftists, have committed the blunder of branding Vivekananda as a mere religious swami and throwing away his priceless contribution from the nationalist treasury.**

The question arises, if my Marxist friends neglect Vivekananda and consider Hinduism as revolting and reactionary, how did I choose to write a book on him? I firmly believed that, by connecting our struggles to where Vivekananda had left us, we could develop our culture and tradition in a true materialistic sense.

There were protests. The so-called Marxists could not appreciate the fact that the Karmakand (rituals) and Gyankand (philosophy) were two sides of the same coin, exactly like the idealistic and the materialistic ideologies. The study of only Marxist-Leninist and Maoist literature tends to develop one-track minds and diehard reactionaries.

The tragedy is that our so-called leftists neither understand Marxism, nor Aadhyatmavad, i.e., spiritualism. They have just learnt by rote some lines of Marxism and taken them as full and final. They make no attempt to realise their true significance and develop a balanced view for our country.

Vivekananda was not an ordinary thinker. **He was an encylopaedia of the knowledge of his time. He deeply probed into the philosophy and the history of not only our own country, but also the whole civilized world. Reading Vivekananda is like swimming in the ocean of enlightenment. In my opinion it is not possible to be a true Marxist without understanding him.** I hope this book will provide a new turn to the thought process of the leftist thinking and will play a positive role.

—Hansraj Rahbar

1

DAREDEVIL AS A BOY

"From my boyhood I was a dare-devil sort of fellow. Otherwise, do you think I could make a tour round the world without a single copper in my pocket?"

—*Vivekananda*

It was the morning of 12th January in 1863. Crowds were heading for a dip in the Ganges, as it was the auspicious day of Makar Sankranti. It was at this hour that a son was born in the celebrated Dutta family of Calcutta, now Kolkata. The boy was named Narendranath who, later on, became famous as Vivekananda. Narendra's mother was Bhubaneshwari Debi. She had already given birth to two daughters and was longing for a son. She used to visit the Shiva temple every morning and evening and pray to Lord Shiva to bless her with a son. It is said that one day, when she was absorbed in her prayers, Lord Shiva appeared before her and, assuming the form of a child, seated Himself in her lap. She, therefore, believed that the birth of the son was a boon from Lord Shiva and, as such, named him Vireshwar. In his home he was known by this name or for short, Bilay.

In Kolkata there were several of Dutta families belonging to the Kayastha caste. These families had produced many able and scholarly persons. One of them was the celebrated historian Romesh Chandra who was a contemporary of Vivekananda. Vivekananda was born in the same family. However, Romain Rolland thinks that he was born in a family of the Kshatriya caste. Perhaps this

Bhuvaneshwari Devi (1841-1911)

misconception was due to a speech made by Vivekananda at Madras on his return from abroad in which he stated:

> I read in the organ of the social reformers that I am a Shudra, and was challenged as to what right a Shudra has to become a Sanyasi. To which I reply: I trace my descent to one, at whose feet every Brahmin offers flowers to the chant of *"Yamai Dharmarajaya Chitraguptayavey namah:"* and who are pure Kshatriyas. If they believe in the mythology these reformers should know that my caste has in the past, apart from rendering other services, ruled half of India for centuries. If my caste is left out of consideration, what will be left of the present day civilization of India? In Bengal alone, my community produced the greatest philosophers, the greatest poets, the greatest historians, the greatest archaeologists, the greatest religious preachers. My blood has furnished India with the greatest of the modern scientists. These detractors ought to have

known a little of their own history, and to have studied their three castes, and learnt that the Brahmins, the Kshatriyas, and the Vaishyas, have equal right to take Sanyas and to study Vedas. This is only by the way that I refer to this. I am not at all hurt if they call me a Shudra. It will rather be a little reparation for the tyranny of my ancestors over the poor. If I am a pariah, I will be all the more glad for I am the disciple of a man, who—the Brahmin of Brahmins—wished to cleanse the house of a Pariah.[1]

Narendra had inherited a rich heritage of thinkers and scientists. His great-grandfather, Rammohan Dutta, was a renowned lawyer at the Supreme Court of Kolkata. The family was noted not only for its wealth and riches but also for its quest for knowledge and interest in scriptures The Dutta family moved with times while, at the same time, retaining its ancient tradition. It was an amalgam of all that was modern and at the same time ancient, signified by its quest for wealth, liberation, enjoyment and renunciation. Durgacharan, the only son of Rammohan, had learnt Sanskrit and Persian, as was in vogue in those days. He had also acquired a working knowledge of English. He had entered the legal profession at a very young age. But, by nature, he was not much inclined to the pursuit of wealth unlike his father. As a young man, Durgacharan was devoted to religion and keen on meeting saintly persons and having discussions on matters spiritual. The result was that, at the young age of 25, he renounced the world and became a Sanyasin, under the influence of some Sanyasins from the North-West. He left behind a remorseful young wife with a son as her only support. When Durgacharan returned to salute his motherland after twelve years according to the custom of Sanyasins, his wife had already died a year back. He went away after blessing his son Vishwanath. He never returned and was no more seen by anyone.

This Vishwanath was the father of Narendranath. He also adopted his paternal profession of a lawyer. But, in

---

1. *Complete Works of Vivekananda.* Vol. III, p. 211.

spite of being busy with his legal profession, he had a great desire to acquire knowledge and took keen interest in discussions about the scriptures. The conflict between Oriental and Western thinkings, which had started during the time of Raja Rammohun Roy, had, by now, sharpened and had reached a decisive stage. The old system of education, which Raja Rammohun Roy wanted to change, had by now been replaced by Macaulay's dispensation. The teaching of Sanskrit and Persian was rendered secondary and English took the place of pride everywhere. What was the type of education that Raja Rammohun Roy wanted to introduce and what was the system, that was actually introduced by Macaulay—we shall discuss in a later chapter. Suffice if to say here that Raja Rammohun Roy wanted to bring about a synthesis between the ancient, and the modern.

This healthy concept was being disregarded and getting distorted. Religious bigotry and obscurantism had been replaced by pedantry resulting from the teaching of Geography, History, Literature and Mathematics. The danger of the Oriental thought being eclipsed by Occidental thought was looming large on the horizon. The Brahmo Samaj, which in reality was an organisation created by this conflict, had been divided into two—Adi (original) Brahmo Samaj and the All India Brahmo Samaj. As a consequence of the conflict between the two, those who belonged to Adi Brahmo Samaj were withdrawing themselves into a shell representing all that was ancient, while those who belonged to the All India Brahmo Samaj were breaking away from past traditions and were leaning towards the West—intoxicated by the modern wave.

The educated Bengali young men were, according to their nature, choosing one or the other of these two concepts as their ideal. But the number of persons, who were not attracted to either of these two concepts, was also growing day by day. They were connected, if at all, with either of the two organisations only formally. They were neither fascinated by what was ancient, nor did they care to show themselves off as being modern. For them the main aim of life was to acquire the comforts of life. Education and scholarly pursuit were, for them, the means of earning wealth and glory. They were neither worried about the ancient nor about the modern. They positively lived in the present.

Narendra's father, Vishwanath, belonged to this third category of people. Apart from learning English literature and history, he had also learnt Persian. He was particularly fond of the poetry of Hafiz. Members of some of the high class Muslim families were among his many clients. Also, as a result of his frequent visits to the cities of Lucknow, Allahabad, Delhi, Lahore, etc., he was in touch with many a respectable Muslim family. Even otherwise, he was quite conversant with the customs of Muslims for which he had a feeling of respect. He had also acquired a good knowledge of the Christian religion by reading the Bible. The only use of this knowledge for him was that it made him more social and helped him to achieve greater success in his lawyer's profession. The one ideal that he followed all through his life was to earn as much as he could and to acquire as many comforts of life as possible. At his home there was a never-ending stream of guests and relatives. There was an army of servants in his household. He maintained horses and horse-carriages and thus led a life full of pomp and show. He spent lavishly and was generous in his charities. He was not worried about saving for a rainy day, nor did he care for the life hereafter. In one word, he was a modern amalgam of enjoyment and renunciation. By nature he was generous, uninhibited and friendly.

In contrast, his wife, Bhubaneshwari Debi, was a woman deeply devoted to religion. Narendra had two brothers and two sisters younger to him. Mother looked after her sons and daughters with great love and affection. She used to read the Ramayana, Mahabharata, Bhagvata and other Puranas regularly. She also kept herself posted with modern thinking through discussions with her husband and sons. Narendra liked to listen to the stories of Ramayana and Mahabharata narrated by his mother. His mother also reciprocated by making him sit in her lap and narrating to him those stories with great interest. Almost daily in the afternoon there was a recitation of the Ramayana and Mahabharata in the Dutta house. Sometimes some old lady of the family and, at other times, Bhubaneshwari Debi herself would recite and the women of the neighbourhood would come and listen to the recitation. Although, by nature, Narendra was restless, yet he used to sit quietly when the recitation programme of the ladies was in progress. He was deeply influenced by the mythological stories so much so that the characters would fill his imagination as living beings. For hours he used to sit spell-bound, listening to the stories.

After listening to the Ramayana so often, Narendra became so much devoted to Lord Rama and Sita that he bought clay idols of the two from the market. He placed the idols in an unused room on the terrace and would sit in contemplation before the idols for hours. Narendra liked the company of his coachman. The coachman was delighted to see that Narendra was so attached to the idols of Sita and Rama. Narendra used to take counsel with the coachman whenever he had some problem or doubt. One day they were talking about marriage. For some reason, the coachman had an aversion to marriage. He drew such a dreadful picture of married life that Narendra was shocked and came crying to his mother. When mother asked him the reason for crying he repeated what the coachman had told him and said to her, "Mother, how can I worship Sitaram? Sita was the wife of Rama." Mother took him in her arms and, wiping his tears, she told him affectionately, "No harm if you do not worship Rama and Sita. From tomorrow you may worship Lord Shiva, my son."

Later on, when his mother became busy in some household work, Narendra went stealthily to the room on the terrace, brought out the idols of Rama and Sita which he had purchased only a few days back and threw them down breaking them into pieces.

Narendra was very naughty and spared nobody from his pranks. His elder sisters would run after him to catch him and give him a reproof. Narendra would suddenly go into the drain and smear himself with mud. The sisters would now desist from catching hold of him for fear of becoming impure. He would clap his hands in glee for having out-smarted them and would challenge her, saying, "Come,

Sri Ramakrishna (1836-1886)

After Sri Ramakrishna's passing away

In California, 1900

At the Parliament of Religions

catch me now."

From his childhood, Narendra refused to observe the prevailing social customs and practices. If his mother chided him on this account, he would innocently ask, "What happens if I touch my body after touching the plate of rice? Why is it necessary to wash the hand if one lifts the glass of water by the left hand and drinks from it? The water does not become soiled?" His mother had no answer to these queries which further encouraged him to defy such customs.

One of the clients of Vishwanath was a Pathan. He had great affection for Narendra. Whenever Narendra came to know of his arrival, he would come running to the Pathan. He would sit in his lap and listen with great interest the stories of camels and elephants of Punjab and Afghanistan. He would often request the Pathan to take him along with him. The Pathan would laugh and tell, "I shall take you with me when you are taller by two fingers." On the very next day Narendra would come to him and would say standing on his toes, "Look, I have grown taller by two fingers. Now take me along with you." Narendra had become so much attached to this Pathan client that he had no hesitation in eating sweets or fruits offered by him. Vishwanath himself was not orthodox and did not care much about caste distinctions and, therefore, he saw nothing wrong in Narendra eating something offered or touched by a Muslim. But other members of the family did object and they used to dissuade Narendra from eating things offered by people of other castes.

But Narendra was not convinced. Distinction based on caste was an enigma to him. He used to think, "Why does one person not eat anything offered by another? What harm will come to a person who eats something offered by a person belonging to a different caste? Will the sky fall on him? Will he die?"

Clients belonging to different communities used to visit the Dutta mansion in connection with their law suits. As was the custom, several silver plated *hookahs* (smoking pipes) were kept in one corner of the sitting room meant for the use of people of different castes. One day Narendra entered the sitting room, wondering about the enigma of caste distinctions. There was no one in the room. Narendra brought the nozzle of one hookah to his lips and had a puff. He looked in the mirror and did not find any change in himself. In spite of smoking from the hookah meant for a different caste, he remained what he was. By chance, Vishwanath Babu entered the room at that moment and asked Narendra, "What are you doing?" Quick came the answer from Narendra, "I was just testing what would happen to me if I do not observe caste distinctions." Vishwanath Babu smiled and, casting an affectionate glance at Narendra went to his study.

As Narendra had been listening regularly to the recitations of Ramayana and Mahabharata, he had learnt parts of these epics by heart. Sometimes he used to entertain the listeners by reciting portions of these epics in his specially sweet voice. He had learnt many a song about the exploits of Rama and Sita and Krishna and Radha from singing mendicants.

Narendra was enchanted by the character of Hanuman in the Ramayana. He used to listen with deep interest to the stories of the heroic deeds of Hanuman. One day his mother told him that Hanuman was immortal and was still alive. From that day he became anxious to see him, but he did not know where to find him. One day when he went to listen to the recitation of Ramayana, he listened to the anecdotes relating to the life of Hanuman narrated in humorous and metaphorical style by the narrator. Suddenly an idea came to Narendra and, approaching the narrator, he said to him, "Panditji, you have just now said that Hanumanji likes bananas and lives in banana orchards. Can I see him in the banana orchards?" The Pandit, in order to please the innocent child, said to him, "Yes, son. You can find him there."

There was an orchard close to the house. Narendra went there, and sitting under a tree, waited for Hanuman. He sat there for quite some time, but Hanuman did not appear. Late in the night, Narendra came back home. He narrated the incident to his mother and asked her why Hanuman had not come. Mother did not want to disillusion the innocent child. She kissed his forehead and said to him,

"Never mind, my child. Possibly Hanuman ji has gone to some place today on an errand for Lord Rama. You may be able to find him on some other day."

No one knows whether Narendra again went to the orchard to look for Hanuman or not. But it is absolutely true that Hanuman always remained his favourite character. As he grew in age, he developed a feeling of greater adoration for Hanuman. A few months before his death, one of his disciples named Saratchandra Chakravarty asked him the question, "What ideal should we follow now?" To this he replied,

"Make the character of Mahavira your ideal. See, how at the command of Ramchandra he crossed the ocean. He had no care for life or death. He was a perfect master of his senses and was wonderfully sagacious. You have now to build your life on this great ideal of personal service. Through that, all the other ideals will gradually manifest in life. Obedience to the Guru without questioning, and strict observance of Brahmacharya—this is the secret of success. On the one hand, Hanuman represents the ideal of service, and on the other, he represents Leonine courage, striking the whole world with awe. He has not the least hesitation in sacrificing his life for the good of Rama. A supreme indifference to everything except the service of Rama, even to the attainment of the status of Brahma and Shiva, the great gods! Only the carrying out of Shri Rama's behest is the one vow of his life! Such whole-hearted devotion is wanted.

"Playing on the *khol* and *kartal* and dancing in the frenzy of *kirtan* has degenerated the whole people. They are, in the first place, a race of dyspeptics and in addition to this, they dance and jump in this way. How can they bear to jump in this way, how can they bear the strain? In trying to imitate the highest Sadhana, the preliminary qualification for which is purity, they have been swallowed in dire *tamas*. In every district and village you may visit, you will find only the sound of *khol* and *kartal* ! Are not drums made in the country?

Are not trumpets and kettledrums available in India? Make the boys hear the deep-toned sound of these instruments. Hearing from boyhood the sound of these effeminate forms of music and listening to the *kirtan*, the country is well nigh converted into a country of imbeciles. What more degradation can you expect? Even the poets' imagination fails to change this picture! The *damaru* and horn have to be sounded, drums are to be beaten, so as to raise the deep and martial notes, and with 'Mahavira, Mahavira' on your lips and shouting 'Har, Har, Bam, Bam' shake the earth."[2]

Hanuman is also regarded as the incarnation of Shiva.

After Narendra completed five years of age, he was taught at home. Later on, he was admitted to the Metropolitan Institute. There Narendra enjoyed the company of many boys of his own age. Soon he organised his own small group of boys. The members of this group used to come to his house every morning and evening to play. The vast courtyard of Dutta Bhavan used to be filled up with the noise they made.

Whenever a boy tried to cheat in the play, Narendra would get annoyed and force his decision. If he found that he was not listened to and if there was a scuffle, he would fearlessly come between the quarrelling boys and prevent the fight. Among his fellows Narendra was second to none in physical strength. They were also impressed by his great courage. He was good at boxing. The boys were afraid of him on this account.

Once he went to attend the Charak Fair along with his friends when he was six years of age. In the fair he purchased clay idols of Lord Shiva. When they were returning home in the evening, a younger boy got separated from the group. Just then a carriage rushed in, which frightened the small boy. Other pedestrians stopped and started shouting, "help! help." Hearing the voice, Narendra looked back and at once took stock of the situation. He did not

---

2. Saradananda, Sri Ramakrishna, the Great Master, p. 750.

hesitate for a moment. He threw aside the idols of Mahadeva, which he was holding, and rushed with lightening speed. He rescued the small boy when he was about to be trampled upon by the horses and wheels.

People were happy to see that the small boy was unhurt. They applauded the courage shown by Narendra.

There is another story of Narendra's great courage and fearlessness.

In the Matia Burj locality of south Calcutta there was a cattle farm which once belonged to the late Nawab Wajid Ali Shah of Lucknow. Narendra was about 7-8 years of age. One day he went to see this cattle farm along with his friends. The boys raised a collection and hired a small boat at the Chandpal Ghat to go there. When they were returning one of the boys vomited in the boat. The boatman, who was a Muslim, got angry and said, "I shall not let any one of you alight from the boat unless you clean my boat." The boys wanted to pay for getting the boat cleaned by someone else, but the boatman did not agree to this. He collected other boatmen on the river bank and was bent upon giving a beating to the boys. Seeing that the quarrel was getting out of control, Narendra quietly got off the boat. None of the boatmen stopped him as he was so young.

On reaching the bank, Narendra started thinking about ways to rescue his friends. He saw two British soldiers going for a walk. He ran towards them and, after saluting them, caught hold of the hand of one of them. He did not know how to speak English, but tried to make them understand the situation by gesturing towards the riverbank and pulling the hand that he was holding. The soldiers were fascinated by the handsome young boy trying to make himself understood. They came to the boat and at once understood the situation. They reprimanded the boatmen and asked them to release the boys forthwith. The boatmen took fright and returned to their respective boats. In this way Narendra rescued his friends. Both the British soldiers were charmed by Narendra. They wanted to take him to the theatre. But Narendra excused himself and returned home with his friends.

It was not possible to prevent Narendra from doing something out of fear.

Another story illustrates this quality:

There was a *Champak* tree in the house of one of his friends who lived close by. Narendra's favourite pastime was to club his feet around one of the branches of this tree and to swing his body to and fro with his hands and head dangling. One day when he was thus swinging from a branch high up in the tree, the grandfather of his friend saw him. The old man was in a panic as he feared that the branch might break. He, however, thought that shouting at Narendra would not dissuade him from indulging in that sport. So he affectionately said to Narendra, "Do not climb on this tree, son, the *Brahmrakshasa* (great demon) lives on it." But Narendra was not impressed. He asked, "Where is the Brahmrakshasa?

I do not see any Brahmrakshasa here." The old man tried to frighten him by saying, "Brahmrakshasa is not visible. He quietly comes and wrings your neck." He also gave a fearsome description of the Brahmrakshasa and gave examples of how the Brahmrakshasa would not tolerate any desecration of the tree on which he lived. Narendra kept quiet and the old man thought that his trick had worked.

But as soon as the old man turned his back, Narendra again climbed higher up on the tree and seated himself on a branch. However, his friend dared not climb the tree. Narendra asked him to come up but the boy refused as he was afraid of the Brahmrakshasa wringing his neck. Narendra chided him saying, "You are a fool. Had there been a Brahmrakshasa on the tree, he would have broken my neck by now."

Narendra retained this quality throughout his life. He never believed in any thing without subjecting it to reason.

Narendra's younger brothers, Mahendra and Bhupendra, were also smart like him, but they were no match to Narendra. When Narendra grew up to become Swami Vivekananda, he said to one of his disciples, "From my boyhood I was a dare-devil sort of fellow. Otherwise, do you think I could make a tour around the world without a single copper in my pocket?"

2

COMING TO RAMAKRISHNA

"As we have spent half of our life in the universities, our mind is filled with alien ideas with alert."

—*Vivekananda*

Narendra suffered from a serious abdominal disease at the age of fourteen. He was in agony for several days and his body became emaciated. At that time his father was sojourning at Raipur in connection with some work and was expected to remain there for quite some time. Therefore, he summoned his family to Raipur thinking that it would be a good change for them. In 1877 Narendra joined his father at Raipur.

Raipur is a city in Madhya Pradesh. At that time it was not connected by railways. The nearest railway station was Nagpur where one could reach via Allahabad and Jabalpur by train. From Nagpur to Raipur one had to undertake a two weeks' journey by bullock cart which passed through a dense forest infested with wild animals. Narendranath later gave an account of this journey saying that he did not feel the rigours of the journey when he saw the beauty of the forest. He saw the peaks of the Vindhya mountains reaching to the sky, trees laden with fruits and flowers and birds in colourful plumes chirping on the trees and occasionally coming down on the ground looking for food. This was a sight which Narendra had never seen before. His mind, which already had the imprint of the stories of the country's glorious past, was now

Sri Ramkṛṣhna (1836-1886)

impressed by its beauty and vastness. This heightened his desire to see more of his country.

Narendra was, then, at a vulnerable age. It was at Raipur that his character was moulded. There being no school at Raipur at that time, Vishwanath himself coached him at home. He had sufficient leisure at Raipur as he had not to attend the courts or to deal with clients. Apart from textbooks, he taught him history, philosophy and literature from various books. He was greatly impressed by Narendra's power of comprehension and derived great pleasure from teaching him. He imparted to his worthy son all the knowledge that he possessed.

Everyday learned people of Raipur used to gather at

the residence of Vishwanath. They used to have discussions on literature, philosophy and other subjects. Points were debated and analysed in detail for hours at a stretch. Narendra was generally present on such occasions and used to listen to discussions with great interest. Occasionally, he was also asked by Vishwanath to give his opinion. In this way he was encouraged to involve himself in the discussions. Although Narendra was still young, he had a clear and analytical mind. Listening to his views gave much pleasure to the elders.

One of the friends of Vishwanath was a celebrated author of Bengali literature. One day, when they were discussing literature Narendra was also invited to join. Narendra soon demonstrated that he had not only read the books of most of the authors, but had also learnt by heart considerable portions from them and was capable of making critical assessment of their literary merit. The author was amazed and also pleased and said to Narendra. "Son, I do hope that some day you will bring honour to the Bengali language."

How true was the prediction of that gentleman!

Narendra stayed at Raipur for two years. During this period, apart from learning a lot from books and discussions referred to above, his adolescent mind was greatly influenced by the personality of his father. One day, for some inexplicable reason Narendra asked his father, "Father, what are you leaving behind for us?" Vishwanath pointed to a mirror hanging on the wall and said, "Go and look at your reflection in the mirror and then you will understand what I am leaving behind for you."

Vishwanath never followed the feudal practice of rebuking his children. He had his own way of reforming them and instilling self-confidence in them. Being rebellious by nature, Narendra spoke harshly to his mother one day. Vishwanath did not reprimand him; instead, he wrote with a piece of charcoal on the wall, "Today Narendra used these harsh words for his mother."

This made Narendra hang his head in shame. He did not forget the lesson throughout his life.

If anyone tried to laugh off his reasoned statement as childish impertinence, he would seethe with rage. At such moments he forgot the consideration of age. He did not spare even the friends of his father while speaking out his mind. Vishwanath never forgave his son for such impertinence. He used to admonish Narendra and warn him to behave in future. In his heart of hearts, however, he was happy that his son had so much of self-confidence.

Vishwanath was also an expert cook. He taught Narendra to cook different kinds of dishes. Later on, Narendra used to entertain his friends by offering them food prepared by himself and much later, when abroad, he often entertained foreigners with different kinds of Indian delicacies. During his two months' stay in the Thousand Islands Park, he often prepared various kinds of Indian food for his disciples.

When Narendra returned to Kolkata from Raipur after two years' stay, he had undergone a mental and physical transformation. Friends were happy to have him among them once again. He was admitted to school and he completed the course of 9th and 10th classes in one year. And yet he was the only student in the school who passed the matriculation examination in first division. This did all his relatives and school authorities proud.

Narendra had a robust body and, at the age of sixteen, looked like a grown-up man of twenty. This was due to the fact that he was regular in physical exercises. He had been practising wrestling from his childhood. Those were the days of political awakening. Surendra Nath Bannerji and Anand Mohan Bose had organised a students' union and they used to exhort the youth to be mentally and physically strong. In the Simla area near Cornwallis Road there was a wrestling ring. It had been started by Nabagopal Mitra who was the founder of the Hindu Fair. Narendranath and his friends used to practise wrestling in this ring. Once he won the first prize in boxing and was awarded a Silver Butterfly. He was also a good cricket player of his time. He was fond of horse-riding. His father had purchased a fine horse for him and he used to go for a ride on that horse. Celebrated writer Romain Rolland in his book on Ramakrishna, has made the following observation about Vivekananda:

> His childhood and boyhood were those of a young prince of the period of European Renaissance. He was gifted with a multiplicity of talents, and cultivated them all. He had a leonine beauty and delicate grace of a fawn. His strong athletic body had further been cultivated by physical exercises. He could wrestle, swim. row and had a passion for riding horses. He was a leader of the youth and the arbiter of fashion. He danced the great religious dances with consummate art. He had a delightful voice which later was to charm the ears of Ramakrishna. He practised vocal and instrumental music for four or five years under famous Hindu and Muslim teachers. He himself composed music and published a documented treatise on the science and philosophy of Indian music.[1]

Narendra learnt music from Ustad Beni, who was a Muslim, and Kansi Ghoshal who was a Hindu. Kansi Ghoshal used to play on the *Pakhawaj* in the music concerts of Adi Brahmo Samaj. It was from him that Narendra learnt to play on Pakhawaj and *Tabla*. Study of history and philosophy was a family tradition inherited by him. His co-disciple has this to say about him:

> When he grew up, he used to start studying text-books only two or three months before the examination. Rest of the time he spent in reading other books of his choice. Thus, before appearing for the Entrance

---

1. Romain Rolland. Ramakrishna, p. 242.

examination, he had practically read all the important books in English and Bengali literature and several books on history. But. as a result of adopting this method, he sometimes had to labour hard immediately before his examinations. One day he said to us in this connection, "I found just two or three days before the examination that the pages of Euclid had not been turned over at all. I then sat up the whole night to study it; I mastered all the four books on the subject in 24 hours and appeared at the examination." Needless to say that he could do so only because he had a robust body and an extraordinary memory by the will of god.[2]

After passing the Matriculation examination, Narendra was admitted to the F.A. class in the General Assembly College. He was then eighteen years old. His brilliance and charming personality attracted the attention of both teachers and students within a short time. He made many students his friends. In fact, it was a matter of pride for the students to be counted among his friends. Priya Nath Sinha, who was one of his fellow students in those days, has written in his reminiscences:

> Narendra studies in the General Assembly College near the Haido Tank. He has passed F.A. from there. Several of his fellow-students adore him for his numerous qualities. They derive so much pleasure from listening to Narendra's song that they flock to his house, whenever they get time. They lose the track of time listening to his reasoned arguments or singing or playing on musical instruments.
>
> These days Narendra goes only twice to his father's house to have his meals. He spends rest of the time in study in his maternal grandmother's house in a lane nearby. It is not that he stays here only to pursue his studies, but he likes to be alone.

The room in which Narendra lived was very small.

---

2. Saradananda, Sri Ramakrishna : The Great Master, p. 721.

Narendra had named it 'Tang' (narrow). Very often, Narendra used to say to his friends. 'Come, let us go to 'Tang.' A typical scene ot the 'Tang' has been described in the following words:

Today Narendra was studying with great application. Just then a friend arrived. It was about 11 o'clock. Narendra had just started reading a book after having his meals. The friend came and said, "put off your studies for the night, let us hear you sing a song or two.

Narendra immediately closed his book and put it aside. He picked up the *Tanpura*. tuned it and said to his friend "Accompany me on the Tabla."

The friend said, "I do not know how to play on the Tabla. I only know to give a beat on the table in school. How can I accompany you on tabla?"

Narendra then himself demonstrated the beats of the sound and told his friend, "Watch carefully, it is not difficult. You will surely be able to play." He explained the rhythm. After an attempt or two the friend was able to accompany him on the Tabla. Then Narendra started singing with gay abandon and made everyone spellbound by singing *Tappa, Dhap, Khyal, Dhrupad* and Bengali, Hindi and Sanskrit songs one after the other.

Narendra was gifted with an extraordinary power of understanding and sharp intellect and was, therefore, able to learn all subjects in a short time. He could thus find enough time to devote to music and to moving about, playing and joking with friends. Other boys misunderstood him for this reason and thought that he had no interest in studies. Those who followed him and wasted their time in play only, had to face dire consequences.

Narendra read the textbooks only to pass the examination. He was more inclined to read books on literature, philosophy and history. Even before he passed the F.A. examination, he had read all about the egoistic philosophy of Descartes, scepticism of Hume and Waine, the theory of evolution propounded by Darwin, apart from

Herbert Spencer's theory of the Survival of the Fittest. His friend, Brijendra Babu, had published his reminiscences of Narendra in *Prabuddha Bharat*, in which he described his restlessness of mind and thirst for knowledge and revealed that Narendra had read the poems of Shelley, the philosophy of Hegel and all about the French Revolution at that age. Apart from this, he was also fond of reading Sanskrit poetry, Upanishads and the works of Raja Rammohun Roy.

At college, Brijendra Babu was senior to Narendra by two or three years, but both liked each other's company. Both of them used to attend meetings of the Philosophical Society. According to Romain Rolland, Brijendra had been influenced by the French Revolution and was an atheist. Later on, he became famous as a scholar. After passing the Matriculation examination, the mental faculties of Narendra had developed so much that it did not take him much time to go through a book. He had revealed his system of studying to his fellow-disciples in the following words:

> Since then, when I took up a book, I did not find it necessary to prod through it line by line in order to understand the author. I could grasp the point by reading the first and the last lines of a paragraph. Gradually that power developed and it was not necessary to read the para also in the aforesaid way. I read the first and the last lines of each page and the content was known. Again, when the author was explaining a particular point of view with argument in any part of his book, I could understand his whole chain of reasoning by merely reading the beginning of his arguments.[3]

The renowned German Vedantist, Paul Deussen, was struck with amazement at this extraordinary power of Narendra when he met him later in his life as Vivekananda. We shall throw more light on this when we discuss their meeting.

---

3. Saradananda, Sri Ramkrishna : The Great Master, p. 721.

Narendra's objective was to discover truth through his studies. Whatever he believed to be the truth, he adhered to it all his life. If anybody differed with him, he would argue with him and would not rest till he had vanquished him with his forceful arguments. Those who were defeated in argument sometimes felt hurt and did not hesitate to call him a despot. But Narendra had no ill-will towards anyone. Nor did he take recourse to unfair means to win an argument. He was frank in stating to others what he felt to be true. He cared little if anybody felt uncomfortable, or held a poor opinion of him or spoke ill of him at his back. His heart was pure, and he himself never spoke ill of anyone at one's back. Gradually, his fellow-students realised the truth about his character and began to listen to him with respect.

William Hasty, the Principal of the General Assembly College, was a learned person apart from being a poet, a philosopher and a thorough gentleman. Narendra, Brijendra, and some of the other talented students used to go to him regularly to study philosophy. Hasty was an admirer of the versatile genius of Narendra and loved him the most. On one occasion, when Narendra analysed a particular theory in detail in a meeting of the Philosophical Club, Hasty was greatly charmed and declared that Narendra was the best student of philosophy and there was no student in any of the universities of Germany and England who was as talented as Narendra.

As he progressed in his studies and grew older, his quest for truth became more pronounced. Many questions were agitating his mind. What is the purpose of human life? Is there a power which controls the material world? Western science and Western philosophy had created many doubts in his mind. Whenever Narendra heard any preacher speaking about God, he would ask him, 'Sir, have you seen God?' The preachers very often prevaricated and, instead of saying 'yes' or 'no,' tried to answer him by expansive injunctions to impress him with their book knowledge. But Narendra was in search of one who had real and direct experience. He had become a sceptic as a result of listening to pedantic and sectarian harangues of preachers.

The critical approach that Narendra had inherited from his father had been sharpened by his knowledge of Western thoughts. He was now in search of a living ideal. This search led him to take the membership of Adi Brahmo Samaj, along with some of his friends.

A few years back, the Brahmo Samaj had been divided into the Adi Brahmo Samaj and the All-India Brahmo Samaj. The former was led by Debendranath Tagore and the latter by Keshab Chandra Sen. Keshab was a good orator and was at that time at the peak of his popularity. Bengali young men were greatly influenced by him. According to Romain Rolland, Narendranath envied Keshab and aspired to become one like him. Still, he did not seek the membership of the All-India Brahmo Samaj, because that organisation had abandoned the ideals and traditions of Raja Rammohun Roy. Keshab and his followers were influenced by Christianity and their conduct was contrary to the high ideals of ancient Hindu religion. From his childhood, Narendra was devoted to these ideals. In spite of being a sceptic, Narendra was not frivolous or disorderly like other young men.

Narendranath used to attend the Sunday prayer meetings of Brahmo Samaj and win the hearts of members by singing Brahmo songs. But he was not in agreement with other members regarding their views about worship. He felt that Brahmo Samaj lacked in dedication and the spirit of renunciation. Narendra used to speak out his mind without fear. Mental peace was still eluding him. One day Debendranath Tagore advised him by saying, 'You have all the signs of a yogi in your physiognomy. You can achieve peace and truth through meditation.'

Narendra was a man of determination. From that very day he started practising meditation. He became frugal in his meals, started sleeping on a mat and wearing a *dhoti* and covering his body with a *chadar*. He started practising

The Holy Mother, Sri Sarada Devi (1853-1920)

At Bosepara Lane, Calcutta (Kolkata) 1897

In Kashmir

Sitting on chairs (left to right) : Swamis Sadananda, Vivekananda, Niranjanananda and Dhirananda

In London, 1896

physical austerities.

Narendra had rented a room in the house of his maternal grandmother close by. Members of his family thought that he was staying away from home to escape disturbance in his studies. Vishwanath Babu never interfered with the freedom of his son. So, Narendra used his time in meditation and worship as soon as he was free from studies and practice of music. Satyendranath Mazumdar has written about these days:

> The days were passing in this way, and his longing for truth also grew with the passage of time. Gradually, he realised that, in order to realise truth which was beyond the senses, it was necessary for him to learn at the feet of one who had himself realised truth. He also avowed that he would realise truth in this very life or would end his life in that attempt.[4]

Surendranath Mittra was a disciple of Ramakrishna Paramahansa and used to live in the Simla Street. One day, in November 1881, he invited Ramakrishna Paramahansa to his house and held a joyous celebration in his honour. Unable to find a good singer, he invited his neighbour Narendranath to sing on the occasion. It was here that Narendranath met Ramakrishna Paramahansa for the first time. As soon as he heard Narendra sing, he recognised his talent. He went to Narendra, talked to him for a while and, before leaving, invited him to come to Dakshineshwar.

As the F.A. examination was ensuing, Narendra got busy in his studies and forgot about the invitation. As soon as the exams were over, his father broached the subject of his marriage. The would-be father-in-law of Narendra was willing to pay a dowry of ten thousand rupees. But Narendra did not want to be tied down by marriage. He used to say to his friends, "I shall not marry. You will see what I become." Vishwanath Babu did not want to put any

---

4. Satyendra Nath Mazumdar, *Vivekananda Charit*, pp. 83-84.

pressure on his son. He asked one of his relatives, Dr. Ramachandra Dutta, to find out the views of Narendra about marriage. When Narendra was approached, he flatly refused to marry as, according to him, marriage would be an obstacle in his achieving the ideal of his life. After listening to his reply Dr. Ramachandra told him, "If you really want to realise truth, you should not waste your time in institutions like Brahmo Samaj. You should go to Sri Ramakrishna in Dakshineshwar."

Narendra now remembered his meeting with Ramakrishna Paramahansa at the house of Surendranath. He went to Dakshineshwar with some of his friends.

Ramakrishna greeted him as an old acquaintance in a normal way. He made Narendra sit on a mat near him and asked him to sing a song. Narendra sang a song of the Brahmo Samaj. According to Narendra, when the song was over, he caught him by the hand and took him into a room and, closing the room from inside, he said, "Is it proper that you should come so late? Should you not have once thought how I was waiting for you? Hearing continually the idle talk of worldly people, my ears have swelled up. From today I shall have peace by talking to you as you are a true recluse." His eyes were filled with tears. Narendra was overwhelmed and kept looking at him. Next moment he stood before him with folded palms and showing him the respect due to God, and said, "I know, my lord, you are one of the seven Rishis. You are that ancient Rishi Nara, a part of Narayana, who had incarnated himself this time, to remove the misery of the sufferings of humanity ...."

Narendra was dumb-struck to hear him speak thus. He thought it was madness. How could he say all this to him who was the son of Vishwanath Dutta. Narendra kept staring at him, totally bewildered. Catching hold of his hand, Ramakrishna Paramahansa said again, "Promise that you will come again and all alone."

Narendra gave his word in order to wriggle out of the peculiar situation but in his heart he decided never to come again.

Then they returned to the sitting room. There Ramakrishna talked like a normal man and there was no trace of madness that he had exhibited a short while ago.

Once in his ecstasy, Ramakrishna had related the story of Narendra's birth to his disciples. The story has been quoted by Romain Rolland in the following words:

One day I found that my mind was soaring high in *samadhi* along a luminous path. It soon transcended the stellar universe and entered the subtle region of ideas. As it ascended higher and higher, I found on both sides of the way ideal forms of gods and goddesses. The mind then reached the outer limits of that region, where a luminous barrier separated the sphere of relative existence from that of the absolute, crossing the barrier where no corporeal being was visible. Even the gods dared not into that sublime realm, and were content to keep their seats far below. But the next moment I saw seven venerable sages seated there in samadhi. It occurred to me that these sages must have surpassed not only men but even the gods in knowledge and holiness, in renunciation and love. Lost in admiration, I was reflecting on their greatness, when I saw a portion of that undifferentiated luminous region condense into the form of a divine child. The child came to one of the sages, tenderly clasped his neck with his lovely arms, and addressing him in a sweet voice, tried to drag his mind down from the state of samadhi. That magic touch roused the sage from the superconscious state, and he fixed his half open eyes upon the wonderful child. His beaming countenance showed that the child must have been the treasure of his heart. In great joy the strange child spoke to him, 'I am going down. You too must go with me.'

The sage remained mute but his tender look expressed his assent. As he kept gazing at the child, he was again immersed in samadhi. I was surprised to find that a fragment of his body and mind was descending to earth in the form of a bright light. No sooner had I seen Narendra than I recognised him to be that sage.[5]

Narendra went again to Dakshineshwar after a month. He found Ramakrishna alone lying on a small bedstead. Narendra says, 'As soon as he saw me he invited me to sit by his side. Soon after I sat down I saw that he was gradually moving towards me. I thought that possibly he would again do something crazy as he did on the previous day. What he did was that he touched the body of Narendra with his right foot and in another moment Narendra felt the identity of the walls, all things and the entire world dissolving into nothingness. He was filled with fear and cried, 'What have you done to me? I have my parents, you know.' Then, keeping the hand of Narendra on his breast he said, 'Let it then cease now.'

Ramakrishna soon became his normal self. As before, he lovingly made Narendra eat something and talked to him about various things joking and showering affection. In the evening when Narendra wanted to take leave of him, he became unhappy and said, 'Promise that you will come again soon.' Narendra could not help but promise as he had done before.

Narendra was amazed at what had happened. While returning home he was trying to solve the riddle. The mental state of Narendra at that time has been described by Swami Saradananda in the following words of Narendra:

"I continued thinking how I could consider that person to be mad who could shatter to pieces the structure of a mind like mine, possessed of a strong will power, and filled with firm impressions, who could refashion

---

5. Romain Rolland, *Ramakrishna*, pp. 329-40.

it after his own pattern like a ball of clay? But how could I regard the manner in which he addressed me and the words that he spoke to me during my first visit to him as otherwise than the ravings of a mad man? Therefore, just as I could not find out the cause of the aforesaid experience, even so, I could not come to any certain conclusion with the help of observation and·investigation about each person and thing I came in contact with. That nature of mine received a severe jolt that day, creating an anguish in my hearts. As a result, there was a firmer determination in my mind to understand thoroughly the nature and power of that wonderful person.[6]

Truly, this was the living ideal whose quest had led Narendra to Dakshineshwar. But being a young man of firm beliefs, Narendra did not accept that remarkable man as his guru till he had properly understood his nature and power.

Now we have to see what the nature of that remarkable man was and what power he possessed. How did Narendra recognise him?, What role was played by that remarkable person in transforming Narendra into what he became as Vivekananda? This question forms an interesting subject of study not only for us but for all those who are the students of the history of Indian philosophy. It is not possible to understand a disciple without understanding his guru. This guru and his disciple—Ramakrishna and Vivekananda are not ordinary individuals; they are epoch-making personalities and they form the historical link in the process of the development of our national thought. Without understanding these two personalities it is not possible to solve the riddle which has been made even more complicated by the so-called spiritualists and which has been constantly disregarded by the so-called leftists.

---

6. Saradananda, *Sri Ramakrishna: The Great Master.* p. 721.

3

THE CONFLICT
AND ACCEPTANCE

*'Truth is achieved only by those who fearlessly enter the temple
of and who, without bargaining, worship it for its sake.'*
—Vivekananda

Ramakrishna Paramahansa was a sage possessing true
knowledge. As a result of his own thinking and his *samadhi*
experiences he had come to the conclusion that there was
an entity which is one and diverse at the same time.
Therefore, according to him, it was futile to quarrel among
ourselves in the name of different religions, e.g., Hinduism,
Islam, Christianity, Vaishnavism, etc., as these religions called
the same entity by various names like Ishwara, Allah, God,
and they were engaged in the pursuit of that entity by
following their own paths.

Ramakrishna felt the need of an organisation through
which he could propagate this ideology. It is for this purpose
that he started initiating disciples in 1884. By the time of
his death in 1886, he had acquired 25 disciples. Narendra
was the best among them and Ramakrishna devoted his
energy to mould him into desired shape. His love the for
Narendra had reached the stage of madness. Priyanath Sinha
has given the following account in his reminiscences:

> Narendra has not visited Ramakrishna for a good
> number of days. So he himself came to his room "Tang"

In Calcutta, 1886

in Calcutta one morning along with Ramlal. On that
morning two fellow students of Narendra, namely,
Haridas Chattopadhyay and Dasharathi Sanyal, were
sitting with him. They used to study and discuss
matters together. Just then they heard someone calling
'Naren' at the door. On hearing that call Narendra
abruptly got up and at once rushed downstairs. His
friends also understood that Sri Ramakrishna had
arrived and that was why Narendra had rushed to
receive him. The friends saw them meeting on the steps
of the staircase. As soon as Sri Ramakrishna saw
Narendra, he was overwhelmed and with tears in his
eyes, asked him. "Why had'nt you come for so many
days?" So saying, he entered the room and sat down.
Thereafter, he took out the sweetmeat—sandesh—which
he had brought, wrapped in the garment covering his
shoulders. He offered him the sweet saying, "eat," "eat."
Whenever he came to meet Narendra, he always
brought some eatables for him. Sometimes he would
send some eatables to Narendra through other people.

The Conflict and Acceptance ∗ 39

Narendra would not eat all the sweets himself. He first offered some to his friends and himself ate some. Thereafter Sri Ramakrishna told him, "I have not heard you sing for so many days. Sing a song for us." Narendra immediately picked up the *Tanpura*, tuned it, and started singing—

"Arise Mother Kundalini"

As soon as the song started, Sri Ramakrishna went into ecstasy. As the song proceeded, he began to feel elevated; his eyes stopped winking, his body became still like a marble statue and he entered into a *Nirvikalpa Samadhi*. Narendra's friends had never before seen anyone going into ecstasy like this. Seeing Ramakrishna in that state, they thought that perhaps Sri Ramakrishna's body was afflicted with pain which had made him unconscious. They were worried. Dasharathi hurriedly brought some water and started splashing it on his face. Seeing all this, Narendra asked them to stop and said, "There is no need for this. He is not unconscious, he is in ecstasy. He will become normal on hearing the song again." Narendra now started singing songs about Goddess Shyama. He also sang some songs about Lord Krishna. While these songs were being sung, Sri Ramakrishna would, by turn, go into ecstasy and regain his normal self. Narendra continued singing for quite some time. At last when he stopped, Sri Ramakrishna said to him, "Will you come with me to Dakshineshwar? You have not been there for so many days. Do come along with me. You may return soon after." Narendra at once got ready to go. He left the books, etc., lying as they were. He replaced the Tanpura carefully and went to Dakshineshwar along with Sri Gurudev.'

If Narendra failed to visit Dakshineshwar for a few days, Ramakrishna would get restless. One day in 1883, he was pacing the verandah restlessly weeping and muttering to himself, 'Mother, I cannot live without seeing him.' After a few moments he composed himself, came into the room, sat down near his disciples and said, 'I wept so much for him and still he has not come.' He was again overwhelmed with emotion and started saying, 'My heart aches so much to see him, I feel as if someone is wringing my heart. He does not understand my pain.' Whenever Narendra came, he would listen to his songs and feed him. Many a time he would go to the city looking for him.

Among his disciples, Ramakrishna loved Narendra the most. When he first saw him at the house of Surendranath, he had recognised him as a young man of character dedicated to truth, who had the qualities of becoming a leader of men. His inner voice had told him that Narendra was the fittest person to propagate the message of 'many paths for many people.' Not only this, his powerful mind had revealed to him that Narendra was one of the seven sages of the celestial world called Nara, a part of Narayana.

When Narendra and Ramakrishna met, they formed their own opinion about each other. Ramakrishna expressed his opinion about Narendra in the following words:

"My Narendra is a coin with no alloy whatsoever, ring it and you hear the finest sound. I see other boys somehow pass two or three examinations with utmost strain. There it ends; they are a spent-up force. But Narendra is not like that. He is the true knower of Brahma. He sees light when he sits for meditation. It is not for nothing that I love Narendra so much."[1]

Sri Ramakrishna loved Narendra for these qualities. He wanted to adopt him and groom him for an epoch-making mission. But Narendra was not the one to be so easily won over. He was a young man of strong mind and his outward behaviour gave the impression of his being arrogant, obstinate, conceited and even profligate. Little did

---

1. Saradananda, *Sri Ramakrishna: The Great Master*, p. 750.

people know how restless was his heart to realise truth and that he was prepared not only to give up all comforts but also his life in order to unravel the mystery of life.

Ramakrishna would accept a disciple only after putting him to test. Although he had guessed that Narendra possessed extraordinary talent, and even though he loved him dearly and could not bear his separation, yet he considered it necessary to put him to test before making him a disciple. He thought that it was possible that he had erred in judging him from appearances. In the same way, Narendra himself was not prepared to accept a person as his Guru unless that person deserved to be so. So he also wanted to test the nature and power of Ramakrishna. Metaphorically speaking, the extraordinary saint and the extraordinary young man were like two stars, each revolving on his own axis, suddenly coming together. Before entering into a relationship of disciple and preceptor, both started evaluating and testing each other.

Before Narendra started visiting Dakshineshwar, he was a member of the Brahmo Samaj, where he had signed a pledge declaring that he will have faith only in one formless God. At Dakshineshwar, Ramakrishna gave him the *Ashtavakra Samhita* to read. But this work propounded beliefs that were in conflict with his existing concepts. This annoyed him and he said, 'I shall not read such books. What can be a greater sin than to call man a God? The Rishis and sages who wrote these books must have had distorted minds; otherwise, how could they have written such things.' Listening to this, Ramakrishna smiled and said to him calmly, 'If you like, you may not just now accept whatever has been said by them. But why do you criticise the Rishis and the sages? On your part, you should go on praying to God as the true entity. Later on, you may put your faith in the shape in which he appears before you.'

Rakhalchandra Ghosh had become a member of Brahmo Samaj along with Narendra. One day Narendra saw him following Ramakrishna into the temple and offering obeisance to idols of gods and goddesses. This was enough for Narendra to go into a rage. He accused Rakhal of violating the pledge he had taken and taking recourse to falsehood. Taken aback Rakhal hung his head. He could not utter any words in reply. But Ramakrishna spoke on his behalf to Narendra, 'If he now feels attracted towards God with a form, what can he do? If you do not like this form of worship, you may not practice it. But what right have you to hurt the feelings of others like this?'

Ramakrishna never forced his views on others and if someone tried to force one's views on others, he always opposed it. It was the time when people in India respected the Guru even more than their parents. But Ramakrishna did not want all this from his disciples. He considered himself as an equal among his disciples. He was like a comrade, a brother to them. He used to talk to them as an intimate friend and never showed himself off as being superior to them.

One day some well-known leaders of Brahmo Samaj like Keshabchandra Sen and Vijaykrishna Goswami called on Ramakrishna. Narendra was also present there. Ramakrishna continued looking at them and talking as if in a trance. But after they had left, he turned to his disciples and said, "Keshab, I saw, has become world-famous on account of the abundance of one power, but Narendra has in him eighteen such powers in the fullest measure. The hearts of Keshab and Vijay, I saw again, are brightened by a light of knowledge like the flame of a lamp; but looking at Narendra I found that the very sun of knowledge had risen in his heart and removed the slightest tinge of 'Maya and delusion.'

Narendra protested strongly against the Master's remark saying, 'Sir, what are you saying? People will regard you as a mad man when they hear it.' The Master was pleased to hear the protest and said affectionately, 'What shall I do, my child? Mother showed me all this: that is why I said so.'

However, Narendra was not convinced. He said. 'Who can say that Mother showed you these things and that they are not a fiction of your imagination? If I had such experiences, I would certainly have taken them as whims of my own brain. Science and philosophy have proved beyond doubt that our eyes, ears and other organs of sense very often deceive us, especially when there is a desire in our mind to see a particular object. You are affectionate to me and want to see me marvel at everything; that is perhaps why such visions appear to you.'

It was against the nature of Narendra to accept something which he believed was not based on reason. He used to weigh every word of Ramakrishna and did not hesitate to express his doubts, if he had any. Ramakrishna, instead of feeling offended, loved him the most for that reason. Even before the coming of Narendra, he had often been heard saying, 'Mother, send someone to me who would doubt my achievements.'

Narendra had studied science and Western philosophy. When he started coming to Dakshineshwar he used to hate superstition and idol worship. At that time not only Ramakrishna's disciples but Ramakrishna also called himself an incarnation of God. He used to tell his disciples, 'He who was Rama and Krishna, is now Ramakrishna.' But Narendra had frankly told him, "Even if the whole world considers you an incarnation, I shall not call you one until I get a proof.'

At this Ramakrishna had smiled and said to his disciples, 'Do not believe anything because I say it. Put everything to test yourselves.'

Narendra did not think much of the concept of Advaita Brahma as was preached by Ramakrishna. He used to make fun of this concept and would say to his friend Hazra, 'Can it ever be possible that the water-pot is God; the cup is God; whatever we see and all of us are God?'

The other devotees and disciples of Ramakrishna were annoyed with Narendra on account of these critical statements of his. In the beginning they thought him to be conceited and arrogant. But Ramakrishna felt very happy with his critical remarks which would send him into ecstasy. Romain Rolland says,

> The keen criticism of Naren, and his passionate arguments filled him with joy. He had a profound respect for his brilliant intellectual sincerity with his tireless quest for the truth. He regarded it as manifestation of Shaiva power, which would finally overcome all illusions.[2]

But at other times the old Master was hurt by his sharp criticism delivered as it was without any consideration for others. Narendra had said to his face, 'How do you know that your realisations are not the creations of your sick brain, mere hallucinations?'

In spite of this, relations between this wonderful man and the extraordinary boy were becoming more and more intimate and full of affection. A couple of incidents fully illustrate this.

Narendra had not visited Dakshineshwar for about two weeks. Ramakrishna was restless to meet him. He decided to go to Calcutta to see him. He thought that even if Narendra was not at home, he would certainly go in the evening to sing in the prayer meeting of Brahmo Samaj. So he went to the Brahmo Temple looking for him. When he reached there, the Acharya was addressing the circle of the Brahmos from the altar. He simple-mindedly entered the temple and went forward towards the Acharya. Many among those present recognised him. People stood up to see him. Whispers became louder.

Reaching near the altar, Ramakrishna suddenly went into a state of ecstasy. This further heightened the curiosity of the people. The eagerness of the congregation to see him increased the disorder and confusion which showed

---

2. Romain Rolland, *Ramakrishna*, p. 213.

no sign of abating. All the gas lights of the Samaj were put out, which, however, made the confusion worse confounded, all rushing towards the door in the dark to get out.

Narendra at once sensed the purpose of his coming. He busied himself in looking after him. When Ramakrishna came out of the samadhi, Narendra brought him out through the back door of the Samaj, and with great difficulty, got him into a carriage and escorted him to Dakshineshwar. Narendra saw that no one of the Samaj showed courtesy to the Master. He was, on the contrary, treated with discourtesy and disregard. Narendra was stung to the quick at this and felt so hurt that, after this incident, he gave up going to the Brahmo Samaj.

Once, in order to test Narendra, Ramakrishna paid him no attention when he came to Dakshineshwar. Neither would he ask him to sing nor would he talk to him. On his part, on such occasions, Narendra showed no concern at being treated like this. He would go back after chatting with other disciples. Among them, he went well particularly with Pratapchandra Hazra. He sometimes spent hours talking to him or arguing with him. In this way, a month passed. One day, after talking to Hazra, Narendra reached and sat near Ramakrishna. When he got up to go, Ramakrishna said to him, 'How do you come here, when I do not talk to you?' At once Narendra replied, 'I like you; that is why I come here, not to talk to you.' This reply of Narendra made Ramakrishna go into ecstasy.

Seeing the Master's love for him, Narendra once said to him, 'King Bharata, we are told in the Puranas, thought day and night of his pet deer; so the deer and he became one after his death. If that is true, you should be aware of the consequences of your thinking much of me and be on your guard.' The Master, simple like a child, said, 'Right you are; ah, my child, what will happen if that be so? For I cannot do without seeing you.' Doubt sprouted, the Master went to Kali Temple to refer the matter to the Divine Mother. He returned shortly afterwards beaming with delight and said. 'Away! Rascal! I shall never give ear to your words. Mother said, "You regard him as Narayan Himself; that is why you love him. The day you do not see Narayan in him, you will not cast even a glance at him."

This is how things went on for three years from 1881 to 1884. When Narendra started visiting Dakshineshwar, he was to appear in the F.A. examination. By that time he had already studied the thoughts of many Western philosophers. While visiting Dakshineshwar, he continued with his study of science and Western philosophy. By the time he passed his B.A., he had become familiar with the thoughts of Descartes, Hume, Bentham, Spinoza, Darwin, Comte and Spencer. In those days, German philosophers were much talked about. Therefore, Narendra read everything about Kant, Fichte, Hegel and Schopenheuer. Apart from this, he attended lectures at the Medical College in order to understand and study the working of the brain and the nervous system. But all this study, instead of quenching his thirst for knowledge, made it even more acute. He had in his heart a strong desire to realise the truth. His mind, which was influenced by the materialism of the West on the one hand and by the spiritualism of Dakhineshwar on the other, was very restless. Narendra preferred to remain a non-believer instead of putting faith in the existence of God without personal experience.

However, it was not easy to decide this way or the other. His family tradition and the prevailing atmosphere in his home were presenting to him two conflicting ideals. On the one hand was the ideal of his grandfather who had renounced everything and become a *sanyasin*. On the other, there was the ideal of his father's love for enjoyment who had established his legal practice, had earned a lot of money, was lavish in his habits and lived his life in great style. His father had been influenced by Western education which taught him to forget the past and live in the present. He did not know Sanskrit and had, therefore, not studied the Gita or the Upanishads, nor did he feel the need of doing so. Although he considered himself to be a free thinker, he never took the trouble to find answers to questions such as what was the relation of the soul to the body? Is there a God or not? His spirituality was confined to the limits of all that was contained in the poetry of Hafiz, the mystic poet of Persian, or the sayings of Christ.

Seeing that Narendra was inclined towards spirituality, one day he gifted him a copy of the Bible and told him, 'It contains everything about religion.' In fact, it was only for fashion or for entertainment that he read Bible or the poetry of Hafiz. His egocentric mind did not find any other practical use for these two works. He was thoroughly self-centred and lived his life only for earning wealth and fame. He believed in living a life of enjoyment above all, and if there was money to spare, for giving charity and thereby achieving virtue. The number of persons like him was growing fast in the educated society of Kolkata. These people had come to believe that all science, freedom of thought and even spirituality was in the West and that nothing except superstition and weakness could be learnt from our ancient Rishis and Shastras. The influence of Western education had even resulted in the division of Brahmo Samaj into two parts. One of them openly criticised Hindu Shastras and considered Christ to be their spiritual ideal. The other part, though it believed in the Gita and the Upanishads, did so only as a means of achieving celebrity status. They lacked the quality of renunciation and devotion to truth. Only the Advaitism of Ramakrishna, which transported people into a state of ecstasy and happiness, was attracting the youth inclined towards renunciation and seeking truth. However, the logical mind of Narendra was restraining him from coming to terms even with this ideal.

Narendra had started visiting Dakshineshwar at the age of 18 years. He was 21 now, when he was appearing for the B.A. examination. It was a settled fact that he had never accepted personal enjoyment as the ideal of his life. His one aim of life was the realisation of truth, and the welfare of society, of the nation and of mankind. In order

At Oakland, February 1900

In Madras (Chennai), February 1897

At Cossipore Garden, 1886

Belgaum, October 1892

to adapt his mind to the pursuit of this ideal, he had melted it in the crucible of knowledge, even as gold is melted in a crucible to give it a the desired shape. However, he had not yet found the ideal person who would take this molten and glittering metal out of the crucible and give it a shape. As yet, he had not given the right to do so even to Ramakrishna.

At that time he was particularly influenced by the Western philosopher Hamilton. Hamilton held the view that human mind did not possess the power to describe the nature of God: it is here that philosophy ends and spiritualism begins. In Dakshineshwar Narendra used to have lengthy discussions with the disciples of Ramakrishna. Perhaps, in this way, he was willy-nilly getting close to the theory of Advaitism. Only a little ground was now left to be covered.

Sometimes, in such a state of mind, real incidents of life play a decisive role. Even before he passed the B.A. examination, he was asked by his father, Vishwanath, to go to the renowned attorney Nimaicharan Bose and learn law from him, so that he could also become a lawyer like his father. Moreover, he also wanted Narendra to be rescued from the influence of Ramakrishna, so that he could get married and become an independent householder. As he knew about the nature of Narendra, he entrusted the task of bringing him round to one of his class-fellows dear to him.

One day, when Narendra was studying in his room preparing for the examination, this friend came to him, and told him sombrely. 'Narendra, give up this madness of religion, worship and the company of saints. Do something which will help you to acquire the comforts of life.' Narendra was, by now, fed up with listening to such talk of the so-called worldly-wise people. He was taken aback when he heard one of his own friends speaking to him in that way. He was silent for a while and then said to his friend, 'My views are quite contrary to yours. I consider *sanyas* to be the highest ideal of life. It is much better to devote one's life to the pursuit of that which is unchangeable—the true, the good and the beautiful—rather than run after the pleasures of a world which is transitory.'

The friend, who had come with the self-imposed duty of bringing round Narendra, said to him excitedly, 'Look Narendra, you can rise a lot in your life with the intelligence and talent that you possess. Ramakrishna of Dakshineshwar has turned your mind. If you care for your welfare, give up the company of that lunatic, otherwise you could be ruined.'

Narendra put aside his books and started pacing the room. The friend continued to have his say and asked several questions about Ramakrishna. Narendra stopped and said to him calmly, "Brother, you do not understand that great man. In fact, I myself have not been able to understand him fully. Still, there is something in him which makes me adore him.'

Many a young man had left the Brahmo Samaj and become disciples of Ramakrishna. When Vijay Goswami also changed his faith and broke away from the general Brahmo Samaj, Vishwanath tried to stop Narendra from going to Ramakrishna. He said to Narendra, 'The ecstasy of samadhi, which you observe is nothing but a symptom of nervous debility. Paramahansa has lost his mental balance due to his rigorous physical practices.'

Narendra did not react to Vishwanath Babu's remarks. He got up and left that place. However, a storm was raging in his mind and he was troubled by questions such as, 'What is this simple-hearted great man? Does he really have a distorted mind? Why does he love a small man like me so much? What is the mystery of all this?'

Narendra was acquainted with most of the leaders of Brahmo Samaj. He was impressed by their scholarship. But for none of them Narendra had as much respect as for Ramakrishna. He now started seeing the different facets of his personality. He asked himself the question, 'Why had he not been able to get any peace of mind even in the prayer meetings of Brahmo Samaj? Had even one of those leaders realised God?'

Satyendranath Mazumdar has written in his book, *Vivekananda Charit*:

One day in his yearning for God, Narendra left his home. Those days Maharshi Debendranath used to live in a boat on the Ganges. Narendra reached the river bank and hastily boarded the boat. The door opened by his forceful push. The Maharshi looked up to see Narendra standing and staring at him like a lunatic. Without giving any time to the Maharshi to think or ask any question, he asked him in a chocked voice, "Sir, have you seen God?" The Maharshi, who was taken by surprise, twice tried to give a reply, but no words came out of his mouth. At last he said, "Narendra, by looking at your eyes I can know that you are a yogi." He reassured Narendra in many ways and said to him that he could acquire knowledge about the Brahma if he practised meditation regularly. Not getting a convincing reply to his question, Narendra returned home....

After returning home, Narendra threw aside books of philosophy and religion. What was the use of such books, if they were of no help in God-realisation? He kept awake all through the night immersed in thought. After passing a night full of agony Narendra rushed to Dakshineshwar as soon as it was dawn. In the company of his Gurudev, he found the ever-cheerful great man preaching in a soft voice, surrounded by his devotees.

There was a storm raging in the heart of Narendra. What would happen if he also said "no" to his question? To whom would he then go? At last, having gone through the agony, he put to Ramakrishna the same question that he had put to many a religious teachers, none of whom had been able to give him a satisfactory reply. He asked, "Master, have you seen God?"

The calm face of the great man brightened with a soft smile. Without any hesitation he replied, "Yes, child, I have seen God. I have seen Him more plainly than I am seeing you now." He heightened the amazement of Narendra a hundredfold by asking him, "Do you also want to see Him? If you follow my advice, I can show Him to you also."[3]

The voice of Ramakrishna had the force of confidence. Narendra mentally accepted Ramakrishna as his Guru, surrendered his freedom to him and started his *sadhana* under his guidance.

Shortly afterwards, his father passed away as a result of heart ailment. His deaih came as a terrible shock to Narendra. Vishwanath had earned a lot of money, but he spent much more than what he earned. Soon after his death, Narendra was besieged by his creditors. Far from being able to repay the debts. Narendra found it difficult even to provide food to the six or seven members of the family. Those who had till now lived in luxury, were now faced with starvation. For the first time Narendra experienced poverty. Narendra was the eldest in his family, therefore, the burden of providing for the family fell on his shoulders. Narendra has given a detailed account of his mental condition at that time and of how he had to run about. Romain Rolland quotes Narendra as follows:

"I almost died of hunger. Barefoot I wandered from office to office, repulsed by all. This was my first contact with realities of life. I discovered that it had no room for the weak, the poor, the deserted. Those who, in

---

3. Satyendranath Mazumdar, *Vivekananda Charit*, pp. 93-94.

the past, would have been proud to help me, turned away their faces, although they possessed the means to do so. The world seemed to me the creation of a devil. One sultry day, when I could hardly stand on my feet. I sat down in the shade of a monument. Several friends were there, and one began to sing a hymn about the abundant grace of God. It was like a blow deliberately aimed at my head. I thought of the pitiable condition of my mother and brothers, and cried, 'Stop singing that song! Such fantasies may sound pleasant in the ears of those who are born with a silver spoon in their mouth, and whose parents are not dying of hunger at home. Oh yes, there was a time when I, too, thought like that. But now when I am faced with all the cruelty of life, it rings in my ears like mockery.' My friend was hurt. He could not make allowance for my terrible distress. More than once, when I saw that there was not enough food to go round at home, I went out telling my mother that I had been invited elsewhere, and I fasted. My affluent friends sometimes asked me to go to their houses to sing, but practically not a single one of them showed any curiosity about my misfortunes; and I kept these to myself."[4]

Narendra's character-building had been influenced the most by his mother. She was a lady of religious inclinations. Even her faith was shaken during this grave crisis. One morning, when Narendra was sitting in his bed and praying, his mother got annoyed and shouted. 'Shut up, boy. From your childhood you have done nothing but chanting the name of God! It is God who has done all this to us.' These words of his mother tore at his heart. He started thinking—is God really there? If He is really there, why does He not listen to all the prayers that I offer to him? Why is there so much evil in the world of Shiva? He was

---

4. Romain Rolland, *Ramakrishna*, p. 262.

reminded of the words of Ishwarchandra Vidyasagar—'If God is really merciful and benevolent, then why should lakhs of people have died in the famine without food?'

His heart was filled with a strong feeling of rebellion against God and he started thinking—if there is God, it is useless to invoke Him, because it will bring no relief.

Narendra was fearless and courageous. It was against his nature to hide his feelings. He started arguing before the people his belief against the existence of God. The result was that Narendra not only earned the notoriety of being anti-God, he was further maligned by people who gave exaggerated accounts of his falling in the company of wicked people, of consuming liquor and possessing a bad moral character. This untruth made Narendra more adamant and he started saying publicly and with pride, 'Some one drinks wine or goes to a prostitute in order to forget his sufferings for a while, I do not consider it evil. The day I come to believe that I can forget my sorrows by such methods, I shall also not hesitate from taking recourse to such conduct.'

Distorted accounts of Narendra's conduct reached the ears of the disciples and devotees of Ramakrishna. In the words of Narendra himself :

"Some came to see me with a view to ascertaining the real state I was in and they let me know that they were ready to believe something at least, if not all, of what they had heard. On knowing that they could regard me so low, I became terribly wounded at heart and proved that it was a great weakness to believe in God for fear of being punished. And quoting Hume, Mill, Bain, Comte and other Western philosophers, I started a fierce argument with them to prove that there was no evidence of the existence of God. Consequently, they went away, as I came to know afterwards, far more convinced of my fall than ever before. I was happy to know that the Master would hear of it from them and would perhaps believe it too. The moment this thought crossed my mind, my heart was filled with a tragic, wounded feeling. I came to the conclusion that there was no harm if he did so, inasmuch as people's opinions, good or bad, were worth so little. Later, however, I was surprised to hear that the Master had heard of it all from them, but had not expressed himself either way at first; but when afterwards Bhabanath wept and said to him, "Sir, it was beyond even our dream that, such would be Narendra's lot," he excitedly said, "Silence! you fellows! Mother has told me, he can never be such. If you mention it again, I will not be able to put up with your presence."[5]

Narendra cared little for others' criticism or praise. Summer came and went by, followed by rains. He failed to get a job in spite of his hunting for it at every possible place. At last he came to the conclusion that he was not born to earn and live like a common man; that he would also have to become a sanyasin like his grandfather. He even fixed the day when he would renounce the world. But on that very day Ramakrishna visited a house close by. Narendra went to see him and he insisted on Narendra accompanying him to Dakshineshwar. In the words of Narendra,

"At Dakshineshwar I was sitting in a room along with others. Just then the Master went into ecstasy looking at me, and all of a sudden he came to me. He caught hold of me with affection and, with tears rolling down, he started singing the following song,

'I am afraid of speaking out to you and equally afraid of not speaking. I have a doubt lest I should lose you.'

"For long I kept back the urge of the strong emotions of my mind, but could no more check their force. My breast, too, was flooded with tears like that of the

5. Saradanand, Sri Ramakrishna: The Great Master, p. 805.

Master. I was quite sure that the Master knew everything. Others were astonished to see that behaviour of ours. Some asked the Master the reason for this after he came back to the normal state. He smiled and answered, 'It is something between ourselves.' Afterwards, sending away all others, he called me at night and said, 'I know, you have come to the world for Mother's work. You can never live a worldly life. But remain in your family for my sake as long as I live. Saying so, the Master immediately began shedding tears again with his voice chocked with emotion."[6]

From Dakshineshwar, Narendra went back home. The worry to make a living again started nagging him. He started earning a little by working at an attorney's office and translating books. But his earnings were not sufficient to support the big family. Worried on this account, Narendra went to Dakshineshwar and insisted on the Master to pray to the Mother for giving relief to his brothers from their sufferings. The Master told him, 'I have already prayed to Mother and requested her to put an end to the sufferings of Narendra. But Mother does not listen to me, as you have no faith in her. Now listen to me. Today it is Tuesday. If you go to the Kali temple tonight, Mother will grant you whatever you ask for. My Mother is the supreme spirit and the *Shakti* of Brahman Himself. There is nothing that she cannot do, if she pleases.'

At the insistence of Ramakrishna, Narendra went to the Kali temple not once, but again and again. But not once could he bring himself upto asking for a boon for his selfish ends. Everytime he entered the temple he felt ashamed of going to the Mother to ask for something for himself. He felt he was being so mean and foolish. In the end, full of shame, he bowed to the Mother and said, 'I ask for

---

6. Saradananda, *Sri Ramakrishna: The Great Master,* p. 806.

nothing else, Mother. Grant me only the boon of knowledge and your devotion.'

One of the disciples of Ramakrishna, Tarapada Ghosh, has given an account of what followed:

"One day at noon I came to Dakshineshwar and saw the Master sitting alone in his room and Narendra sleeping on one side, outside the room. The Master's face was beaming with delight. No sooner had I approached and bowed down to him, he pointed to Narendra and said, 'Look here, that boy is very good; his name is Narendra; he had not accepted the divine Mother before, it was only last night that he did. He was in straitened circumstances. I, therefore, advised him to ask Mother for money; he, however, could not ask her for it; he said he felt ashamed. Coming back from the temple, he asked me to teach him a song addressed to Mother. He sang that song the whole night. So, he is sleeping now (smiling with joy). Narendra has accepted Kali; it is very good, is that not so?' Seeing that he was happy like a child on account of that, I said, 'Yes, Sir, it is very good.' A little afterwards, he smiled and said again, 'Narendra has accepted Mother; it is very good; what do you say?' He thus expressed his joy, saying it over and over again.

"When Narendra awoke, he came and sat beside the Master in the room at about four in the afternoon. It seemed that Narendra would now take leave of him and return to Calcutta. But the Master entered into ecstasy as soon as he saw him, and touching Narendra's body with that of his, sat almost on his lap, saying, 'What I see is that this (his body) I am and this (Narendra's body) too, I am. Truly I say, I see no difference. Just as the water of the Ganges seems to be divided into two parts when a stick is placed in it, but actually there are no divisions; one whole mass of water exists; so it is here. Do you understand, what is there except Mother?'

"We continued talking till it was eight o'clock. Seeing that the Master was, to some extent, his normal self, Narendra and I took his leave and returned to Calcutta on foot. Afterwards on many occasions we heard Narendra say, 'Ever since our first meeting, it was Master alone, and no one else, not even my own mother and brothers, who always had uniform faith in me. That faith and that love of his bound me to him for ever. It was the Master alone who knew how to love and he did love; while others of the world but feign love for the sake of their self-interest'."[7]

Narendra, who earlier hated idol-worship, ultimately put his faith in idol-worship. It was a case of love prevailing over reason. Later on, as Vivekananda, he wrote a letter to Miss Mary Hale from Los Angeles on 18th June, 1900:

Kali worship is not a necessary step in any religion. The Upanishads teach us all that there is of religion. Kali worship is my special fad, you never heard me preach it, or read of my preaching it in India. I only preach what is good for universal humanity. If there is any curious method which applies entirely to me, I keep it a secret and there it ends. I must not explain to you what Kali worship is, as I never taught it to anybody.[8]

In his teachings, he only attached importance to principles, as is clear from his letter of 14th April, 1896 written from New York to Swami Trigunatitananda:

That Ramakrishna Paramahansa is God, that sort of thing has no go in countries like this.... That will make our movement a little sect. You should keep aloof from

7. Saradananda, *Sri Ramakrishna: The Great Master*, p. 809.
8. *Complete Works of Vivekananda*, Vol. III, p. 522.

such an attempt. At the same time' if people worship him as God, no harm. Neither encourage nor discourage them. The masses will always have the person; the higher ones, the principles, we want both. But principles are universal, not persons. Therefore stick to the principles he taught—People think whatever they like of his person.[9]

Writing a long letter to his fellow disciples from England on 27th April 1896, he, further elucidated the principles:

About doctrines and so forth I have only to say this: if anyone accepts Paramahansa Dev as *avatar* etc., it is all right; if he does not do so, it is just the same. The truth about it is that in point of character, Paramahansa Dev beats all previous records, and as regards teaching, he was more liberal, more original, and more progressive than all his predecessors. In other words, the older teachers were rather one-sided, while the teaching of this new incarnation or teacher is that the best point of yoga, devotion, knowledge, and work must be combined now so as to form a new society...the older ones were no doubt good, but this is the new religion of this age—the synthesis of yoga, knowledge, devotion to all, down to the very lowest, without distinction of age or sex. The previous incarnations were all right, but they have been synthesised in the person of Ramakrishna.[10]

Now the question arises, if God takes the form of an incarnation, in what sense can one incarnation be said to be more progressive than a previous one? Vivekananda himself replied to this question. He told one of his disciples once:

---

9. *Ibid.* Vol. IV, p. 324.
10. *Ibid.* Vol. IV, p. 493.

The people may call a Guru an avatar, they may have any idea of him they like. But incarnations of God are not born anywhere and everywhere and at all seasons. At Dacca itself I heard there were three or four *avatars*.[11]

In fact, Vivekananda understands an *avatar* to be a teacher. It is true that one teacher is followed by another who is more progressive. They have contributed to the progress of thought whether about the spiritual or the material world. About his Guru, Ramakrishna, he says:

Ramakrishna used to consider himself as an incarnation in the ordinary sense of the term, though I could not understand it. I used to say that he was Brahma in the Vedantic sense; but just before his passing away, when he was finding it difficult to breathe, as I was cogitating in my mind whether he would even in that state of pain, claim to be an incarnation, he said to me: 'He who was Rama and Krishna, has now actually become but not in your Vedantic sense.'[12]

Before we proceed further with the story of Narendra, let us know Vivekananda's views about God realisation, so as not to leave room for any doubt. He said:

"If you ask me, 'Is there any God?' and I say 'Yes,' you immediately ask my grounds for saying so, and poor me has to exercise all his powers to provide you with some reason. If you had come to Christ and said, 'Is there any God?' he would have said, 'Yes' and if you had asked, 'Is there any proof?' He would have replied, 'Behold the Lord is before you.' And thus, you see, it is a direct perception, and not at all ratiocination of reason."[13]

---

11. *Ibid*, Vol. VII, p. 411.
12. *Ibid*, Vol. VII. p. 411.
13. *Ibid*. Vol. IV, p.125.

He also says:

These great teachers are the living gods on earth. Whom else should we worship? I try to get an idea of God in my mind, and I find what a false little thing I conceive, it would be a sin to worship that God. I open my eyes and look at the actual life of the great ones of the earth. They are higher than any conception of God that I could form.[14]

According to the Vedantic theory every man is essentially a soul and can, therefore, call himself God. We shall analyse this theory in the chapter entitled 'Spiritual Advaitism versus Material Advaitism.' As every theory takes a concrete shape in the lives of individuals, as such, the life story of Narendra, i.e., Vivekananda, is a proper medium for understanding this theory. We, therefore, proceed with the story of his life.

After sometime, a branch of the Metropolitan School was opened in the Champatala locality. Narendra was appointed the Headmaster of this school on the recommendation of Ishwarchandra Vidyasagar. In this way, the problem of providing for the family was solved.

During this period of adversity, some of his relatives had given a lot of trouble to Narendra and the members of his family. They had taken possession of Narendra's ancestral house by fraudulent means. Narendra, along with his mother and brothers, had to seek shelter in his maternal grandmother's house. Narendra had to fight a legal battle with his relatives, and the case went upto the High Court, before he could get back the possession of the house.

All the disciples of Ramakrishna had come to him by 1884. He was warning them away from attachment to sex, wealth and the pleasures of life and was guiding them towards the path of devotion. One day Ramakrishna was sitting surrounded by his disciples. Narendra was also

---

14. *Ibid*, p.124.

present. While they were talking about sundry matters in a jovial mood, they started talking about religion. Ramakrishna told them that the essence of religion was devotion to God's name, compassion for living beings and worship according to the Vaishnava traditions. He further elaborated the point by saying that one should show compassion for living beings believing that all creation belongs to Shiva who is the supreme being. After saying this, he went into ecstasy and started mumbling, 'Who art thou to show compassion to living beings, thyself being a mere insect. It is not compassion that thou shouldst show them. Rather, thou shouldst serve them thinking them to be none other than the Lord Himself.'

Although these words, spoken in ecstasy, were heard by all the disciples, only Narendra among them could understand the hidden meaning. Coming out of the room, he said to Sivananda: 'Today, I have heard a great truth spoken. I shall be announcing this living truth before all in the world.' He further elaborated by saying, 'From whatever has been said by the Master in ecstasy today, I have learnt that Vedanta can be brought into the home. The first thing that we should understand is that it is God alone, who is present before us in the form of living beings and all creation. Therefore, serving God in the form of living- beings is devotion of the highest order.'

Subsequently, he presented this idea in the following words in a letter written to Saratchandra on 3rd July, 1897:

> Our principle, therefore, should be love and not compassion. The application of the word compassion even to Shiva seems to be rash and vain.[15]

In those days Narendra was following the path of *sadhana* as shown by the Paramahansa. Sometimes he would sit in meditation under the trees for days and nights. Ramakrishna, noticing the devotion with which he was

_____

15. *Ibid*. Vol. V, p. 103.

practising sadhana, called him one day and said to him, 'Look, I achieved eight kinds of perfection through hard sadhana. I have not ever been able to make use of any of them. I pass them on to you. You will find them of use in future.'

Narendra asked, 'Master, will they be of any help in realising God?'

Ramakrishna replied, 'No, that may not happen. But no earthly desire will remain unfulfilled.'

To this Narendra replied unhesitatingly, 'Sir, in that case I don't need them.'

In 1885, Ramakrishna was afflicted with cancer of the throat. He was being treated by Dr. Mahendralal Sircar. But the disease showed no signs of abating and became more acute. He was kept first in a house in Kolkata, then in a garden house in Kashipur. Narendra gave up his teaching job in the month of August and started living in the Kashipur house along with other disciples. Apart from nursing his Guru, he utilised his time in studying works such as the Upanishads, *Ashtavakra Samhita, Panchadashi, Viveka Chudamani*, etc. As Narendra had advanced a lot in his practice of meditation, there was a strong desire in his heart to be able to enter into Nirvikalpa samadhi. He knew that the Paramahansa did not want him to try for such a samadhi, yet he gathered courage one day and approached the Master with this wish.

Ramakrishna cast an affectionate look at him and asked, 'Narendra, what do you want?'

Narendra replied, 'Master, I want that I should remain immersed in the sea of true happiness through Nirvikalpa samadhi like Shukdeva.'

Ramakrishna, though he loved Narendra the most, got angry and said, 'Do you not feel ashamed of saying this again and again? The time will come when you will grow, and like a banyan tree, give cover of peace to others. On the contrary, today you are worried only about your own salvation. Has the standard of your ideal fallen so low?'

Tears welled up in Narendra's eyes and he said with great persuasion, 'I can have no peace of mind unless I can achieve Nirvikalpa samadhi and I shall not be able to do anything else without this.

'It is not of your own volition that you will do those things. Mother will hold you by the neck to do all that. You may not willingly do it, but your bones will do it.'

However, he could not refuse the request of Narendra altogether. In the end he said, 'All right, go. You shall achieve Nirvikalpa samadhi.'

One evervmg, while sitting for meditation, Narendra entered into Nirvikalpa *samadhi* all of a sudden. When the other disciples saw him in that state, they thought he was dead. They ran to Ramakrishna. But Ramakrishna remained quiet on hearing about his condition. After some time, Narendra was back to his normal self. His face was now glowing with happiness. He came to Ramakrishna and bowed before him. Ramakrishna said, 'This is enough for now. It is all locked and the key will be with Mother. The lock will be opened again when you have finished your work.'

Thereafter, devotional songs continued for days and nights. Narendra continued singing, with great emotion, songs about the doings of Lord Krishna and Sita. Ramakrishna was praying to Goddess Kali: 'Mother, hide his realisation of Advaita under the shadow of your *maya*. I have yet to get him do many things.'

A bond of affection had bound the twelve disciples who had left their homes and were staying at Kashipur to nurse their Master. One day in that house of Kashipur, The Ramakrishna Sangha was founded. Ramakrishna adorned the young disciples with saffron clothes and initiated them to the order of *sanyasins*. He addressed their leader Narendra and asked: 'Will all of you be able to put aside your pride and go to the streets with a begging bowl?'

Vivekananda as a Wandering Monk

In Kashmir

(Left to right) : Miss MacLeod, Mrs. Ole Bull, Swami Vivekananda, Sister Nivedita

At Shillong, 1901

In London, May 1896

All of them at once set out to beg for alms. In the garb of sanyasins, they went begging in the streets of Kolkata, a city where they had been born and where they had started their education with rosy dreams about the future. All that they got in alms, they brought and placed before the Master and accepted the *prasad* given by him. That day, there was no limit to the joy of Ramakrishna.

Though Ramakrishna felt better for a while, yet later his condition continued to deteriorate. Romain Rolland has written:

> Naren directed their activities and their prayers. They begged the Master to join them in praying for his recovery, and the visit of a Pandit, who shared their faith, gave them an opportunity to renew their entreaties. 'The Scriptures,' said the Pandit to Ramakrishna, 'declare that saints like you can cure themselves by their will-power.'

> Ramakrishna replied, 'My mind has been given to God once and for all. Would you have me ask it back?'

> His disciples reproached him for not wishing to be restored to health.

> 'Do you think my sufferings are voluntary? I wish to recover, but that depends on the Mother.'

> 'Then pray to Her.'

> 'It is easy for you to say that, but I cannot speak these words,' said the Master sweetly 'I will try what I can do.'

> They left him alone for several hours. When they returned, the Master said, 'I said to Her, "Mother, I can eat nothing because of my suffering. Make it possible for me to eat a little.' She pointed out to me of you all and said, 'What! thou canst eat through all these

mouths!' I was ashamed and could not utter another word.

Several days later he said: 'My teaching is almost finished. I cannot instruct people any longer; for I see the whole world is filled with the Lord. So I ask myself, Whom can I teach'?"[16]

The great man gave up his mortal frame on Sunday, the 15th August, 1886.

Ramakrishna had passed on all his knowledge and his mantle to Vivekananda as his worthy successor. We shall see a little later how Vivekananda added to this inheritance. Romain Rolland has described the role that Ramakrishna played in grooming Narendra to become Vivekananda. He says:

The torrent forming the remarkable destiny of Vivekananda would have been lost in the bowels of the earth, if Ramakrishna's glance had not, as with one blow of an axe, split the rock barring its course, so that, through the breach thus made, the river of his soul could flow.[17]

Ramakrishna was afraid that if Narendra was not equipped with the knowledge of Vedanta, his talent would remain one-sided and that he might use such talent in founding his own religion or sect.

In other words, had Narendra not come into contact with Ramakrishna Paramahansa, perhaps the harmony between the past and the present forms of *Dvaita*, *Vishishtadvaita* and *Advaita* and between the past and the future would not have developed in his mind. But what was to be, had to be. As we shall see, the synthesis of the historical past with historical future, was inevitable.

---

16. Romain Rolland, *Ramakrishna*, pp. 265-66.
17. *Ibid*, p. 219.

4

UNDERSTANDING INDIA

"Our greatest national sin is the disregard of the masses."
                                                    -Vivekananda

Narendra was now the leader of the Ramakrishna Sangh. He was soon to become famous as Vivekananda. While departing from this world, Ramakrishna Paramahansa had entrusted his disciples to the care of Narendra. He had told him: 'Take care of these boys.'

Very soon, after the death of their Guru, the boys had to vacate the garden-house of Kashipur. There were two kinds of people among the disciples of Ramakrishna. The first included those who had entered the monastic order and had become sanyasins. They were twelve in number, Narendra being one of them. The second included those who were householders. Now the question arose: where were the young sanyasins to be lodged. For this purpose, Surendranath rented a house in the Baranagar locality. The ground floor of this building was not habitable. Therefore, the sanyasins started living in the three rooms on the upper floor. Surendranath also volunteered to arrange for their food and other necessities. The young sanyasins were satisfied with whatever they got. They never spoke to Surendranath about their needs. They had no utensils or plates. They were happy to eat the frugal meals consisting of rice and boiled vegetables using leaves as plates. Despite all this, they regularly practised meditation, worship and

Probably at Belgaum, October 1892

chanting. They uséd to collect quite a crowd whenever they sang devotional songs with fervour.

Quite often, householder devotees also visited this monastery at Baranagar. They used to discuss matters relating to religion with their fellow disciples and talked to them about Sri Ramakrishna. Apart from them, lay persons and strangers would also come there out of curiosity. They would argue with the young sanyasins and tried to test them. There were some among such people who used to make fun of the sanyasins and would criticise them in a crude manner. The parents of young sanyasins also came to persuade them to return home. They tried to convince them about the superiority of the life of a householder and the bright future that awaited them there. Vivekananda described the situation in a speech that he once made about his life and his aims. He said:

> We had no friends who would listen to the few boys, with their crank notions! Nobody. At least in India, boys are nobodies. Just think of it—a dozen boys, telling people of sublime ideas, saying they are determined to work these ideas out in life. Why? Everybody laughed. From laughter, it became serious, then it became persecution.... And the more we were derided, the more determined we became.[1]

As the family fortunes continued to be in bad shape, Vivekananda continued to live at his house although he passed most of the time in the monastery and looked after the education of his fellow disciples. Litigation about the house had still not concluded. His relations, the opposite party, had filed an appeal. The appeal was yet to be decided. All this necessitated Vivekananda's living at home. Moreover, he was the only bread-winner in the family. Some other sanyasins also, following the example of Vivekananda, returned to their homes and started preparing for the examinations. The danger of the monastery breaking up loomed large. Narendra was shaken by the thought that, with the breaking up of the monastery, he will not be able to accomplish the task that Sri Ramakrishna had entrusted to him. Indeed, if the Sangh broke up, Ramakrishna's views would scatter. He says: 'With that belief came the realisation that it is better that a few persons suffer than that such ideas should die out of the world.' He felt that even if his mother and brothers died, it was a sacrifice that had to be made as nothing great could ever be achieved without making sacrifices. One had to carve out one's heart, as it were, and offer it, dripping with blood, at the altar of worship.

---

1. *Complete Works of Vivekananda*, Vol. VIII, p. 80.

Although they knew what had to be done in that situation, yet it was difficult for them to do what was required to be done. Man is bound by numerous influences—it is not possible to break all the bonds at one go. Even Vivekananda, with his robust physique, could not break them. However, he started living in the monastery permanently from December 1886; now aged 23-24 years. He had banished all family problems from his mind.

The doubts that others had started entertaining about Vivekananda, disappeared after he started living in the monastery at Baranagar. The other young sanyasins, who had started living with their families, also returned to the monastery. All of them, under active supervision of Vivekananda devoted themselves wholly to the study of the Vedas, Puranas, and Bhagwat, etc., and the practice of meditation, chanting and living the hard and austere life of a sanyasin. Vivekananda used to wake them up early in the morning calling them, 'Children of bliss.' He used to make them sit with him and read out to them sometimes from the Gita and sometimes from a book on Christ by Thomas A. Kempis. Romain Rolland says:

He made this period of solitude a school of severe education and of higher spiritual bearing. The superiority of his genius and his knowledge had, from the very beginning, given him a tacit but definite procedure over his companions, although many of them were older than he....

Naren resolutely undertook the conduct of the young seminary and did not permit it to indulge in idle worship. He kept its members ever on the alert, he kept their minds constantly active; he read them the great books of human thought; he explained to them the evolution of the universal mind; he forced them to dry but impassioned discussion of all the great philosophical and religious problems; he led them indefatigably towards the wide horizons of boundless truth, which surpass all the limits of schools and races, and embrace and unify of all specific truths.[2]

A year and a half passed in this way. But soon a new tendency among the sanyasins raised its head. For how long could the young sanyasins, who were full of zeal and fired with curiosity, engage themselves in colourless debates and the study of lifeless books. Although the learning of books is an essential part of one's education, yet books contain only the compilation of human experience. The young sanyasins were dying to go out of the confines of the monastery and acquire knowledge from personal experience which, to them appeared more appealing. Their Guru, Ramakrishna Paramahansa, had read no books. He had acquired all his knowledge about the Shastras and about our culture by the word of mouth and had imparted this knowledge to his devotees by the word of mouth in his own lively and metaphorical language. How could his disciples limit themselves to bookish knowledge reducing themselves to lifeless individuals without any ideal? So two of the sanyasins quietly slipped out and went on a pilgrimage. Then one day, when Vivekananda had gone to Kolkata on some errand, one of the young sanyasins named Saradaprasanna (later known as Swami Trigunatitananda) secretly left the monastery. This made Vivekananda very restless. Full of anxiety, he said to Rakhal, 'Why did you let him go? Look, I find myself in a precarious situation. I came here after breaking all the bonds of the world. But here also I made for myself another world full of *maya*. My heart is full of anxiety for this boy.'

Saradaprasanna had left behind a letter which someone brought to Vivekananda. He had written: 'I am going to Vrindavan on foot. It has become impossible for me to live here. Who knows when my mind would change? I often dream of my parents, my home and my relatives. I am

---

2. Romain Rolland, *Vivekananda*, p. 12.

being tempted by maya. I have suffered a lot, so much so that once or twice I was compelled to go home to meet my family members. It would not be proper to continue here any more. There is no alternative to my going away to some other country to save myself from the clutches of maya.'

On reading the letter, Vivekananda received a great shock, as if a chain had been broken. He thought: 'All these boys are wanting to go out on pilgrimage. In this way the monastery will close down one day. Let it be so. Who am I to keep them chained here?' He had himself been bitten for the last two years by the same wanderlust. Why was he now hesitating to break this chain? It bound him to the monastery when he had already broken one chain that had bound him to the world? He was finding himself chained to the monastery by the bonds of maya. So he also decided to break this bond in spite of all the persuasions of his fellow-disciples. After obtaining the blessings of Mother (Ramakrishna's widow Saradamani), he also left on a pilgrimage.

It was, however, decided that a part of the group would always remain at the monastery. Shashi (Swami Ramakrishnananda) was the one amongst them who never left the monastery. He was the faithful guardian of the monastery, its immobile axis. Other fellow-disciples would leave and would return after their wanderings to the nest which was guarded by Shashi.

It was in 1888 that Vivekananda set out from Baranagar as a *parivrajaka*—a wandering monk. While passing through Bihar and Uttar Pradesh, he reached Kashi, the main centre of pilgrimage. He decided to spend some time there and, therefore, started living in the Dwarkadas Ashram. He devoted himself to a daily routine of meditation, worship and discussion on the Shastras. One day, someone introduced him to Pandit Bhudeva Mukhopadhyaya. Bhudeva was so captivated by the erudition of Vivekananda that he confided to that person his belief that Vivekananda would be a great man one day, as he possessed such deep insight at such a young age.

At Varanasi, in those days Swami Bhaskarananda was greatly valued for his erudition. One day Vivekananda visited his Ashram. Swami Bhaskarananda was sitting surrounded by his devotees and disciples. He gave a sermon to Vivekananda on the ideal of life as a sanyasin and asserted that no one had ever been able to wholly give up the temptations of wealth and sex. Vivekananda contradicted him by saying, 'Sir, there are several sanyasins who are completely free from the temptations of sex and wealth.' He cited the example of Ramakrishna Paramahansa. Bhaskarananda laughed and said to him: 'You are still a child. At this age you would not understand the matter.' However, when he started criticising the character of Ramakrishna, Vivekananda firmly and fearlessly contradicted him. Bhaskarananda was held in great awe by people, so much so that even the Rajas and Maharajas and great scholars considered it a privilege to be able to touch his feet. He was taken aback by the audacity and arguments of the young sanyasin, Vivekananda. Bhaskarananda was a large-hearted sanyasin. He praised Vivekananda in the presence of his disciples and devotees, saying, 'He is blessed by Saraswati in his speech. His heart is illumined by knowledge.' However, Vivekananda left the place, as he could not tolerate disrespect being shown to his Guru.

After spending some days at Kashi, Vivekananda returned to the monastery at Baranagar. Satyendranath Mazumdar has written:

Varanasi is the heart of the Hindu India. Here people from Madras, Punjab, Bengal, Gujarat, Maharashtra, United Provinces, etc., gather together in the temple of Lord Vishwanath, impelled by one common sentiment despite the disparity in their lifestyles and language. The city of Kashi abounds in people who have strayed from the path of doing good to others, those who are mindlessly observing rituals for outward show. Living even amongst such people, Vivekananda absorbed the great tradition of our religion that has been preserved through the ages. Hence we find him returning to the monastery at Baranagar and encouraging his fellow disciples to take upon themselves the task of publicising that great heritage. He exhorted them to see India, to understand it and to find out what was the pain, what was the void that was being felt by lakhs of its men and women in various stages of life that was drawing them to a great but unfulfilled greed. To this end he exhorted them not only to give up self interest, but also their entire self, even their desire for salvation.[3]

When Vivekananda returned to Kashi again, he was introduced by his fellow disciple, Akhawandra, to Prabhdadas Mitra. Prabhdadas Mitra was a great scholar of Sanskrit language, literature and the Vedantic philosophy. Vivekananda was highly impressed by the erudition of Prabhdadas and developed a feeling of great respect for him. This can be judged from the letter written to him from Baranagar by Vivekananda on 17th August, 1889:

> You have expressed embarrassment in your last letter on being addressed reverentially. But the blame attaches not to me but to your own excellent qualities. I had written in one letter before that, from the way I feel attracted by your lofty virtues, it seems we had some affinity from previous births. I make no distinction between a householder and a sanyasin in this respect. For all time my head will bow low in reverence whenever I see greatness, goodness of heart and peace. My prayer is that, among the many people embracing sanyasa nowadays, greedy of honour, posing

---

3. Satyendranath Mazumdar, *Vivekananda Charit*, p. 146.

renunciation for the sake of and fallen off from the ideal on both sides, may at least one in a lakh become an enlightened soul like you! Those Brahmin fellow-disciples of mine who have heard of your noble virtues send you their respectful salutations.[4]

After this, whenever Swami Vivekananda had any doubt or problem about the Shastras, he always sought the guidance of Prabhdadas. However, eight years later, on 30th May, 1897, he wrote to him from Almora:

Though for a long time I had no direct correspondence with you, yet I have often been receiving from others almost all the news about you. Sometime ago you kindly sent me to England a copy of a translation of the Gita. The cover only bore a line of your handwriting. The few words in acknowledgement of this gift, I am told, raised doubts in your mind about my old affection towards you.

Please know these doubts to be groundless. The reason for that laconic acknowledgement is that I was given to see, during four or five years, only that one line of your handwriting on the cover of an English Gita, from which fact I thought: when you have no leisure to write more, would you have leisure enough to read much? Secondly, I learnt, you were particularly the friend of white-skinned missionaries of the Hindu religion and the roguish, black natives were repelling! There was apprehension in my mind on that score. Thirdly, I am a Mlechchha, *Shudra*, and so forth; I eat anything and everything, and with anybody and everybody—and that too in public, both abroad and in India. Besides, my views have gone quite perverse. I visualise only one attributeless, absolute Brahman, I can see in some particular individuals the special manifestations of that Brahman. If such individuals are

---

4. *Complete Works of Vivekananda,* Vol. VII. p. 411.

called by the name of God, I can understand. But my mind does not feel inclined towards intellectual theorisings such as this postulated creator and the like.[5]

When intellectual differences occur, old bonds are bound to weaken. It is wiser to break such bonds and follow the chosen path.

In August 1888, Swami Vivekananda left Kashi for a pilgrimage. After passing through many places in north India, he reached Ayodhya situated on the banks of river Saryu. In this city his childhood memories were revived. He was greatly attached to the story of Ramayana which he had heard from his mother and Mahavira was his hero. At Ayodhya he passed his days in the company of Ramayat sanyasins; then he walked through Lucknow and Agra towards Vrindavan.

At Agra and Fatehpur Sikri, he had a look at the Mughal architecture. On the way to Vrindavan he saw a man smoking a pipe on the roadside. He felt the desire to have a puff and requested the man to let him share a smoke and extended his hand for the pipe. But the man, bound by custom, refused saying, 'Sir, I am a *bhangi* by caste.' On hearing him say that he was a bhangi or *mehtar* by caste, Vivekananda, in obedience to the custom inherited by him from birth, withdrew his hand and hastily moved on. He had hardly gone a few steps when he was overwhelmed with a feeling of self-reproach. He asked hismself, 'Why this hatred for a mehtar when you have entered sanyasa after relinquishing your caste, your lineage and dignity? Why this feeling of caste superiority? He immediately retraced his steps and came back to that man. He made him fill up the pipe with tobacco and had a smoke with great love and relish. After that, through his journeys, he passed many nights in the huts of the low caste bhangis and chamars and banished all thoughts of untouchability from his mind.

---

5. *Ibid.* Vol. VI, p. 393.

From Vrindavan he came to Hathras where he had a chance meeting with the young railway station master Saratchandra Gupta. Sarat took him to his house and Vivekananda spent a few days with the family of Sarat. When the time came for him to depart, Sarat was not prepared to part company with him. After seeking his father's permission, he became a sanyasi in and followed Vivekananda with a staff and a begging bowl in his hands. He was the first disciple of Vivekananda whom he named Swami Sadananda after initiating him into the order of the monks. Later on, on being called by his Guru, Swami Sadananda went to America and helped him in the task of propagating the Vedantic philosophy.

The Guru and the disciple set out together on their journey. However, Sadananda was not used to the hard life of a sanyasin and the rigours of the journey, and fell ill. Vivekananda carried him on his shoulders and wandered through the inhospitable terrain. Ultimately, he also fell ill and returned to Hathras along with his disciple. He was nursed back to health by the Gupta family and some enthusiastic young men. He came back to the monastery at Baranagar in August 1888. He was soon followed by Sadananda who joined the Ramakrishna Sangha.

For one year, Vivekananda stayed in the Baranagar monastery and at the house of Balram Basu in Kolkata. He spent the time in the study of Vedanta, the Grammar of Panini and the Shastras along with his fellow-disciples. During this period he wrote letters to Prabhdadas Mitra which shed light on his life, his work and his mental condition at that time. Prabhdadas had presented copies of Vedanta and 'Ashtadhyayi' to the sanyasins. Acknowledging receipt of these works, Vivekananda wrote to Prabhdadas on 19th November, 1888:

By sending your gift of the Vedanta, you have laid under life-long obligation not only myself, but also the whole group of Ramakrishna's sanyasins. They all bow to you in respect. It is not for my own sake alone, that I asked of you a copy of Panini's Grammar. A good deal of study, in fact, is given to Sanskrit scriptures in this Math. The Vedas may well be said to have fallen quite out of vogue in Bengal. Many here in this Math are conversant with Sanskrit and they have a mind to master the Samhita portions of the Vedas. They are of the opinion that what has to be done, must be done to a finish. So, believing that a full measure of proficiency in the Vedic language is impossible without first mastering Panini's Grammar, which is the best available for the purpose. A copy of the latter was felt to be a necessity. The grammatical work *Mugdhabodha* is superior in many respects to *Laghu Kaumudi*. You are yourself, however, a deeply learned man and are, therefore, the best judge in the matter. So, if you consider Panini's *Ashtadhyayi* to be the most suitable in our case, you will lay us under a debt of life-long gratitude by sending us the same (provided you feel it convenient and feel inclined). This Math is not wanting in men of perseverance, talent, and penetrative intellect.[6]

During these days, apart from the Vedas, Vivekananda made a deep study of the Upanishads and Shankara Bhashya. He continued to write to Prabhdadas Mitra to seek clarifications of doubts that arose in his mind. In his letter of the 17th August, 1889, he raised twelve questions out of which we quote three which throw light on Vivekananda's line of thinking:

If the Vedas are eternal, then what are the meanings and justification of such specifications as 'this for the age of Kali' and 'that for the age of Dwapar' and so forth? The same God who gave out the Vedas, became Buddha again to annul them; which of these

---

6. *Ibid.* Vol. V, p. 182.

dispensations is to be obeyed? Which of these remains authoritative, the earlier or the later one?

The Tantra says, in the Kaliyuga the Veda mantras are futile. So which behest of God, the Shiva, is to be followed?

Vyasa makes out in the Vedanta Sutras that it is wrong to worship the divine manifestation, Vasudeva, Sankarshana, etc., and again that very Vyasa expatiates on the great merits of that worship in the Bhagavata? Was this Vyasa a mad man?

On 13th December he wrote:

I have received the pamphlet written by you. A kind of scientific Advaitism has been spreading in Europe ever since the theory of conservation of energy was discovered, but all that is Parinamavada, evolution by real modification. It is good you have cleared the distinction between this and Shankar's Vivartavada (progressive manifestation by unreal superimposition). I can't appreciate your citing Spencer's parody on the German transcendentalists; he himself is fed much on their doles. It is doubtful whether your opponent, Gough, understands his Hegel sufficiently. Any way, your rejoinder is very pointed and unbeatable.

Again, he wrote on himself on 4th July:

But with me it is a different malady this time. I have not lost faith in benign providence—nor am ever going to lose it. My faith in scriptures is unshaken. But by the will of God, the last six or seven years of my life have been full of constant struggle with hindrances and obstacles of all sorts. I have been vouchsafed the ideal Shastras; I have seen the ideal man, and yet find myself unable to get on with anything to the end— this is my profound misery.

And particularly I see no chance of success while remaining near Calcutta. In Calcutta live my mother and two brothers. I am the eldest; the second is preparing for the Arts examination and the third is young.[7]

Referring to the poverty of the family and the litigation about the house he writes:

Living near Calcutta, I have to witness their adversity, and the quality of Rajas prevailing, my egotism sometimes develops into a form of desire that rises to plunge me into action; in such moments, a fierce struggle ensues in my mind. So I wrote that the state of my mind was terrible. Now their law-suit has come to an end. So bless me that, after a stay here in Calcutta for a few days more to settle matters, I may bid adieu to this place for ever.[8]

In the meantime, Vivekananda undertook short journeys. In February 1889 he visited Kamarpukur, the birth-place of Ramakrishna and Jairamabati, the birth-place of Mother Saradamani. While returning, he fell ill and was in bed for quite some time. In July he visited Simultala and towards the end of December, Vaidyanath and Allahabad. In 1890 he visited Ghazipur twice. This is important and of interest and needs to be narrated in some detail.

Vivekananda reached Ghazipur on 21st January, 1890. At this place, there was a famous Sadhu who used to live in a cave. His name was Pavhari Baba. Vivekananda was very anxious to meet the Sadhu. He, however, was not getting the opportunity to meet him. On 31st January he wrote to Prabhdadas Mitra:

It is so very difficult to meet Babaji. He does not step out of his home, and, when willing to speak at all, he just comes near the door to speak from inside.

I have come away with having just a view of his garden house with chimneys tapering above and encircled by

7. *Ibid.* Vol. VI, p. 175.
8. *Ibid*, p. 170.

high walls—no means of admittance within. People say there are cave-like rooms where he dwells, and he only knows what he does there, for nobody has had a peep. I had to come away one day sorely used up with waiting and waiting, but shall take my chance again.[9]

This is followed by letters of 4th and 7th February:

. . .through supreme good luck, I have obtained an interview with Babaji. A great sage indeed! It is very surprising that in this atheistic age also, a symbol of marvellous power born of Bhakti and yoga exists! I have sought refuge in his grace, and he has given me assurance—a thing very few may be fortunate enough to obtain. It is Babaji's wish that I stay on for some days here, and he would do me some good. So following this saint's bidding, I shall remain here for some time. No doubt, this will give much pleasure to you also. I don't mention them in a letter, but the incidents are wonderful indeed. I shall tell you when we meet. Unless one is face to face with such men, faith in the scriptures does not grow in all its real integrity.[10]

What was this strange fact, only Prabhdadas Mitra must have come to know. However, the next letter went on to say:

I was very happy. Babaji is a Vaishnava, the embodiment, so to speak, of yoga, *bhakti* and humility. His dwelling has walls on all sides with a few doors in them. Inside these walls, there is one long underground cave wherein he lays himself up in samadhi. He talks to others only when he comes out of the cave. Nobody knows what he eats, and so they call him Pavhari Baba (he who lives on air). Once he

---

9. *Ibid*. Vol. VI, p. 189.
10. *Ibid*. Vol. VI, p. 189.

did not come out for five years, and people thought that he had given up the body. Now again he is out, but this time he does not see people, and talks from behind the door. Such sweetness in speech I have never come across. He does not give a direct reply to questions but says, 'What does this servant know?' But as he talks, words come out of his mouth like fire-like luminaries. On my pressing him very much, he said, 'Favour me highly by staying here for some days.' But he never speaks in this way; so from this I understood he meant to reassure me; and whenever I insist, he asks me to stay on. So I wait in hope. He is a learned man no doubt, but nothing in him betrays this. He acts according to scriptures from the full moon day to the last day of the moon; sacrificial oblations go on. So it is sure, he is not retiring into the cave during this period. How can I ask his permission, for he never gives a direct reply; he goes on multiplying such expressions as 'this servant,' 'my fortune' and so on.[11]

Later Vivekananda also wrote a long article on Pavhari Baba which has been included in his Complete Works. In this article, he has described the figure and narrated the story of his death in these words:

In appearance he was tall and rather fleshy, had but one eye, and looked much younger than his real age. His voice was the sweetest we have ever heard. For the last ten years or more of his life, he had withdrawn himself entirely from the gaze of mankind. A few potatoes and a little butter were placed behind the door of his room, and sometimes during the night it was taken in when he was not in samadhi and was in the room on the ground floor. When inside his cave, he did not require even that. Thus, this silent life went

---

11. *Ibid*, p. 190.

on, witnessing the science of yoga, and a living example of purity, humility and love....

As we have said already, whenever smoke from inside became visible from outside, it indicated his coming out of samadhi. One day, this smoke smelled of burning flesh. The people around could not guess what was happening; but when the smell became overpowering, and the smoke was seen to rise up in volumes, they broke open the door, and found that the great yogi had offered himself as the last oblation to his sacrificial fire, and very soon a heap of ashes was all that remained of his body.

Let us remember the words of Kalidasa: 'Fools blame the actions of the great, because they are extraordinary and their reasons past the comprehension of ordinary mortals'.[12]

No one knows how many remarkable persons like him have been produced by our country. Whether we agree with them or not, no one can deny their strength of character and single-minded devotion. These are the men who have kept the lamp of knowledge burning with their life's blood as it were, who have protected this lamp from being extinguished by the storms that have raged. It is such people who have sustained, among the masses, a feeling of unwavering faith in the culture and traditions of this country.

Satyendranath Mazumdar has thrown some light on the relations of Baba and Vivekananda and on what the latter sought from the former:

As the relations between the two became intimate, Swamiji was charmed by the great sage Pavhari Baba. He thought to himself, "Why is it that I have not got any peace of mind in spite of having been favoured by Sri Ramakrishna so much? It is possible that I may

---

12. *Ibid.* Vol. IV, p. 294.

achieve peace of mind with the help of this person possessing the knowledge about Brahman.

Swamiji had heard that Pavhari Baba had achieved perfection through the practice of yoga. So he felt a desire to receive suitable instruction from him.

At dead of night, Swamiji got ready to go into the cave of Pavhari Baba. But as soon as the question of choosing between Ramakrishna and Pavhari Baba arose in his mind, all his enthusiasm subsided. He sat down on the earth with a heart full of turmoil and a mind full of doubts ... he raised his tearful eyes only to see a divine image appearing before him. It was the image of none other than the godman of Dakshineshwar who was the ideal of Vivekananda's life. Vivekananda continued sitting on the ground for an hour like a statue carved out of stone. The day dawned. He was wondering in his mind whether his having seen Sri Ramakrishna was not fiction and the manifestation of the weakness of his mind! So the next night he again got ready to go to Pavhari Baba. But on the next night also, the same effulgent image appeared before him. This happened not once or twice but continuously for 21 days. In the end he could no longer resist and fell to the ground writhing in agony saying, 'O my master Ramakrishna, I shall go to no other being. You alone are my master. I am your slave. Please pardon me for my mental weakness."[13]

Vivekananda had, in every sense, acknowledged Ramakrishna as his guru and no one could take the place of Ramakrishna in his heart. He wrote the following poem[14] later on-which was inspired by the above-mentioned incident:

'I indulge in childish pranks with you Master!
And sometimes, in a fit of anger

---

13. Satyendranath Mazumdar, Vivekananda Charit, pp. 161-62.
14. Translated from the Hindi version.

Try to run away from you.
But when night falls
I see you standing at the head of my bed
Mutely, with eyes full of tears
You look at my face.
Just then my mood changes.
I fall on your feet but I do not ask for pardon.
You show no anger.
I am your son.
Tell me, who else will tolerate such
    impertinence?
You are my Master, my soul-mate.
Sometimes I look and find—
You are I and I am you.

How demeaning the desire for peace to the agonised heart! Was it not escapism? How was it possible for Narendra, that is, Vivekananda, who was so dedicated and firm of dedication, to become so weak? He was reminded of the words of his Guru who had said, 'Your Nirvikalpa Samadhi has now been kept under lock and key and will be restored to you only after the completion of your work.'

Had his Guru not warned him against entertaining a feeling of superiority by thinking of showing compassion to living beings? Had the Guru not charged him to serve every living being as the image of the Lord? Had he not, after hearing these words of the Master, said, 'Today I have realised a great truth. I shall announce this living truth before the world.' How could he now go back on his words? If he also, in order to bring tranquillity to his troubled heart, shut himself up in a cave like Pavhari Baba and ultimately burn his body in the sacrificial fire, how would he be able to fulfil his earlier resolve of bringing the Vedanta of the forests into the homes and serving Lord Himself in the form of living beings?

Decidedly, the path of Pavhari Baba was not the path for Vivekananda. In the religious seminar that used to be held in Ghazipur on Sundays, he always talked about uplifting the country, the society and the nation, and personal tranquillity and liberation was never the goal of his life. Many a time, he had even asked Pavhari Baba the question as to why he did not come out of his cave to save the world. If the Baba did not come out of his cave, why should Vivekananda enter that cave? He returned from Ghazipur with his heart full of fire, which he expressed to Prabhdadas Mitra by telling him, 'I shall burst on the society like a bomb and the society will follow me.'

Vivekananda had now resolved to undertake a journey of the entire country from the Himalayas to Kanyakumari. He had also resolved not to return to the monastery before completing his journey a round the country. All the persuasion of his fellow disciples failed to deter him.

He set out on his journey in July 1890 accompanied by Akhandananda, another fellow-disciple. From Bhagalpur, he went to Devghar and from there to Kashi. As the Himalayas were beckoning him, he did not stay long at Kashi. He reached Almora, passing through Ayodhya, Nainital, Badrinath and Kedarnath. On getting the news of his arrival, Saradananda and Kripananda also joined him there. In this way most of the sanyasins of the Baranagar monastery left the monastery on pilgrimages. Vivekananda stayed at several places in the Himalayas for six to seven months and enjoyed the natural beauty of the mountains. Finally, he came down for his journey towards Kanyakumari. While he was staying in a garden in Meerut, several other fellow-disciples also joined him there one by one. The garden has now turned into a mini-monastery. They passed the days in meditation, singing of devotional songs, chanting of *mantras*, discussing Vedanta and Shastras and giving religious discourses to visitors. One day Vivekananda realised that he was again getting tied down to a routine after having broken all previous bonds. So he collected his fellow-disciples and told them of his resolve to proceed soon on a journey alone and forbade them to follow him.

In February 1891 he started on his journey alone. Romain Rolland has given an account of this journey in the following words:

"His itinerary led him through Rajputana, Alwar (February to March, 1891), Jaipur, Ajmer, Khetri, Ahmedabad and Kathiawar (end of September), Junagarh and Gujarat, Porbander (a stay of between eight and nine months), Dwarka, Palitana—the city of temples close to the Gulf of Cambay, the state of Baroda, Khandwa, Bombay, Poona, Belgaum (October, 1892), Bangalore in the state of Mysore, Cochin, Malabar, the state of Travancore, Trivandrum, Madura.... He travelled to the extreme point of the immense pyramid, where is the Benaras of southern India, Rameswaram of Ramayana, and beyond to Kanyakumari, the sanctuary of the Great Goddess (end of 1892).

From north to south the ancient land of India was full of gods; yet the unbroken chain of their countless arms formed only one God. He realised their unity of flesh and spirit. He realised it also in communion with the beings of all castes and all outcastes. And he taught them to realise it. He took the message of mutual understanding from one person to the other, to the sceptics; to the intellectuals obsessed with the abstract, he preached respect for images and idol gods,—do young men, the duty of studying the grand old books of the past, the Vedas, the Puranas, the ancient annals, and still move the people of today—to all religions, love for Mother India and a passion to dedicate themselves to her redemption.

He received no less than he gave. His vast spirit, never for a single day, failed to widen its knowledge and its experience, and it assimilated all the rivers of thought scattered and buried in the soil of India, for the source seemed to him identical. As far removed from the blind devotion of the orthodox, who were engulfed in the muddy stench of stagnant waters, as from the misguided rationalism of the reformers of the Brahmo Samaj, who with the best intentions were busy in drying up the mystic fountains of hidden energy, Vivekananda wished to preserve and to harmonise them all by drawing the whole entangled reservoir of the waters of a whole continent possessed by a deeply religious soul.

He desired more than this... everywhere he carried with him the Imitation of Christ. Side by side with the Bhagavad Gita, he spread the thought of Jesus; and he urged young people to study the science of the West.[15]

Vivekananda described the rigours of these journeys in one of his speeches, entitled 'My Life and Mission,' in the following words:

So things went on ... sometimes one meal at nine in the evening, another time a meal at eight in the morning, another after two days, another after three days—and always the poorest and the worst thing. Who is going to give to the beggar the good things he has? And then, they have not much in India. And most of the time walking, climbing snow peaks, sometimes ten miles of hard mountain-climbing, just to get a meal. They eat unleavened bread in India and sometimes they have it stored away for twenty to thirty days, until it is harder than bricks and then they will give a square of that. I would have to go from house to house to collect sufficient food for one meal. And then the bread was so hard. It made my mouth bleed to eat it. Literally, you can break your teeth in that bread. Then I would put it in a pot and pour over it water from the river. For months and months, I existed that way—but it was telling on my health.[16]

---

15. Romain Rolland, Vivekananda, pp. 24-26.
16. Complete Works of Vivekananda, Vol. VIII, p. 84.

In this journey Vivekananda saw numerous faces of the masses of India. He not only stayed in the huts and hovels of the poor, but also in the palaces of princes and Nawabs, who smothered him with their hospitality. He also became the guest of scholars with whom he had learned discourses and was honoured by them. He also spent his time in the company of thieves and criminals and discovered, among them, many a man possessing excellent qualities of character, who could have blossomed into greatness, given a proper environment.

The journeys were a great source of education for Vivekananda. A couple of incidents are sufficient to illustrate this.

Once he was staying with the Maharaja of Khetri who was his great admirers. One day during a programme of entertainment in his court, Vivekananda rose to go out, as soon as the court-dancer got up to give her puerformance. The Maharaja tried unsuccessfully to prsuade him to stay. The dancer was stung by the contempt shown by the young sanyasin for her. She sang:

"O Lord, look not upon my shortcomings! Thy name, O Lord, is even-sightedness ....'

Vivekananda got the message that the girl tried to convey. He was completely overwhelmed. It was a lesson that he never forgot in his life. He, at once, returned to the hall where she was performing and, after apologising to her, listened to her song and watched her dance performance.

In the Himalayas he lived among the Tibetans, who practise polyandry. He was the guest of a family of six brothers, who shared the same wife and, in his neophytic zeal, he tried to show them the immorality of polyandry. But it was they who were scandalised by his views. 'What selfishness!' they said. To wish to keep one woman all to oneself!...'

The above incident taught him a lesson about the

relativity of virtue; it taught him that moral values continue to change with the change of lands and the times; and then these can vary with the differences in circumstances even within the same countries and times.

During this journey, as also in his journeys abroad, one by one, his prejudices disappeared. This brought him closer to people. He has referred to the changes, that gradually affected him, in his letter of 6th July, 1896:

> At twenty years of age I was the most unsympathetic, uncompromising fanatic; I would not walk on the footpath on the theatre side of the street in Calcutta. At thirtythree I can live in the same house with prostitutes.

Everywhere he shared the privations and the insults of the oppressed classes. While Ramakrishna, in a state of ecstasy, saw the effulgent Goddess Kali herself appear before him, Vivekananda, during his journeys saw Mother India in the misery and nakedness of her people. Once he wept bitterly and cried, 'O my country! O my country!' when he read in a Calcutta newspaper about the death of a person from starvation.

Even earlier, he had once wept bitterly on hearing about the death of Balram Basu, a householder who was one of the devotees of Ramakrishna. On seeing him in such a state, Pramada Babu had said to him, 'It does not behove a sanyasin like you to feel so grieved.' Vivekananda had answered him by asking him: 'Do you think a sanyasin has no heart? Sanyasins, by nature, are more sympathetic to others than a common man. As for myself, I am no more than a man. Even otherwise, he was a fellow-disciple of mine. What is strange about my being grief-stricken at his loss? I do not want the life of a sanyasin devoid of all feelings like a piece of stone.'

As a sanyasin, Vivekananda ever remained sensitive with his heart becoming softer with the passage of time. All through his life he felt for the exploited, the repressed and the poverty-stricken people, whose sufferings caused him great anguish.

In September, 1892, when he was going to Pune by train, three Maharashtrian young men were travelling in the same compartment with him. They were having an animated discussion about sanyas. Two among them, who were convinced about the superiority of the Western style of living, were, in the fashion of reformers like Ranade, criticising *sanyas* as hypocrisy calling it an exercise in futility. But the third young man was contradicting them and was extolling the virtues of the ancient institution of sanyas. For some time, Vivekananda listened to their arguments and counter-arguments. Later on, he also joined the conversation supporting the stand taken by the third young man. Very calmly he explained to the young men that the sanyasins, roaming from one part of the country to the other, had, in fact, given publicity to the high ideals of Indian life throughout the length and breadth of the country. It was the sanyasins who were the loftiest manifestation of Indian culture and who had, through the tradition of discipleship, protected the highest national ideals in times of adversity. There was no doubt, however, that the institution of sanyas had been debased and brought into disrepute by some self-serving hypocrites, but the institution itself could not be blamed for that reason.

The three young men were greatly impressed by the learning of this sanyasin who spoke English. When the train reached Pune railway station, the third young man took Swamiji to his home. Vivekananda was happy to find that the young man possessed a good knowledge of the Vedas and the Shastras and passed several days in his house revealing to him the mysteries of the Vedas. This young man was no other than Bal Gangadhar Tilak who was, in fact, seven years senior to Vivekananda.

Bhupendranath Datta has written that, he was told by Basudev at Pune, that he was present at Pune when Vivekananda and Tilak had their discussions. Between them, they decided that Tilak would do the work of bringing about national awakening in the political field while Vivekananda would work for such an awakening through the medium of religion.

Vivekananda had studied a part of *Mahabhashya* by Sankaracharya with the help of Narayandas during his journey through Rajputana. He studied the remaining portions with the help of Pandit Sankara Pandurang who was a reputed scholar of Porbandar. After completing the study of *Mahabhashya*, he took up the study of *Vedanta Sutra* of Vyasa. In the meantime, a seminar of scholars was held there. In this seminar, the participating scholars differed on many points. Vivekananda spoke in a sweet voice and chaste Sanskrit and explained to the scholars how the different schools of Vedantic thought were complementary to one another instead of being contradictory. He said that the different Vedanta shastras were not a mere collection of a number of philosophical doctrines, they were rather the embodiment of truth realised by the *sadhakas* in different situations. The scholars attending the seminar were spellbound and amazed after listening to an altogether novel exposition of Vedantic thought by Vivekananda.

After the seminar, his teacher Pandit Sankara Pandurang, said to Vivekananda, 'Swamiji, I don't think that you will be able to achieve anything in this country through the propagation of religion. Do not waste your time and energy here: better go to Western countries. People there know how to honour talent and ability. You will certainly achieve success there on account of your catholic views.'

Swamiji paused a little and replied, 'Yes, one morning, when I was standing by the sea-coast and looking at the dancing of the waves, a thought suddenly struck me that I should go across this disturbed sea to distant lands. Let us see when my wish is fulfilled.'

Later on when he was a guest in the royal palace of Mysore, he learnt about the Parliament of Religions that was proposed to be held at Chicago. The Maharaja of Mysore was prepared to bear the expenses of his journey there. However, Swamiji told the Maharaja that he had resolved to go on a pilgrimage of the country from the Himalayas to Kanyakumari; he would think about the proposal only after completing it.

In October he left Mysore. When he reached Kanyakumari in December passing through Cochin and Madurai, he was very tired. He had no money left to pay for his boat-fare at the last leg of his journey. So he jumped into the sea and swam across the strait infested with sharks. Climbing on to the terrace of the tower at land's end, he looked around and his heart was filled with joy.

With the sea in front of him, one by one, the panorama of the mountains, the plains, the rivers, the palaces, the temples, the hovels of his sacred motherland swayed before his eyes. He saw India, the land of religion, savaged by famines, pestilence, disease and misery. On the one hand, there were those who were intoxicated with wealth and power and who, after sucking the blood of the poor, were living the life of inebriation and luxury; on the other were countless starving men, women and children in tattered clothes, their faces bearing the stamp of perennial frustration, piercing the skies with their cry for food. The masses belonging to the lower classes, deprived of education and learning, had lost all faith in the Sanatana Dharma—the ancient religion—as a result of the heartless and unkindly treatment meted out to them by the priestly class. Not only this, thousands of people were accusing the Hindu religion itself and were ready to embrace other religions; millions of people, having fallen into the deep abyss of ignorance, were without hope and faith and lacked moral strength. The so-called educated classes, instead of showing any sympathy, were living a life of licence under the influence of Western education, and were abandoning those poor people and founding new sects and social orders, thereby damaging the core of Hindu religion. Religion had been reduced to the spectacle of evil practices and a collection of lifeless rules of conduct. The result was that religion had become a big cremation ground where hope, enterprise, joy and zeal lay buried in ruins.

... he started thinking what the thousands of sanyasins,

who were sustained by the food given by these people, were doing for them. Were they teaching them only philosophy? A curse on them! Sri Ramakrishna used to say that there could be no religion on an empty stomach and the provision of ordinary meals and coarse clothes to the people is a must. There is enough religion in them. What was needed was the expansion of education, the provision of food and clothes. But how could it be made possible? To do something in this regard, the first requirement was of men and the second of money.[17]

Vivekananda, now sitting on a rock in Kanyakumari at the end of 1892, though not different outwardly from the man who started on his pilgrimage in the beginning of 1888 from the Baranagar monastery, was certainly a man who had undergone a vast change. The great mental development that he had attained over a small period of four years, was only possible through mass contact. He had felt the pulse of every inch of the country with his body and had come into direct contact with the problems thereof. The truth realised by him through the knowledge of books, and in the realm of imagination, had now been concretised in the realm of reality.

He had set out on his pilgrimage with the intention of awakening India from her slumber and bringing about unity through the teachings of Vedanta among various castes, sects and religions of the country as, indeed, that was the task entrusted to him by Sri Ramakrishna Paramahansa.

But during his journey, he saw with his own eyes that the enfeebled masses of India were groping in the darkness of ignorance and were suffering from starvation. In such a situation religion was secondary. The first priority was to remove their ignorance and hunger.

During his journey he went to the doors of the wealthy,

_____
17. *Vivekananda Charit*, pp. 198-99.

the Rajas and Maharajas and implored them to help the poor and the miserable. But no one paid any heed to him; they only gave him lip sympathy.

It was now that he thought of going to the Western countries which had an abundance of wealth but lack of religion. He thought of imparting to them the knowledge of Vedanta and asking them in return to give money for the illiterate and poor people of India. This is how he would be able to get money.

In this way, his future plans were made. He swam back to the shores of Kanyakumari after resolving to go to Chicago to attend the Parliament of Religions. He reached Madras, now Chennai passing through Pondicherry which was under the possession of the French. He had many disciples in Chennai. He revealed his plans to them and started making preparations for going abroad.

Many Rajas and Maharajas offered him help for his foreign visit. But he told his disciples that he was going abroad as a representative of the poor people of the country and, therefore, it would be appropriate to accept financial help only from the middle classes.

He did not inform his fellow-disciples at Baranagar about his plans. But, by coincidence, just before his departure, he happened to meet Abhayananda and Suryananda at a railway station near Mumbai. He poured out his feelings to them:

I have now travelled all over India.... But alas, it was agonising to me, my brothers, to see with my own eyes the terrible poverty and misery of the masses, and I could not restrain my tears! It is now my firm conviction that it is futile to preach religion among them without first trying to remove their poverty and sufferings. It is for this reason— to find more means for the salvation of poor India—that I am now going to America.'

He boarded the ship, bound for America, at Mumbai on 31st May, 1893. He was dressed in a silken gown and was wearing a saffron turban.

5

TRAVELS ABROAD

'Expansion is life and contraction is death.'
                                        Vivekananda

As a sanyasin walking through the length and breadth of India, Vivekananda had carried with him only a staff and a bowl in addition to some books. Now, on his journey to other countries, he had the botheration of carrying so much baggage consisting of trunks, suitcases, beddings and clothes. As was his nature, he soon became friendly with the passengers on board the ship and also got to know the captain of the ship. Gradually, he also got accustomed to the European customs and the variety of food served on the ship. He has given a detailed description of his journey to Alasingha Perumal, one of his disciples at Chennai. It would be interesting to quote his own words. He wrote from Yokohama (Japan) on 10th July, 1893:

'Excuse me for not keeping you constantly informed of my activities. One is so busy everyday, especially myself who is quite new to the life of possessing things and taking care of them. That consumes so much of my energy. It is really an awful botheration.'

'From Bombay, we reached Colombo. Our steamer remained in port for nearly the whole day, and we took the opportunity of getting off to have a look at the town. We drove through the streets and the one thing

I remember the most, there is a very gigantic *murti* (image) of Lord Buddha in a reclining posture, entering *nirvana*....

The next station was Penang, which is only a strip of land along the sea in Malay Peninsula. The Malayans are all Mohammedans, and in old days were noted pirates and quite a dread to merchants. But now the leviathan guns of modern battleships have forced the Malayans to give up piracy and to look for peaceful pursuits. On our way from Penang to Singapore, we had glimpses of Sumatra with its high mountains, and the captain pointed out to me several places as the favourite haunts of pirates in days gone by. Singapore is the capital of straits settlements. It has a fine botanical garden with the most splendid collection of palms. The beautiful fan-like palm, called the traveller's palm, grows here in abundance, and the bread-fruit tree is found everywhere. The celebrated mangosteen is as plentiful here as mangoes in Madras. But mangoes are mangoes and no other fruit can stand comparison to them. Even though the place is very near the equator, yet the people here are not half as dark as the people of Madras. Singapore has a fine museum too....

Hong Kong is next. You feel that you have reached China, the Chinese element predominates so much. All labour, all trade seems to be in the Chinese hands. And Hong Kong is real China. As soon as the steamer casts anchor, you are besieged by hundreds of Chinese boats to carry you to the land. These boats, with two helms are rather peculiar. The boatman lives in the boat with his family. Almost always, the wife is at the helms, managing one with her hands and the other with one of her feet. And in ninety per cent cases, you find a baby tied to her back, with the hands and feet of the little child left free. It is a quaint sight to see little babies swinging very quietly on their mother's back, whilst she is now setting with might and main, now pushing heavy loads, or jumping with wonderful agility from boat to boat. And all this amidst such a rush of boats and steam-launches coming in and going out. Baby John is every moment put to the risk of his little head pulverised, pigtail and all; but he does not care a fig. This busy life seems to have no charm for him, and he is quite content to learn the anatomy of a bit of a rice-cake, given to him from time to time, by the madly busy mother. The Chinese child is quite a philosopher and calmly goes to work at an age when your Indian boy can hardly crawl on fours. He has learnt the philosophy of necessity too well. Their extreme poverty is one of the causes why the Chinese and the Indians have remained in a state of mummified civilization. To an ordinary Hindu or Chinese, everyday necessity is too hideous to allow him to think of anything else.

The letter brings into focus the mental and emotional make-up of Vivekananda when he set out for his journey abroad. He was gifted with a penetrating insight, a large heart full of feelings, a love of beauty, a respect for labour and the power of objective analysis. While reading his account of the journey, the reader feels as if he is floating in a great ocean of consciousness.

From Hong Kong, Swami Vivekananda went to Canton at a distance of eighty miles. He goes on to write,

We landed on a strip of land given by the Chinese government to foreigners to live in. Around us, on both sides of the river for miles and miles in the big city—a wilderness of human beings, pushing, struggling, surging, roaring ... but the Chinese ladies can never be seen. They have got as strict a zenana as the Hindus of northern India; only the women of the labouring classes can be seen. Even among these, one sees now and then a woman with feet smaller than those of your youngest child, and, of course, they cannot be said to walk, but hobble.'

He returned to Hong Kong and from there came to Nagasaki, the first part of Japan. From Nagasaki, he went to Kobe by ship and proceeded by land route to Osaka to have a glimpse of the interior of Japan. Writing about this part, he says:

'I have seen three big cities in the interior—Osaka, a great manufacturing town, Kyoto, the former Capital, and Tokyo, the present Capital. Tokyo is nearly twice the size of Calcutta with nearly double the population."

Japan was also like Germany—a capitalist country with all the zeal and energy. It was competing with Western countries in every field. Exactly twelve years later, it defeated Tsarist Russia in a war.

Vivekananda has described the emerging and expanding power of Japan in the following words:

"The Japanese seem now to have fully awakened to the necessity of the present times. They have now a thoroughly organised army equipped with guns, which one of their own officers has invented, and which is said to be second to none. And, they are continually increasing their navy. I have seen a tunnel nearly a mile long, bored by a Japanese engineer.

The factories are simply a sight to see. The Japanese are bent upon producing everything they want in their own country. There is a Japanese line of steamers plying between China and Japan, which shortly intends running between Bombay and Yokohama.

Another passage presents a picture of Japanese national life:

'The short-statured, fair-skinned, quaintly dressed Japs,

their movements, attitudes, gestures, everything is pictur-esque. Japan is the land of beauty. Almost every house has a garden at the back, very nicely laid out according to Japanese fashion with small shrubs, grassy plots, small water-bodies and small stone bridges, which are so pleasant to see.'

While observing the prosperity of Japan, he was reminded of his own tattered country with its self-centred educated class. The grief of his heart was poured into the following words:

I cannot write about what I have in my mind regarding Japs in one short letter. Only I wish a number of our young men pay a visit to Japan every year. To the Japanese, India is still the dreamland of everything high and good. And what are you? .. .Talking twaddle all your lives, vain talkers, what are you? Come, see these people and then go and hide your faces in shame. A race of dotards, you lose your caste if you come out! Sitting down these hundreds of years with an ever-increasing load of crystallised superstition on your heads, for hundreds of years spending all your energy discussing the touchability or untouchability of this food or that, with all humanity crushed out of you by the continuous social tyranny of ages—what are you? And what are you doing now?... promenading the sea-shores with books in your hands—repeating undigested stray bits of Europeon brain work....'

All through his long journey, which took him to many lands, he never for a moment forgot his motherland.

Now he boarded the ship, bound for America, which passed through the northern part of the Pacific Ocean to reach Vancouver. From there, he reached Chicago after a three-day rail journey via Canada. Because of his strange saffron clothes, he became a subject of curiosity for onlookers.

They not only stared at him with curiosity, but often surrounded and teased him. Children would make fun of him and follow him. Right from Vancouver, he had also to face cheats and tricksters who victimised him whenever they got a chance. The coolies charged him exhorbitant rates. In the hotels also he felt similarly bothered. He wrote:

> ...on an average it cost me £1 every day, even a cigar here costs eight annas of our money. The Americans are so rich that they spend lavishly and have by law kept the price of everything so high that no other nation on earth can approach it. Every common coolie earns nine or ten rupees a day, and spends it all. All the rosy ideas we had before starting have melted, and I have now to struggle against an impossible situation. A hundred times I had a mind to leave this country and go back to India.

The reason for this disillusionment was that, right from 1890 America was facing economic crises which had become acute in 1893. During this one year 15,000 firms, banks and small factories were declared insolvent. Thousands of workers were rendered unemployed or had to accept reduced wages. Vivekananda had gone to America to raise funds for the poor, but found the country facing a depression.

At that time, a world fair was being held at Chicago in the Jackson Park close to Michigan Lake. The fair had been organised to mark the fourth centenary of Columbus discovering America. Therefore, it was named World Columbus Exhibition. The exhibition, which started from the 1st of May, 1893, continued for six months and came to a close in November. It was housed in 400 big buildings which had taken about two years to construct. The participants included 46 countries and all the States of America. The exhibition highlighted the progress made by the Western countries in the field of science, industry and arts during the 400 years after Columbus.

The Parliament of Religions had also been convened

to coincide with the fair. Besides, separate conferences were held on various fields of human endeavour, like education, philosophy, education and other social matters. These conferences were attended by about seven lakh persons and about six thousand papers were presented.

Vivekananda stayed in Chicago for eleven days and visited the fair every day. He was filled with child-like joy on seeing new inventions, various kinds of big and small machines and strange things of various kinds. The buildings, in which the exhibition was housed, were fine specimens of architecture. In the big square, in the midst of the main buildings, was the Statue of Liberty on one side of which was a big fountain and on the other a column of pillars. The chief attraction of the fair was the Feris Wheel especially designed by the renowned engineer W.G. Feris for the fair. Even after visiting the fair every day for about ten or eleven days, Vivekananda wanted to see more of it.

Vivekananda was always attracted by science and whatever was new. When he went to Switzerland from England along with the Seviers couple, he saw with great interest, an art exhibition that was being held there. After going round the exhibition all day, he was delighted to see a balloon which was a new exhibit. He wanted to have a ride in the balloon. The Seviers advised him against it, as a ride in a balloon was not risk-free. But Swamiji would have none of it. He not only had a ride in the balloon himself, but made the Seviers also to give him company. The balloon rose high into the clear sky. Swamiji was delighted to see the beautiful sight of sunset from the sky. After the balloon landed on the ground, they all had a group photograph taken.

A sidelight of the fair was an interesting incident which he narrated in a lively style as follows:

In Chicago the other day, a funny thing happened. The Raja of Kapurthala was here, and he was being lionised by a section of the Chicago society. I once met the

Raja in the fair grounds, but he was too big to speak to a poor fakir. There was an eccentric dhoti-clad Maratha Brahman selling pictures drawn on paper with nails. This fellow told the reporters all sorts of things against the Raja—that he was a man of low caste, that these Rajas were nothing but slaves, and that they generally led immoral lives, etc., etc. And these truthful (?) editors, for whom America is known, wanted to give to the boy's stories some weight; and so the next day they wrote huge columns in their papers about the description of a man of wisdom from India, meaning me—extolling me to the skies, and putting all sorts of words in my mouth, which I never dreamt of, and ascribing to me all those remarks made by the Maratha Brahman about the Raja of Kapurthala. And it was such a good brushing that Chicago society gave up the Raja in hot haste .... These newspaper editors made capital out of me to give my countrymen a brushing. That shows, however, that in this country intellect carries more weight than all the pomp of money and title.

One day he learnt that the Parliament of Religions would not be held before the month of September and also that no one could participate in the conference unless he was sponsored by some organisation and also that the last date for seeking participation in the conference as a delegate was over. He found that it was impossible for him to participate in the conference as a representative of the Hindu religion.

By now, he had spent most of his money on his two-week stay in a hotel. He also did not possess suitable clothes to face the cold of that country. Disappointed and worried, he came to Boston. Whatever might happen, he wanted to stay on in America to propagate Vedanta. When he was returning from Boston, he by chance became acquainted with an old lady in the train. When she learnt that he was Vivekananda—a sanyasin who had come to America from

India to propagate Vedanta—she took him to her home in a village nearby and made him welcome there. He has referred to this incident in one of his letters: 'I have an advantage in living with her in saving for sometime my expenditure of £1 per day, and she has the advantage of inviting her friends over here, and showing them a curio from India.'

Swamiji benefited from his stay in the house of the old lady in another way also. The lady took him to a women's meeting, where he made his first speech. Accepting the advice of women, he changed the style of his dress. He got a long black coat made for himself for general use, sparing the saffron cloak and turban to be worn while addressing meetings. He also got to know Mrs. Johnson who was the superintendent of the women's prison. Along with her, he visited the prison which was known as a 'reformatory', where prisoners were treated well in an effort to make them useful members of society. Swamiji has given a detailed account of this visit in one of his letters.

In the house of the old lady he also became acquainted with Professor J.H. Wright—teacher of Greek language in the Harvard University. The professor was greatly impressed by Swamiji. He suggested that Vivekananda must attend the Parliament of Religions. He gave him a letter of introduction to the President of the conference, Dr. Burrows, who was his personal friend. Armed with this letter, Swamiji again set out for Chicago, the Professor having also paid for the railway fare.

Vivekananda returned to Chicago in high spirits. The train was late and he had lost the address of the office of the Parliament of Religions somewhere on the way. He was faced with the problem of finding out the office in the big city. He asked some of the passers-by about the site of the office but they turned away scornfully thinking him to be a Negro. Night had already fallen and it was snowing. He had no place to pass the night. He saw an empty packing case lying near the goods godown. He crawled into the case and passed the night in it. As the day dawned, he came out into the streets. He was feeling the pangs of hunger. He went from door to door in the hope of getting some alms. But he was in America and not in India! He was repulsed from every house. Some hastily shut their doors on his face and some even used force to drive him away.

At last, when he got tired, he sat down by the road-side. He was observed by an extremely beautiful lady from the window of a big house across the street. She was struck by his strange appearance. She came out to him and asked him if he was a delegate to the Parliament of Religions. Swamiji told the lady about his predicament and enquired from her the location of the office of Dr. Burrows. The lady took him into her house and offered herself to take him there after lunch. That lady was Miss Mary Hale who, along with her mother, later became a great devotee of Swamiji and proved very helpful to him.

After lunch and some rest, Miss Hale took him to the office of the Parliament of Religions. There he was admitted as a delegate representing Hindu religion. Arrangements were made for his stay as a guest in the building, where other delegates were staying.

The role of Vivekananda in the conference, the opposition offered to him by the orthodox Indians and the Christian missionaries and his propagation of religion in America and Britain will be discussed separately in the next chapter, as we do not want to mix the same with his own experiences in the Western world.

Vivekananda spent two and a half years, from August 1893 to August 1895 and from November 1895 to April 1896, in America. He was thoroughly disillusioned. His first impression of the country was that it was an ideal country for deceit and cheating where 99.9 per cent people tried to take undue advantage of others. He felt like a fish out of water. Still he did not let his mind be affected by it and always kept his goal before him.

Gradually he got acquainted with good people and earned the respect and affection of many of them. After his success in the Parliament of Religions, the number of his admirers and devotees swelled. He toured all over the country making speeches. People opened their doors to him and made him their guest, wherever he went. As his contacts with life and people grew, he analysed objectively the evils and virtues of America as a nation. A letter written to his fellow-disciples on 25th September, 1894 brings out the objectivity with which he analysed the people of America and their customs:

Here, in summer, they go to the seaside—I also did the same. They have got almost a mania for boating and yachting. The yacht is a kind of light vessel which everyone, young and old, who has the means, possesses. They set sail in them every day to the sea, and return home to eat and drink and dance—while music continues day and night. Pianos render it a botheration to stay in their houses.

I shall now tell you something about W.G. Hale, on whose address you send me letters. He and his wife are an old couple, having two daughters, two nieces and a son. The son lives abroad for his living. The daughters live at home. In this country, relationship is through the girls. The son marries and no longer belongs to the family, but the daughter's husband pays frequent visits to his father-in-law's home. They say:

'Son is son till he gets a wife.

The daughter is daughter all her life.'

'All the four girls are young and not yet married. Marriage is a very troublesome matter here. In the first place, one must have a husband after one's heart. Secondly, he must be a moneyed man. Such combination is hard to find. Though beautiful and graceful they will probably remain unmarried; they are now inclined to renunciation through my contact and are busy meditating on Brahma.

The two daughters are blondes that is, having golden hair, while the two nieces are brunettes, that is, of dark hair. They are well-versed in all sorts of arts. The nieces are not so rich, they conduct a kindergarten school; but the daughters do not earn. Many girls of this country earn their living. Nobody depends upon others. Even millionaires' sons earn their living, but they marry and have separate establishments of their own. The daughters call me brother, and I address their mother as mother. All my things are at their place, and they look after them, wherever I go. Here the boys go in search of a living while quite young, and the girls are educated in the universities. So you will find that in a meeting there will be 99 per cent girls. Boys here are no match to girls.

It is indeed interesting that a sanyasin gave such a lively description of American society ninety years ago. He goes to say in the same letter that he was struck dumb with wonder at seeing the women of America. He himself could not do even a quarter of all the work that they did. They were handsome like Lakshmi—the Goddess of Fortune—and wise as Saraswati—the Goddess of Learning. He would die a contented man if he could create a thousand women in his country who could match them. Only then the males of his country would deserve to be called men. Not to speak of the women of our country, even our males stand no comparison to the women of America.

Vivekananda discovered how one city of America was different from another: 'I am going to live for a few months in New York. That city is the head, hand and purse of the country. Of course, Boston is called the Brahmanical city, and here in America there are hundreds of thousands that sympathise with me....' However, after visiting Paris and London, he wrote to a friend saying that New York looked very dirty and poor as compared to the clean and beautiful cities of Europe.

Vivekananda tried his best to remove a common misconception about America that family life in that country was permissive. He testified to having seen examples of happy family life there. He found the women of America as pure as snow, exceptionally educated and advanced— mentally and morally. About life in general in that country, he wrote:

It is as cold here, as it is hot. The summer is not a bit less hot than in Calcutta. And how to describe the cold in winter! The whole country is covered with snow, three or four feet deep, nay, six or seven feet at places. In the southern parts there is no snow. Snow, however, is a thing of little consequence here. It snows when the mercury touches 32° F. In Calcutta the temperature scarcely comes down to 6°. It occasionally approaches zero in England. But here, the mercury drops to minus 40 or 50. In Canada, in the north, mercury freezes. They have, then, to use the alcohol thermometer. When it is too cold, that is, when the mercury stands even below 20° F, it does not snow. I used to think that it must get exceedingly cold as soon as the snow falls, but it is not so. It snows on comparatively less cold days. Extreme cold produces a sort of intoxication. No vehicles ply; only the sledge, which is without wheels, slides on the ground! Everything is frozen stiff—even an elephant can walk on rivers, canals and lakes. The massive Falls of Niagra, of such tremendous velocity, have frozen to marble! But I am fine. I was a little afraid at first, but necessity makes me travel by rail to the borders of Canada one day, and the next day finds me lecturing in South America! The carriages are kept quite warm, like your own room, by means of steam pipes, outside there are masses of snow, spotlessly white—oh, the beauty of it!

I was mortally afraid that my nose and ears would drop off, but to this day they are intact. I have to go out, however, dressed in a heap of warm clothes surmounted by a fur coat, with boots encased in a woollen jacket, and so on. No sooner than you breathe out, than the breath freezes on the beard and the moustache! Notwithstanding all this, the fun of it is that they won't drink water indoors without putting a lump of ice into it. This is because it is warm indoors. Every room and staircase is kept warm by steam pipes. They have no match in arts and appliances, in enjoyment and luxury, in making money and spendingit.

The foregoing samples have been cited not with a view to highlighting the material progress and prosperity of America, but to illustrate the versatile genius and the writing prowess of Vivekananda. This would help us to understand his wide and objective vision. It would also help us to understand the process of development of science; to what extent Vivekananda reconciled his religious preaching to material progress and, in so doing, to what extent he widened his own thinking. This is what should be particularly understood. We shall attempt to do that in our next chapter.

In his own words, Vivekananda was not travelling for sightseeing or as an aimless tourist. He had gone to America for the sole purpose of finding a remedy for the poverty of India. That is why he did not, for a moment, forget his country or her poor people. The progress and prosperity of America always reminded him of the poor and the destitutes in India and filled his heart with agony:

A country where millions of people live on plants, and a million or two of sadhus and crores and crores of Brahmans suck the blood of these poor people, without even the least effort for their amelioration—is that a country or hell? Is that a religion or the devil's dance? My brother, here is one thing for you to understand fully—I have travelled all over India, and seen this country too—can there be an effect without a cause? Can there be punishment without sin?

He observed, a

'The whole difference between the West and the East is this: They are each a nation, we are not. Civilization and education here is universal, it penetrates into the masses; the higher classes in India and America are the same, but the difference is infinite between the lower classes of the two countries. We crippled the lower classes by depriving them of education and civilization; we did not allow them to remain a part of the nation. The result was that the defeat of a handful of upper class people, living a life of luxury, at the hands of foreign invaders, became a national defeat. The lower classes, as long as they were being exploited, were the least concerned with the victory or defeat of either of them. This made it easier for them to conquer India.

Vivekananda realised that worldly and material education is needed for making India one nation. Not merely eyes, but ears too, are the medium of education. He was of the view that educated young men should go from village to village and door to door and relate to the illiterate masses of the country the story of the progress achieved by different nations. They should carry a globe and maps with them and, through their talks, they should impart, to the people, knowledge of Geography, Mathematics, History, etc. Priority was required to be given to making the life of the nation dynamic. The wheel of progress once set in motion, would not stop. We have seen that Vivekananda went to America only when he had lost all hope, after touring all over the country, of getting any financial help from the wealthy and the Rajas and Maharajas for getting his plans through. In America also the simple-hearted Swami met with disappointment and he wrote that in America, too, there was class-discrimination, even though the Americans criticised the caste differences in India. According to Americans themselves, the all-powerful dollar there could make every mare go.

The economic crisis of 1893 had become even more critical in 1894. This was a very bad year for America. The number of unemployed in 1894 had surpassed all previous records in that country. The poor and the destitute were moving in groups from place to place in search for food and employment. In August there was a big strike by the railway workers and in the Pullman Company. Although the reformist trade union leaders were urging the striking workers to remain peaceful by telling them that whosoever harmed property or violated laws was an enemy and not a friend of the workers, yet the workers became violent and property was damaged on a large scale. A large number of workers were put behind bars after going through legal formalities in courts. Vivekananda saw all this with his own eyes; he also saw inhuman atrocities on Negroes and the hateful spectacle of racial discrimination.

In his speech at Chennai, Vivekananda referred to the civil war in America. He was of the view that the condition of slaves, after the civil war, was much worse than what it was before the civil war. Before the civil war, the poor Negroes at least belonged to some one and were looked after by that person in his own interest. But after the civil war, no one felt concerned about them; they were being burnt alive or shot for minor offences; there was no law against their killing. Why was it that the Negroes were being treated worse than humans, worse than even animals, simply because they were Negroes?

The ruling classes of America, who had declared liberty to be their national ideal, had become expansionist for the past fifty years. They were now competing with the European countries in their race to become an imperialist power. This was the reason for a border dispute with Venezuela, in which Britain had to give in due to her preoccupation in South Africa. This was also the reason for a war with Spain and the American occupation of Cuba and Philippines. The 'open-door' policy adopted with regard to China was also the result of this policy. The dollar-kings of America were getting richer by exploiting the workers of other countries and of their own country. How could they be expected to give financial aid for providing secular education to the poor and illiterate masses of India? They could only encourage religious fundamentalism and that was what they have always been doing.

Vivekananda reached Paris from New York on 23rd August along with a wealthy friend, Franeis Legett. Vivekananda stayed in Paris, which was the highest centre of art, culture and enjoyment, for about two weeks to attend the marriage of Mr. Legett. Thereafter, he proceeded to England.

Writing to Miss Josephine McLeod about his safe arrival in London, Vivekananda informed her that he met many retired generals who had returned from India and who treated him with respect. He did not find every black man being treated as a Negro there. Nor was he stared at in wonder. Writing to Mrs. Legett a month later, he again praised the English as being generous of heart. He found that they did not hate the blacks with the exception of some Anglo-Indians. He was not hooted in the streets which made him wonder if the complexion of his face had not become white.

He also found that some thinkers in England believed that the only solution to the social problem was the caste system of the Hindus and for that reason he surmised that they must be hating the socialists and social democrats. He also found that highly educated Englishmen took much interest in Indian thought, but not many women did that.

He found England to be more conservative than America.

In England, Vivekananda started taking classes and felt encouraged with the initial success of his work there. He wrote to Alasingha Perumal on 18th November, 1895.

...In England I can definitely do more work than in America. I am astonished myself at it. The English do not talk much in the newspapers; they work silently. I am sure of more work in England than in America. Bands and bands come and I have not sufficient room for seating them; so they squat on the floor, ladies and all. I tell them to imagine that they are under the sky of India, under a spreading banyan tree. And they like the idea.

The feeling of hatred and defiance towards Britain that Vivekananda had due to colonising India and their atrocities here, vanished after he came to England. He went to America in the beginning of December but returned to England in April, 1896. Later, he spoke about his feelings about England, in a speech in Kolkata where some of his English disciples were also present :

No one ever landed on English soil with more hatred in his heart for a race than I did for the English.... Now there is none amongst you ... who loves the English people more than I do...

He considered his work in England important for the reason that he made out in his letter of 6th July to Francis Legget:

The British Empire, with all its drawbacks, is the greatest machine that ever existed for the dissemination of ideas. I mean to put my ideas in the centre of this machine, and they will spread all over the world...

Continuous hard work exhausted him and he went to Switzerland for rest for two months. From there he wrote to Goodwin:

I am much refreshed now. I look out of the window and see huge glaciers just before me and feel that I am in the Himalayas. I am quite calm. My nerves have regained their normal strength.

From Switzerland he visited Germany at the invitation of the renowned Sanskrit scholar, Paul Deussen. He reached Kiel where Prof. Deussen was a Professor of Sanskrit in the university, after passing through several big cities and capitals. They had discussions about the Upanishads, Vedantic philosophy and the *Shankara Bhashya*. In the course of their discussions, the professor had to go out for some time. When he returned, he found Swami Vivekananda turning the pages of a book of poetry. The Swami was so immersed in the book that he did not notice that the professor had returned. When he put aside the book after going through it, he saw the professor sitting nearby. He apologised for not noticing him because of his being immersed in the book. However, from Prof. Deussen's look, he guessed that the professor did not believe that he had really gone through the book in such a short time. To remove his doubt, Swamiji started quoting poems from the book.

Upon Prof. Deussen's surprise as to how he could memorise a book of two hundred pages in half an hour unless he had read it earlier, Vivekananda assured him that he had seen the book for the first time and that he could memorise every book that he read because of the concentration with which he did it.

Swamiji had read a lot and, because of his capacity to memorise everything that he read, he was like a walking encyclopaedia. This was the main reason for the extraordinary success achieved by him in the Parliament of Religions.

In 1900, he undertook his second journey to the West. He was impressed by what he saw of Germany as an emerging nation. He writes :

Germany is fast multiplying her population and the

Germans are exceptionally hardy. Today Germany is dictating the whole of Europe; her place is above all! Long before other nations, Germany has given her men and women compulsory education, making illiteracy punishable by law; and today she is enjoying the fruits of this tree. The German army is foremost in reputation, and Germany has vowed to gain superiority in her navy also. German industry has beaten even England. German merchandise and Germans themselves are slowly obtaining a monopoly even in the English colonies. At the behest of the German Emperor, all the nations have ungrudgingly submitted to the lead of the German Generalissimo in the battlefields of China.

In 1900, a secret organisation of Chinese peasants and artisans known as Yo Ho Twan (organisation for purity and peace) started an armed struggle to throw out the foreigners from China. The struggle received wide support from the Chinese people. This struggle is known as Boxer Rebellion in history. The power of Yo Ho Twan and the wide support that it received from the people can be gauged from the fact that they surrounded the allied forces of Britain, America, Russia, France, and Japan at Long Fang and decimated them. All the imperialist powers became demoralised at the victory of these rebels and they felt that their domination in China was coming to an end. Therefore, in order to suppress the rebellion, rightist powers, which included Britain, America, Japan, Germany, Russia, France, Italy, Austria and Hungary, organised a common front in August that year under the command of the Germans. The struggle continued for one year. Although the rebels fought with great courage, yet, ultimately, the feudal Ching Government of China surrendered before the imperialists.

Vivekananda referred to this rebellion in his reminiscences of his visit to Europe. It brings out the fact that Vivekananda was keenly studying the developments in the world. He was as far-sighted as he was wide of vision. In August 1893, he was staying as a guest of Prof. J.H. Wright in a village in New England in America. There he had discussions with some selected intellectuals which was recorded by Mrs. Wright in a report entitled, 'Revenge of History.' Some portions are quoted below which testify to the farsightedness of Swamiji and to his love for humanity and a strong feeling of hatred for imperialism. The report says:

"It was the other day," he said, in his musical voice, "only just the other day, not more than four hundred years ago." And then followed tales of cruelty and oppression, of a patient race and a suffering people, and of a judgement to come!

"Ah, the English," he said, "Only just a little while ago, they were savages.... The vermin crawled on the ladies' bodies.. .and they scented themselves to disguise the abominable odour of their persons. Most horrible! Even now they are barely emerging from their barbarism."

"Nonsense," said one of the scandalised hearers, "that was at least five hundred years ago."

"And I did not say 'a little while ago?' What are a few hundred years when you look at the antiquity of the human soul?" Then with a turn of tone, quite reasonable and gentle, "They are quite savage," he said. "The frightful cold, the want and privation of their northern climate," going on more quickly and warmly, "has made them wild. They only think of killing! Where is their religion? They take the name of that Holy One, they claim to love their fellow men, they civilize—by Christianity!—No! In their hearts there is nothing but evil and even violence. 'I love you my brother, I love you!'... and all the while they cut his throat! Their hands are red with blood"... .Then, going on more slowly, his beautiful voice deepening till it sounded like a bell, "But the judgement of God will fall upon them. 'Vengeance is mine; I will repay,' said the Lord, and destruction is coming. What are your Christians? Not one third of the world. Look at the Chinese, millions of them. They are the vengeance of God that will descend upon you. There will be another invasion of the Huns," adding, with a chuckle, "they will sweep over Europe, they will not leave one brick standing upon another. Men, women, children all will be annihilated and dark ages will come again." His voice was indescribably sad and pitiful; then suddenly and flippantly, dropping the sneer, "Me,—I don't care! the world will rise up better from it, but it is coming. The·vengeance of God is coming soon.

His words seem no doubt somewhat emotional. But how correct was his thinking! We have seen how British Imperialism has suffered, it has shrunk and is confined to a corner. China has truly emerged as a world power. The age that we are living in, a century after the death of Vivekananda, is the age of total destruction of imperialism; and revolution is the main current of history today. The world will certainly emerge in a better shape from the existing chaos and upheavals that beset it.

6

AT THE PARLIAMENT
OF RELIGIONS

*The greater the opposition, the better. Does a river acquire
its velocity unless there is resistance? The newer and better
a thing is, the more opposition it will meet with at the outset.
It is opposition which is a forerunner of success. Where there
is no opposition there is no success either.*

—*Vivekananda*

Before leaving for America, Vivekananda had held discussions
with members of the Literary Society, Triplicane, at Chennai.
They had been greatly impressed by his views and, ultimately,
it was at their insistence and by their efforts that
Vivekananda was sent to Chicago to attend the Parliament
of Religions as a representative of the Hindu religion. Four
years later, after he returned to his country, he spoke to
the members of the Society and his speech is worth quoting:

> Before Buddhism, Vedanta had penetrated into China,
> into Persia, and the Islands of the Eastern Archipelago.
> Again, when the mighty mind of the Greek had linked
> the different parts of the Eastern world together, there
> came Indian thought, and Christianity with all its
> bloated civilization, is but a collection of little bits of
> Indian thought. Ours is the religion, of which Buddhism,
> with all its greatness, is a rebel child, and of which
> Christianity is a patchy imitation. One of these cycles

has again arrived. There is the tremendous power of England which has linked the different parts of the world together. English roads are no more contented like Roman roads to run over lands. They have also ploughed deep in all directions. From ocean to ocean run the roads of England. Every part of the world has been linked to every other part, and electricity plays a most marvellous role as the new messenger. Under all these circumstances we find India again reviving and ready to play her part in the progress and civilisation of the world. And that I have been forced, as it were, by nature, to go over to America and England to preach religion, is the result. Everyone ought to have seen that the time has arrived. Every thing looks propitious, and Indian thought, philosophical and spiritual, must once more go over and conquer the world. The problem before us is, therefore, assuming larger proportions everyday. It is not only that we must revive our own country—that is a small matter; I am a man of imagination and my idea is the conquest of the world by the Hindu race."[1]

The above speech presents a clear picture of all that Vivekananda saw and learnt; the extraordinary success achieved by him at the Parliament of Religions and the evolution of his own thinking during his four years' stay abroad. While going to America he had declared that he was going to seek financial assistance for the starving people of India. It was the expression of an objective which was much inferior, which was illusory and a distorted image of a vague consciousness. It was good that the Parliament of Religions began one month after he had reached America. He had enough time to see the real face of Western life, and to know about the greed of Western people for money. He was soon disillusioned on that account. However, his main objective of going abroad was to cross swords with

1. Complete Works of Vivekananda. Vol. III. pp. 275-8.

the Christian missionaries with whose assistance the imperialists had mounted cultural aggression against us with a view to consolidating their political conquest. Suffice it to say that, at Chicago, Vivekananda became the spokesman of the awakening of a new consciousness to fight against the Christian missionaries. When he got up to address the Parliament of Religions on 11th September 1893, this was the single objective in his mind. We shall see how he stormed the citadel of the Christian missionaries by giving a fitting reply to their propaganda and defeating them in debate.

Vivekananda gave an account of the opening day of the Parliament of Religions in a letter to Alasinga Perumal in the following words:

> On the morning of the inauguration of the Parliament, we all assembled in a building called the Art Palace, where one huge, and other smaller temporary halls had been erected for the sittings of the Parliament. Men from all nations were there. From India were Mazumdar of the Brahmo Samaj and Nagarkar of Bombay, Vir Chand Gandhi representing the Jains, and Chakravarthy representing Theosophy with Mrs. Annie Besant. Of these, Mazumdar and I were, of course, old friends, and Chakravarthy knew me by name. There was a grand procession, and we were all marshalled on to the dais. Imagine a hall below and a huge gallery above, packed with six and seven thousand men and women representing the best culture of the country and on the dais, the learned men of all the nations of the earth. And I, who never spoke in public in my life, to address this august assemblage! It was opened in great form with music and ceremony and speeches; then the delegates were introduced one by one and they stepped up and spoke. Of course my heart was fluttering and my tongue nearly dried up; I was so nervous, and could not venture to speak in the morning. Mazumdar made a nice speech—Chakravarthy a nicer

one, and they were much applauded. They were all prepared and came with readymade speeches. I was a fool and had none, but bowed down to Devi Saraswati and stepped up, and Dr. Burrows introduced me. I made a short speech. I addressed the assembly as, "Sisters and Brothers of America,"—a deafening applause of two minutes followed and then I proceeded, and when it was finished I sat down, almost exhausted with emotion. The next day all the papers announced that my speech was the hit of the day, and I became known to the whole of America. Truly has it been said by the great commentator Sridhara, "It is he who makes the dumb a fluent speaker: His name be praised." From that day I became a celebrity and the day I read my paper on Hinduism, the hall was packed as it had never been before. I quote to you from one of the papers: "Ladies, ladies, ladies packing every place—filling every corner, they patiently waited while the papers that separated them from Vivekananda were read," etc.

The Indian sanyasin had broken new ground by addressing the audience not merely as ladies and gentlemen, but as brothers and sisters, which was suggestive of intimacy. This sentiment was reciprocated by a continuous applause. The words also carried the message of universal brotherhood, of large-heartedness. Behind these words was also a dignified confidence. These words were followed by the expression of the sentiments in the following terms in a voice that was musical:

It fills my heart with joy unspeakable to rise in response to this warm and cordial welcome which you have given us. I thank you in the name of the most ancient order of monks in the world; I thank you in the name of the religion, and I thank you in the name of the millions and millions of the Hindu people of all classes and sects.'

Before proceeding to America, Vivekananda had travelled all around the country, talking to scholars and, after studying the Shastras and the country's history, had fully understood their contribution to the country's great past and to human civilization in general. His words reflected the strength of our tradition and national glory when he said:

'I am proud to belong to a nation which has sheltered the persecuted and the refugees of all religions and all nations of the earth. I am proud to tell you that we have gathered in our bosom the purest remnant of the Israelites, who came to Southern India and took refuge with us in the very year in which their holy temple was shattered to pieces by Roman tyranny. I am proud to belong to the religion which has sheltered and is still fostering the remnants of the Grand Zoroastrian nation.'

The one and a half page speech ended with the following words:

'Sectarianism, bigotry, and its horrible descendent, fanaticism, have long possessed this beautiful earth. They have filled the earth with violence, drenched it often and often with human blood, destroyed civilizations and sent whole nations to despair. Had it not been for these horrible demons, human society would have been far more advanced than it is now. But their time has come; and I fervently hope that the bell that tolled this morning in honour of this convention may be the death-knell of all fanaticism, of all persecutions with the sword or with the pen and of all uncharitable feelings between persons, wending their way to the same goal.'

Vivekananda exhibited great courage and genius in a foreign land. He was possessed of a handsome figure, attractive features and there was an extraordinary sparkle in his eyes. Surely, the dignity of this Indian sanyasin must have been a sight to watch!

The speech delivered by the Swami on the 19th September on Hindu religion was his best speech. In this speech he gave a rational interpretation of Vedantic philosophy on the one hand, and, on the other, he attacked the basic concept of Christian religion which holds that the original sin committed by Adam led to the fall of Adam and Eve to the earth and the beginning of the creation and that, by nature, man is sinful and has to repent for his sins and needs the help of Christ and the Church for that purpose.

He sought the permission of the audience to address them endearingly as children of immortal bliss and said:

"Children of immortal bliss"—what a sweet, what a hopeful name! Allow me to call you, brethren, by that sweet name—heirs of immortal bliss—yea, the Hindu refuses to call you sinners. Ye are the children of God, the sharers of immortal bliss, holy and perfect beings. Ye divinities on earth—sinners! It is a sin to call a man so; it is a standing libel on human nature. Come up, O lions, and shake off the delusion that you are sheep; you are souls immortal, spirits free, blest and eternal; ye are not matter, ye are not bodies; matter is your servant, and not you the servant of matter.'

Vivekananda gave a fitting reply to the calumny that is heaped upon us by the Christian preachers that we are idolaters, barbarian and uncivilized by narrating an anecdote in a lighter vein:

'I remember, as a boy, hearing a Christian missionary preach to a crowd in India. Among other sweet things he was telling them, one was that, if he gave a blow to their idol with his stick, what could it do? One of the hearers sharply answered, "If I abuse your God, what can you do?" "You would be punished," said the preacher, "when you die." "So my idol will punish you, when you die," retorted the Hindu.'

Vivekananda was speaking boldly and had not gone there to make polite and flattering statements, as the other speakers had done by saying, 'Christianity and Western civilization have taught us a lot.' He was in no way ashamed of idol worship and, rather, made it a basis for repeated counter attack. He called the morality, spirituality and quest for love of an idol-worshipper to be exemplary and said:

'Superstition is a great enemy of man, but bigotry is worse. Why does a Christian go to church? Why is the cross holy? Why is the face turned towards the sky in prayer? Why are there so many images in the Catholic Church? Why are there so many images in the mind of Protestants when they pray? My brother, we can no more think about anything without a mental image, than we can live without breathing. By the law of association the material image calls up the mental idea and *vice versa*. This is why the Hindu uses an external symbol, when he worships. He will tell you, it helps to keep his mind fixed on the Being to whom he prays. He knows, as you do, that the image is not God, is not omnipresent. After all, how much does the omnipresent mean to almost the whole world? It stands merely as a word, a symbol. Has God superficial area? If not, when we repeat the word "omnipresent," we think of the extended sky or of space, that is all.'

This speech of the Swami raised a hornet's nest. Some of the delegates to the Parliament of Religions started berating him. They declared that most of the Hindus were unaware of the importance of soul as enunciated by Vivekananda, and that he was bluffing the Western world by giving a subtle philosophical interpretation of idol-worship which the Hindu idolater could not even dream of. They also gave currency to a propaganda that Vivekananda was born in a low caste, that he had been excommunicated and was a man of no consequence and had no *locus standi* to speak on religion. A "reverend" gentleman coming from India went to the extent of asking the organisers of the Parliament of Religions to expel that characterless young man from the Parliament. The officials did not accede to this demand. However, Vivekananda was asked to reply to the objections raised by his recalcitrant.

Vivekananda was already prepared for this. In the meeting of the 22nd September he boldly demolished the allegations of his opponents. Later on, while speaking on the Hindu religion on the 25th September, he stopped in the middle of his speech and asked those of his audience to raise their hands who had direct knowledge of the Hindu religion and Shastras. Only three or four out of about seven thousand people raised their hands. The warrior-saint asked them in ridicule, how they could then criticise his religion when they knew nothing about it.

In the Parliament of Religions, Vivekananda was the representative of the poor and downtrodden of India whom the Christian priests were trying to lure into Christianity. Addressing these priests in his brief speech on 25th September he said:

Christians must always be ready for good criticism. You Christians, who are so fond of sending out missionaries to save the soul of the heathen—why do you not try to save their bodies from starvation? In India, during the terrible famines, thousands died of hunger, yet you Christians did nothing. You erect churches all through India, but the crying evil in the East is not religion—they have enough religion—but it is bread that the suffering millions of burning India cry out for with parched throats. They ask for bread. But we give them stones. It is an insult to a starving people to offer them religion; it is an insult to a starving man to teach him metaphysics. In India a priest that preached for money would lose caste and be spat upon by the people. I came here to seek aid for my impoverished people, and I fully realised how difficult it was to get help for heathens from the Christian in a Christian land.

Commenting upon these developments, *Iowa Times* wrote on 29th September, 1893:

The Parliament of Religions reached a point where sharp ascerbities developed. The thin veil of courtesy was maintained, of course, but behind it was ill-feeling. Rev. Joseph Cook criticised the Hindoos sharply and was more sharply criticised in turn. He said that to speak of the universe, that was not created, is almost impardonable nonsense, and the Asiatics retorted that a universe which had a beginning is a self-evident absurdity. Bishop J.P. Newman, firing at long range from the banks of Ohio, declared that the Orientals have insulted all the Christians of the United States by their misrepresentation of the missionaries, and the Orientals with their provokingly calm and supercilious smile, replied that this was simply the Bishop's ignorance.'

This 'calm and supercilious' smile belonged to none other than Vivekananda. He was the chief spokesman of the Orientals. In the cool and deep voice of a teacher, he met the shallow charges of the Bishops, though tinged with a bit of sarcasm. In the valedictory session of the Parliament, held on the 27th December, he gave a short speech and said:

My thanks to this enlightened audience for their uniform kindness to me and for their appreciation of every thought that tends to smoothen the friction of religions. A few jarring notes were heard from time to time. My special thanks to them, for they have, by their striking contrast, made general harmony, the sweeter.

These words, besides snubbing the Bishops for the mean tactics adopted by them, conveyed the universal message of striking a harmony of all religions and sects with the scientific consciousness of the West. This was what was preached by Ramakrishna Paramahansa, when he spoke of as many paths as there were sects. It was in this context that Vivekananda further said:

The seed is put in the ground, and earth and air and water are placed around it. Does the seed become the earth, or the air, or the water? No. It becomes a plant, it develops after the law of its own growth, assimilates the air, the earth, and the water, converts them into plant substance, and grows into a plant.

Similar is the case with religion. The Christian is not to become a Hindu or a Buddhist, nor a Hindu or a Buddhist to become a Christian. But each must assimilate the spirit of the others and yet preserve his individuality and grow according to his own law of growth.'

The discerning among the audience, proclaimed Vivekananda to be the best speaker at the Parliament of Religions. His speeches were reproduced in full in the newspapers and reviewed with appreciation. In his letter written on 15th November, 1894, exactly one year after the Parliament, he gave an account of this to Haridas Desai:

I spoke at the Parliament of Religions, and with what effect. I may quote to you from a few newspapers and magazines ready at hand. I need not be self-conceited, but to you in confidence I am bound to say, because of your love, that no Hindu made such an impression in America, and if my country has done nothing, it has done this that the Americans have come to know that India even today produced men at whose feet even the most civilised nations must learn lessons of religion and morality. Don't you think that it is enough to say for the Hindu nation sending over here this sanyasin? You would have the details from Virchand Gandhi.

These I quote from the journals: "But eloquent as were many of the brief speeches, no one expressed as well the spirit of Parliament (of Religions) and its limitations as the Hindu monk. I copy his address in full, but I can only suggest its effect upon the audience; for he is an orator by divine right, and his strong intelligent face with its picturesque setting of yellow and orange was hardly less interesting than these earnest words and the rich rhythmical utterances he gave them." (Here the speech is quoted in *New York Critique*.)

He has preached in clubs and churches until his faith has become familiar to us .... His culture, his eloquence, and his fascinating personality have given us a new idea of Hindu civilization....

His fine, intelligent face and his deep musical voice, prepossessing one at once in his favour.... He speaks without notes, presenting his facts and conclusions with greatest art and the most convincing sincerity, and rising often to rich inspiring eloquence.

Vivekananda is undoubtedly the greatest figure in the Parliament of Religions. After hearing him we feel how foolish it is to send missionaries to this learned nation. —*Herald* (the largest paper here).

I cease from quoting lest you think me conceited; but this was necessary to you who have become nearly frogs in the well and would not see how the world is going on elsewhere. I do not mean you personally, my noble friend, but our nation in general.

His extraordinary popularity led one private company

to make him an offer to arrange for his lectures in various cities. Vivekananda thought it to be a golden opportunity for achieving his objective of propagating the universal ideal of world religion. By this arrangement, he also hoped to collect sufficient funds for implementing his plans in India. He, therefore, signed a contract with the company for lecture programmes to be arranged by it.

Under this arrangement, Vivekananda got the opportunity of lecturing in most of the big cities of the various states. He collected large crowds of listeners, wherever he went in spite of the entry fee being rather high. By his lectures, Vivekananda was achieving a dual purpose. On the one hand, he gave a liberal interpretation of his own religion and propagated the message of world brotherhood and, on the other, he exposed the shortcomings and narrowness of the Christian religion by way of contrast. He also did not hesitate to expose the foolish and wicked propaganda carried on by the Christian missionaries against India.

However, he was now faced with difficulties. Firstly, the atmosphere in American cities was different from what he had found in the Parliament of Religions. In the cities the audience generally consisted of people who were superstitious and narrow-minded who tended to become rowdy. Secondly, the Christian missionaries, who wanted to harm the popularity of Vivekananda, started sending men who came prepared to disturb the meetings. Vivekananda at once saw through the game of the imperialists. But he was not the man to be frightened and displayed his characteristic courage. Romain Rolland has written:

His first feeling of attraction and admiration for the formidable power of the young republic had faded. Vivekananda almost at once fell foul of the brutality, the inhumanity, the littleness of spirit, the narrow fanaticism, the monumental ignorance, the crushing incomprehension, so frank and sure of itself with regard to all who thought, who believed, who regarded life differently from the paragon nation of the human race.... And so he had no patience. He had nothing. He stigmatised the vices and crimes of the Western civilization with its characteristics of violence, pillage and destruction. Once, when he was to speak at Boston on a beautiful religious subject particularly dear to him, he felt such repulsion at the sight of his audience, the artificial and cruel crowd of men of affairs and of the world that he refused to yield them the key of his sanctuary, and brusquely changing the subject, he inveighed furiously against a civilization represented by such foxes and wolves. The scandal was terrific. Hundreds noisily left the hall and the Press was furious.[2]

He was especially bitter against false Christianity and religious hyprocrisy:

"With all your brag and boasting, where has your Christianity succeeded without the sword? Yours is a religion preached in the name of luxury. It is all hypocrisy that I have heard in this country. All this prosperity, all this from Christ! Those who call upon Christ care for nothing but to amass riches! Christ would not have found a stone on which to lay his head among you.... You are not Christians. Return to Christ![3]

This public speech led to an explosion of anger and opposition. The American missionaries were already defaming him by calling him a cheat and fraud. They were visiting homes and telling people that back at home he had a harem full of wives and an army of children and that he was only posing as a sanyasin in America. In India also the Christian missionaries and, out of jealousy, the Brahmo Samaj representative to the Parliament of Religions—Pratap Chandra Mazumdar—were carrying on false propaganda against Vivekananda that he was staying in big hotels of

---

2. Romain Rolland, Life of Vivekananda, pp. 46-47.
3. Ibid, p. 47.

America, that he was eating all kinds of prohibited food and was leading a life of luxury in America. The fanatic and orthodox Hindus also encouraged this sort of propaganda. Vivekananda's disciples, as also his fellow-disciples, who were not aware of the facts, were taken aback by such propaganda here and abroad. They wrote to the Swami about it and also sent him cuttings of newspapers which had written against him. He replied to a disciple at Chennai on 24th January, 1894;

> Your letters have reached me. I am surprised that so much about me has reached you. The criticism of the paper you mention is not to be taken as the attitude of the American people. That paper is almost unknown here and belongs to what they call a 'blue-nose presbyterian paper,' very bigoted. The American people, and many of the clergy are very hospitable to me. That paper wanted a little notoriety by attacking a man who was being lionised by society. That trick is well known here, and they do not think anything of it. Of course, our Indian missionaries may try to make capital out of it. If they do, tell them, "Mark, Jew, a judgement has come upon you!" Their old building is tottering to its foundation and must come down in spite of their hysterical shrieks. I pity them—if their means of living fine lives in India is cut down by the influx of Oriental religions here. But not one of their leading clergy is ever against me. Well, when I am in the pond, I must bathe thoroughly.[4]

In another letter he had said to the orthodox Hindus that if they were so worried about his losing his religion (by eating Western food) why did they not send a cook and provisions for him from India? When they were not prepared to spend money for this, what was the use of their making irrelevant statements? But the opposition

---

4. *Complete Works of Vivekananda*, Vol. V, p. 24.

continued to gather momentum. The Christian missionaries, fanatic Hindus, Theosophists, Reformists, Brahmo Samajists and the reactionary political elements—all gathered together to oppose him. Vivekananda did not have a one-track mind. He soon realised that the time had now come and the false propaganda could no longer be treated with disregard, but had to be utilised for propagating his own objective. In order to strike the iron when it was hot, he wrote to Alasinga Perumal in his letter of 9th April 1894:

> Of course, the orthodox clergymen are against me; and seeing that it is not easy to grapple with me, they try to hinder, abuse and vilify me in every way; and Mazumdar has come to their help. He must have gone mad with jealousy. He has told them that I was a big fraud, and a rogue! And again in Calcutta he is telling them that I am leading a most sinful life in America, specially unchaste! Lord bless him! My brother, no good thing can be done without obstruction. It is only those who persevere to the end that succeed ... I believe that the Satya Yuga (Golden Age) will come when there will be one caste, one Veda, and peace and harmony. This idea of Satya Yuga is what would revive India. Believe it. On thing may be done if you can. Can you convene a big meeting in Madras, getting Ramnad or any such big fellow as the President, and pass a resolution to your entire satisfaction at my representation of Hinduism here, and send it to the *Chicago Herald, Inter Ocean*, and the *New York Sun*, and the *Commercial Advertiser of Detroit* (Michigan). Chicago is in Illinois. *New York Sun* requires no introduction. Detroit is in the State of Michigan. Send copies to Dr. Burrows, Chairman of the Parliament of Religions, Chicago. I have forgotten his number. One copy to Mrs. J.J. Bagley of Detroit, Washington Ave.

> Try to make the meetings as big as possible. Get hold of all the big bugs who must join it for their religion

and country. Try to get a letter from the Mysore Maharaja and the Dewan approving the meetings and their purpose—so of Khetri—in fact, as big and noisy as you can.

The resolution would be of such a nature that the Hindu community of Madras, who sent me over, is expressing its entire satisfaction in my work, etc.[5]

Consequently, big meetings were held in cities like Chennai and Calcutta where Vivekananda's efforts were not only praised, but were also declared to be a matter of pride for the country for which he was felicitated. The reports of these meetings were published in the newspapers of India and America and an account of the meetings was also sent to the persons named by Vivekananda. In this way the false propaganda of the Christian priests was exposed. Vivekananda not only wanted to silence these priests, but he also wanted to awaken the conscience of the Indian people. Accordingly, he wrote a letter on 18th November, 1894 to Pyare Mohan Mukherjee who had presided over the Calcutta meeting which had been held to felicitate him:

Give and take is the law; and if India wants to raise herself once more, it is absolutely necessary that she brings out her treasures and throws them back among the nations of the earth, and in return, be ready to receive what others have to give her. Expansion is life, contraction is death. Love is life, and hatred is death. We commence to die the day we begin to hate other races, and nothing can prevent our death unless we come back to expansion, which is life.

We must mix, therefore, with all the races of the earth. And every Hindu that goes out to travel in foreign parts renders more service to his country than hundreds

---

5. Complete Works of Vivekananda, Vol. V, p. 31.

of men who are bundles of superstition and selfishness, and whose one aim in life seems to be like that of a dog in the manger. The wonderful structures of national life, which the Western nations have raised, are supported by the strong pillars of character, and until we can produce large numbers of such men of character, it is useless to fret and fume against this or that power.

Do such people deserve liberty, as are not ready to give it to others? Let us calmly and in manly fashion go to work, instead of dissipating our energy in unnecessary frettings and turnings. I for one thoroughly believe that no power on earth can withhold from any one anything he really deserves. The past was great no doubt, but I sincerely believe that the future will be still more glorious.[6]

It is not possible to achieve progress without knowing our weaknesses and without learning from others. However, self-criticism should be resorted to only in the presence of our own people; and to the enemy we must always present a united front. This was the strategy adopted by Vivekananda. Before the opponents of the Hindu religion, he even justified idol-worship by giving a philosophical interpretation thereof, but did not hesitate to unburden himself and express his agony to his own people. This was the reason why the liberal bourgeois class and its intellectuals adored him, gave him all honour and accepted him as their religious and cultural leader, and they do so even today. Consequently, on his return to India he was given a big welcome everywhere. And speaking before his own people, he did not hesitate from unburdening himself and said in his Chennai speech:

With all my faults, I think I have a little bit of boldness. I had a message from India to the West, and boldly

6. *Complete Works of Vivekananda*, Vol. IV, p. 365.

gave it to the American and English people. I want, before going into the subject of the day, to speak a few bold words to you all. There have been certain circumstances growing round me, tending to thwart me, oppose my progress, and crush me out of existence if they could. Thank God they have failed, as such attempts will always fail. But there has been, for the last three years, a certain amount of misunderstanding, and so long as I was in foreign lands, I held my peace and did not even speak one word; but now, standing upon the soil of my motherland, I want to give a few words of explanation. Not that I care what the result will be of these words. I care very little, for I am the same *sanyasin* that entered your city about four years ago with this staff and *kamandalu*; the same broad world is before me.[7]

When the enemies of the country and the enemies of the nation do not find it possible to give a straight and open fight, they try to disguise themselves and infiltrate into our ranks. They pose as our well-wishers and try to give a subtle turn to our thinking, trying to turn our victory into defeat, trying to obliterate us. When the Theosophists failed in their open attacks, and when the Indians pronounced Vivekananda to be their religious leader, the Theosophists adopted the same tactics. They started saying that they helped and facilitated Vivekananda in every way. However, Vivekananda was wise enough not to be taken in by these tactics of his enemies, who were now parading as his friends: Continuing his speech, he said:

Without further preface let me begin. First of all, I have to say a few words about the Theosophical Society. It goes without saying that a certain amount of good work has been done in India by the Society; as such every Hindu is grateful to it, and especially to Mrs.

7. *Ibid*. Vol. IV, p. 207.

Besant; for though I know very little of her, yet, what little I know, has impressed me with the idea that she is a sincere well-wisher of this motherland of ours, and that she is doing the best in her power to raise our country. For that, eternal gratitude of every Indian is hers, and all blessing be on her for ever.

But that is one thing and joining the society of Theosophists is another. Regard and estimation and love are one thing, and swallowing everything one has to say, without reasoning, without criticising, without analysing, is quite another. There is a report going round that the Theosophists helped the little achievements of mine in America and England. I have to tell you plainly that every word of it is wrong, every word of it is untrue. We hear so much talk in this world, of liberal ideas and sympathy with differences of opinion. That is very good, but as a fact, we find that one sympathises with another only so long as the other believes in everything he has to say, but as soon as he dares to differ, that sympathy is gone, that love vanishes. There are others, again, who have their own axes to grind, and if anything arises in a country which prevents the grinding of them, their hearts burn, any amount of hatred comes out, and they do not know what to do. What harm does it do to the Christian missionary that the Hindus are trying to cleanse their own houses? What injury will it do to the Brahmo Samaj and other reform bodies that the Hindus are trying their best to reform themselves? Why should they stand in opposition? Why should they be the greatest enemies of these movements? Why? I ask. It seems to me that their hatred and jealousy are so bitter that no why or how can be asked there.

Four years ago, when I, a poor, unknown, friendless sanyasin was going to America, going beyond blue waters to America without any introductions or friends there, I called on the leader of the Theosophical Society. Naturally I thought that he, being an American and lover of India, perhaps will give me a letter of introduction to somebody there. He asked me, 'Will you join my Society?' 'No,' I replied, 'How can I ? For I do not believe in most of your doctrines.' 'Then, I am sorry, I can not do anything for you,' he answered. That was not paving the way for me. I reached America, as you know, through the help of a few friends of Madras. Most of them are present here. Only one is absent, Mr. Justice Subramania Iyer, to whom my deepest gratitude is due. He has the insight of a genius and is one of the staunchest friends I have in this life, a true friend indeed, a true child of India.

I arrived in America several months before the Parliament of Religions began. The money I had with me was little, and it was soon spent. Winter approached, and I had only thin summer clothes. I did not know what to do in that cold, dreary climate, for if I went to beg in the streets, the result would have been that I would have been sent to jail. There I was with the last few dollars in my pocket. I sent a wire to my friends in Madras. This came to be known to the Theosophists, and one of them wrote, 'Now the devil is going to die, God bless us all.' Was that paving the way for me? I would not have mentioned this now; but, as my countrymen wanted to know, it must come out. For three years I have not opened my lips about these things; silence has been my motto; but today the thing has come out. That was not all. I saw some Theosophists in the Parliament of Religions, and I wanted to talk and mix with them. I remember the looks of scorn which were on their faces, as much as to say, "What business has this worm to be here in the midst of gods?" After I had got name and fame at the Parliament of Religions there, came tremendous work for me. But at every turn the Theosophists tried to cry me down. Theosophists were advised not to come and hear my lectures, for thereby they would lose all sympathy of the Society, because the laws of the esoteric section declare that any man who joins the esoteric section should receive instruction from *Kuthumi* and *Moria*, of course through their visible representatives—Mr. Judge and Mrs. Besant—so that, to join the esoteric section, means to surrender one's independence'.[8]

The Swami had seen through the guile of these enemies parading as friends. He had in his heart great hatred and anger for them. In a letter to someone he narrated how the Theosophists were trying to flatter him as he had now been acknowledged a leader in India. He also wrote that had his health not been bad, he would have seen to it that those hypocrites were wiped out in India.

In spite of being sharply rebuked by Vivekananda and in spite of the expression of unqualified hatred he had for them, the Theosophists tried to utilise his popularity for their own benefit. Their cunning and guileful leader Annie Besant published an eulogy of Vivekananda in the *Brahmavadin* of March 1914—twelve years after his death. She praised his magnetic personality, calling him a warrior monk, who though being the youngest delegate present at the Parliament of Religions, was the best exponent of the most ancient religion of the world and of its glorious tales. Instead of enunciating his true role of being the exponent of the national goal, she only described him as the best exponent of the oldest religions of the world and in her opinion his speeches were no more than religious talks, though unmatched. In this way, she tried in a subtle manner to demolish the very ground on which Vivekananda stood.

---

8. *Ibid.* Vol. IV, pp. 207-8.

This eulogy was nothing more than an unfriendly act in the guise of a friend. We are, however, sorry to say that those who do not understand the phenomenon of a struggle "that takes place between thesis and anti-thesis within the same ideology, will not be able to understand this subtle difference. But Vivekananda very well understood the clash between thesis and anti-thesis and, therefore, he rejected the false praise of Theosophists and other jackals wearing the deer's skin. He never forgave them for their sins against the Indian nation and against humanity. He had realised the eternal truth that our survival was possible only by eliminating these unfriendly elements.

Therefore, he stood like a rock and faced the storm of opposition. The opposing associations and sects tried to bring him round to their side through fear and temptation. But Vivekananda remained unmoved. He declared that he was a true devotee of truth and insisted upon truth, that truth never compromised with untruth, that he was prepared to fight with the world in order to revindicate truth and that truth shall ultimately prevail.

At that time, the population of America was about six crore. One third of them were Christians and Theosophists numbered only 650. The Christians were further divided into sects such as Catholics, Protestants, Presbytarians and Syrian Christians. The followers of Christianity were generally those who were clever and knew the ways of the world; they were not concerned with the philosophical subtleties of religion; they led a life of pleasure and took to religion only out of the fear of being consumed by the fires of hell and to get a seat reserved for themselves in heaven. These people personified all that was mean, they were the embodiment of foolishness and prided in their ignorance. Vivekananda suddenly developed great hatred for such people. Those who were thoughtful among the Christians, respected Vivekananda and derived much pleasure from listening to his discourses and exchanging views with him. Most of the Americans were influenced by the Darwin and Herbert Spencer's theories of evolution and agnosticism and by the new scientific inventions. As such they were sceptic, rationalists and non-believers and rejected religion and religious deeds as thuggery and bad influence. All of them were members of the Free Thinkers Society. These people were also opposed to Vivekananda and were very active in ridiculing him.

Although indirectly they strengthened the hands of the Christian missionaries against Vivekananda, yet their opposition was not selfish and was of a different kind. Once they invited Vivekananda to address their meeting and Vivekananda readily accepted their invitation. Vivekananda had himself once passed through the mental stage through which all these people were passing. After his speech, he replied to their queries and they were so impressed by his well-reasoned replies that many of them became his disciples.

Lenin, in the Foreword to his book On Religion had said:

> We said at the beginning of this Foreword that Marxism cannot be conceived without atheism. We would add here that atheism without Marxism is incomplete and inconsistent. The decline of the bourgeois free thinkers' movement offers an instructive confirmation of this argument. Wherever materialism in science fails to develop into historical materialism—that is, into Marxism, it ends up in idealism and superstition.[9]

One of the persons belonging to this group of rationalists was Robert Ingersol who, though against religion, had wide knowledge of literature and philosophy. He was a popular speaker and used to earn a lot from his lectures. After this meeting, he became a great friend of Vivekananda. It was

---

9. Lenin, On Religion.

an unusual friendship between a materialist and a sanyasin. But both were learned and, at their first meeting, they had discovered each other's erudition.

In this way Vivekananda slowly won the recognition of the great and the thinking people of the new world. He had by now realised the futility of lecturing to heterogeneous crowds of people while the lecture company was taking him from place to place like a circus animal to earn maximum amount of money through his lectures. It was never the sole objective of Vivekananda to earn money. With the help of friends he terminated his contract with the lecture company and started taking classes on Vedanta in New York free of charge. This no doubt meant a financial loss to him, but his selflessness won recognition in the eyes of every one.

In New York, his lectures on Raj Yoga became so popular that his small room used to be crowded with philosophers, scientists and teachers of the city on the day of his lecture. In May 1895 he dictated his famous commentary on Raj Yoga to Miss S.E. Waldo (who later came to be known as Sister Haridasi) to which he also added a commentary on Patanjali's *Yoga Sutra*. The book became so popular that, within a few weeks, three editions of the same were published.

This exercise earned for him many disciples and helpers. Now it was necessary for him to take some rest after the hard work that he had put in for the last one and a half years. He, therefore, spent a few days in the Thousand Island Park where a lady disciple had a beautiful hut on the banks of St. Lawrence river. He passed his days with his disciples in this hut with all of them cooking their meals together.

One of the disciples, Miss E.S. Waldo, has given an account of the few weeks passed by Vivekananda and his disciples in the idyllic place. All the time was spent in spiritual discourses forgetting the material world. Vivekananda was a storehouse of Hindu Puranic lore and he narrated these stories to illustrate the philosophical thought he wanted to emphasise in his discourses.

The American disciples of Vivekananda had a cultural history of not more than three hundred years. They had no mythology of their own, nor had they inherited any philosophical thought or rich cultural tradition. Their only inheritance were the accounts of the travels of Marco Polo and Columbus or thoughts gathered from here and there in Europe. This accounts for the shallowness of American thought. America's art and literature are full of subjects that are only hilarious or comical. Even the history of America, which is in two parts, is full of cartoons. In no other country's history will you find so many cartoons or so much importance given to cartoons. In fact, this new world in America consisted of an amalgam of civilized and semi-civilized races belonging to the countries of Europe such as England, Germany, Spain, etc. The lives of American people totally lacked in the innocence of imagination, which is a typical characteristic of the period of infancy of the human race. It is not difficult to imagine how much interest the stories of Vivekananda, drawn from the Vedas, Upanishads and Puranas, must have generated in the minds of these Americans seeking respite from worldly pleasures. One day Vivekananda told his disciples:

> This is a great land, but I would not like to live here. Americans think too much of money. They give it preference over everything else. Your people have much to learn. When your nation is as old as ours, you will be wiser."[10]

It is worth recording in this context that the celebrated philosopher, William James, was so impressed by his book

10. Complete Works of Vivekananda, Vol. V, p. 328.

on Raj Yoga that he came to meet Vivekananda after reading it. James was the exponent of the theory of Pragmatism according to which truth has only a utilitarian value for dealing with the prevailing situation and achieving the objective. The new ruling class, which was engaged in the race for expanding its trade and empire, adopted this theory as its principle and is still holding on to it. This ruling class considered Raj Yoga also to be of purely utilitarian value as a means of achieving material capability. "A giant with the brain of a child, the Americans are only interested, as a rule, in ideas which they can turn to their advantage. Metaphysics and religion are transmuted into false applied sciences, their object being the attainment of power, riches and health—the kingdom of the world."[11] How could Vivekananda tolerate this attitude. He publicly condemned this tendency based on selfishness and profit motive. This gave the Bishops another opportunity to berate Vivekananda and they charged him with carrying on political propaganda in the garb of religion.

From August to December, 1895, he was in England. Thereafter, he returned to America where he devoted himself to taking classes on Karma Yoga and Bhakti Yoga and lecturing in cities like New York, Boston and Detroit. A Vedanta society was set up under the chairmanship of Francis Legget which, for some time, remained the centre of Vedantic movement in New York. However, this centre did not last long and, out of the many disciples he had made, all proved worthless, barring a few.

In April 1896 Vivekananda returned to England and remained there till the end of the year before coming back home. In England he met scholars like Max Mueller who understood India. After his meeting with Vivekananda, Max Mueller wrote an article and, later on, a book about

---

11. Romain Rolland, Vivekananda, p. 86.

Ramakrishna Paramahansa. Once someone asked Vivekananda in England that, if his ancestors were so eager to impart religion to others, why did they not come to England to preach religion. To this Vivekananda replied: 'Because at that time Englishmen were barbarians, living in the caves and covering their bodies with leaves. How could any one come to preach religion to them?'

However, Vivekananda had no complaints against the British. He wrote to Francis Legget, The work is growing silently, yet surely in England. Almost every other man or woman came to me and talked to me about the work.'

In another letter, addressed to Mrs. Ole Bull, he praised the generosity of the British people and narrated how he collected a subscription of £150 from his class within about three minutes for a new building, wherein the next programme was to be conducted in the coming winter.

The four disciples who accompanied him to India— the Sevier couple, Goodwin and Sister Nivedita—were all from England. The Seviers were quite rich. It was with their efforts that the Mayavati Ashram was set up at Almora. Goodwin was good at shorthand. He offered his free services. It was he who recorded most of Vivekananda's speeches which are now our invaluable treasure.

Sister Nivedita's name (originally Miss Margaret Noble) is inseparable from that of Vivekananda even as the names of Bala and Mardana are inseparable from that of Guru Nanak. She was a learned lady of strong character. She played the same role in the history of our freedom movement which was played by B. Vyohen in the Chinese revolution, whose life was dedicated for organising the revolutionary movement. It is regrettable that we glorify such people as Hume and Annie Besant, who were our enemies in the garb of friends, but we have forgotten Sister Nivedita who sacrificed her life for breaking the shackles of slavery. Miss Hale was the personification of the tenderest sympathy that Vivekananda received in America. Vivekananda showered all his love on her by adopting her as his sister. Nivedita was the sister of the whole nation of ours and it is our national duty to continue paying homage to her.

It is worth noting how Vivekananda's own personality was shaped as a result of his four years of stay in America and England where he continuously engaged himself in preaching and propaganda. The methodology adopted by him there was explained by him to Alasinga Perumal in his letter of 17th February, 1896:

> To put the Hindu ideas into English and then make out of dry Philosophy and intricate Mythology and queer startling Psychology, a religion which shall be easy, simple, popular and at the same time meet the requirements of the highest minds, is a task only those can understand who have attempted it. The abstract Advaita must become living, poetic in every day life; out of hopelessly intricate mythology must come concrete moral forms; and out of bewildering Yogism must come the most scientific and practical psychology— and all this must be put in a form so that a child may grasp it. That is my life's work.[12]

It was, however, not an easy task. While trying to explain himself to the intelligent audiences of England and America, he himself went through a process in which his own knowledge grew and his vision widened. In another letter to Perumal he wrote:'

> Now I will tell you my discovery. All of religion is contained in the Vedanta, that is, in the three stages of the Vedanta philosophy, the Dvaita, Vishishtadvaita, and Advaita, one comes after the other. These are the three stages of spiritual growth in man. Each one is necessary. This is the essential of religion. The Vedanta, applied to the various ethnic customs and creeds of

---

12. *Ibid.* Vol. VI, p. 80.

India, is Hinduism. The first stage, i.e. Dvaita, applied to the ideas of the ethnic groups of Europe, is Christianity, as applied to the Semitic group Mohammedanism. The Advaita as applied in its yoga-perception form, is Buddhism etc. Now by religion is meant the Vedanta; the applications must vary according to the different needs, surroundings and other circumstances of different nations.[13]

This discovery had filled him with a new zeal which he expressed in a letter to Miss Mary Hale in May, 1896:

I like to see new things. I do not care a fig to loaf about old ruins and mope a life out about old histories and keep sighing about the ancients. I have too much vigour in my blood for that. In America is the place, the people, the opportunity for everything. I have become horribly radical. I am just going to India to see what I can do in that awfulness of conservative jelly-fish, and start a new thing, entirely new, simple, strong, new and fresh as the first born baby.[14]

In other words, the fire, which Vivekananda had carried in his heart, became even stronger after coming into contact with Western science and turned into a roaring flame. It was this flame that Vivekananda carried in his soul when he returned home from England, in the beginning of 1897, after passing through Rome.

---

13. *Ibid.*
14. Complete Works of Vivekananda, Vol. VIII, p. 498.

7

VEDANTA AND UNIVERSAL BROTHERHOOD

Work for the welfare of the entire human race. Give up the pride of being a pure Hindu that you entertain in your narrow confines.

—Vivekananda

Vivekananda returned home after four years of stay abroad. He reached Colombo and Pamban amidst tumultous welcome by the Indians residing in Sri Lanka. He received a similar great welcome wherever he went on the Indian soil—at Ramnad, Madurai, Chennai, Kolkata and other places. In the procession that was taken out at Ramnad and Rameshwaram, the local Raja himself pulled Vivekananda's chariot according to the ancient custom. Vivekananda felt greatly elated by the honour that was bestowed upon him and wrote to his adopted sister, Mary Hale, on 28th April:

'The whole country here rose like a man to receive me. Hundreds of thousands of persons, shouting and cheering at every place, Rajas drawing my carriage, arches all over the streets of the capitals with blazing mottos etc.!!'

It was quite by coincidence that at that very time Dr. Burrows, the President of the Parliament of Religions, came to India to preach Christianity. He however, did not succeed in his mission. Vivekananda referred to him in the above letter and said:

Dr. Burrows has reached America by this time I hope, poor man! He came here to preach the most bigoted Christianity, with the usual result that nobody listened to him. Of course, they received him very kindly; but it is my letter that did it. I could not put brains into him! Moreover, he seems to be a queer sort of man. I hear that he was mad at the national rejoicings over my coming home. You ought to have sent a brainier man any way, for the Parliament of Religions has been made a farce of in the Hindu mind by Dr. Burrows. On matters metaphysical, no nation on earth can hold a candle to the Hindus, and curiously all the fellows that came over here from Christian land have that one antiquated foolishness of an argument that because the Christians are powerful and rich and the Hindus are not, so Christianity must be better than Hinduism. To which the Hindus very aptly retort that, that is the very reason why Hinduism is a religion and Christianity is not, because, in this beastly world, it is blackguardism alone which prospers, virtue always suffers.[1]

In this context, another incident is worth mentioning. When Vivekananda reached Kolkata, that region was in the grip of a famine. People thought that it would be better to save the money to be spent on the welcome and donate it to the famine relief fund. But he preferred his procession to be taken out. When one of his disciples asked him the reason for this the Swami replied:

"Why, I wished rather that a great enthusiasm should be stirred up. Don't you see, without some such thing how could the people be drawn towards Sri Ramakrishna and be fired in his name? Was this ovation done for me personally? See, how much thirst has been created in the minds of men to know about him! Now they will come to know of him gradually, and

1. *Ibid.* Vol. VI, p. 389.

will not that be conducive to the good of the country? If the people do not know him who came for the welfare of the country, how can good befall them? When they know what he really was, then men—real men—will be made, and when there be such men, how long will it take to drive away famines, etc., from the land?"[2]

The good of the nation was at the top of his agenda. He had shed his individuality and merged his personality with the nation. The only objective of his life was to raise and reawaken the conscience of the nation. On his second visit abroad in 1900, he spoke about his life-mission on 27th January in the Shakespeare Club, Pasedona:

Now, to understand what I have been trying to do, in my small way, I will take you, in imagination, to India. We have no time to go into all the details and all the ramifications of the subject; nor is it possible for you to understand all the complexities in a foreign race in this short time. Suffice it to say, I will at least try to give you a little picture of what India is like.

It is like a gigantic building all tumbled down in ruins. At first sight, then, there is little hope. It is a nation gone and ruined. But if you wait and study, then you see something beyond that. The truth is that so long as the principle, the ideal, of which the outer man is the expression, is not hurt or destroyed, the man lives, and there is hope for that nation. If your coat is stolen twenty times, that is no reason why you should be destroyed. You can get a new coat. The coat is unessential. The fact that a rich man is robbed does not hurt the vitality of the man, it does not mean death. The man will survive.

Standing on this principle, we look in and see—what? India is no longer a political power, it is an enslaved

2. *Ibid.* Vol. V, pp. 266-67

race. Indians have no say, no voice in their own government; they are three hundred millions of slaves— nothing more! The average income of a man in India is two shillings a month. The common fate of the vast mass of the people is starvation, so that, with the least decrease in income, 'millions die. A little famine means death. So there, too, when I look on that side of India; I see ruin—hopeless ruin.

But we find that the Indian race never stood for wealth. Although they acquired immense wealth, perhaps more than any other nation acquired, yet the nation did not stand for wealth. It was a powerful race for ages, yet we find that the nation never stood for power, never went out of the country to conquer. Quite content within their own boundaries, they never fought anybody. The Indian nation never stood for imperial glory. Wealth and power, then, were not the ideals of the race.

What then? Whether they were wrong or right—that is not the question we discuss—that nation, among all the children of men, has believed, and believed intensely, that this life is not real. The real is God, and they must cling unto that God through thick and thin. In the midst of their degradation, religion came first. The Hindu man drinks religiously, sleeps religiously, walks religiously, marries religiously, robs religiously.

Did you ever see such a country? If you want to get up a gang of robbers, the leader will have to preach some sort of religion, then formulate some bogus metaphysics, and say that this method is the clearest and quickest way to God. Then he finds a following, otherwise not. This shows that the vitality of the race, the mission of the race is religion; and because that has not been touched, therefore the race lives?[3]

The political and cultural battles are fought through

---

3. Complete Works of Vivekananda, Vol. VIII, pp. 73-74.

religion, too. We do not have to go far for an example. The European bourgeois class fought its battle against feudalism through the medium of religion. Who does not know that Catholicism was the religion of the dying feudalism and Protestantism the religion of rising capitalism? Protestants were burnt at the stakes but, eventually, they were the winners. Engels has written:

> The ineradicability of the protestant heresy corresponded to the invincibility of the rising burghers. When these burghers had become sufficiently strengthened, their struggle against the feudal nobility, which till then had been predominantly loyal, began to assume national dimensions. The first great action occurred in Germany.

> The so-called Reformation .... But, beside the German Luther, appeared the Frenchman Calvin. With true French acuity he put the bourgeois character of the Reformation in the forefront, republicanised and democratised the church. While the Lutheran Reformation in Germany degenerated and reduced the country to rack and ruin, the Calvinist Reformation served as a banner for the republicans in Geneva, in Holland and in Scotland, freed Holland from Spain and from the German Empire and provided the ideological costume for the second act of the bourgeois revolution.[4]

From this Engels concludes,

> And we see therefore: religion, once formed, always contains traditional material, just as in all ideological domains tradition forms a great conservative force.

The capitalist class that came into being in our country in the first half of the nineteenth century was the main

---

4. Ludwig Faeurbach, pp. 70-71.

power behind the reformist movement and the renaissance. The capitalist class was by itself incapable of giving a fight to the foreign ruler in the political and economic fields. Its culture was also under attack from within and without. How was this attack to be faced?—this was the serious problem. How could this class assert that the civilisation inherited by it from its ancestors was better than the industrial civilization of the foreign rulers?—this was the question. By way of solution, the nationalist bourgeois class declared that their civilisation was essentially based on spiritualism, that it had never been their goal, nor would it ever be in future, to run after material gains and that the main objective of life for them was renunciation and asceticism. That is why we find Vivekananda, the spokesman of national awakening, proudly proclaiming:

> I have seen a little of the world, travelling among the races of the East and the West, and everywhere I find among nations one great ideal which forms the backbone, so to speak, of that race. With some it is politics, with others it is social culture; others again may have intellectual culture and so on for their national background. But, this, our motherland has religion and religion alone for its basis, for its backbone, for the bedrock upon which the whole building of its life has been based?[5]

It was only Vivekananda who was capable of giving such a beautiful and poetic definition of our national ideal just as, in an equally capable manner, he had given a subtle interpretation of idol worship.

He further added that just as the good and great men of other nations proudly traced their lineage to some leader of a big gang of robbers who used to hide themselves in caves and come out to rob passersby, in the same way, we Hindus take pride in the fact that we are the successors

---

5. Complete Works of Vivekananda, Vol. VI, p. 80.

of those sages and great souls who used to live in caves devoting themselves to the realisation of God and surviving on a frugal diet of fruits and flowers. Even though we have fallen from our path, yet we can regain that old glory, if we once again devote ourselves to the ideal of religion.

In this context, it is interesting to recall an incident when Vivekananda was referring to the glory of India. Some one from the audience asked, 'What have you Hindus done? You have never conquered a single nation.' The Swami replied that it was not as if the Hindus could not conquer. In fact they did not conquer; they did not conquer because they were not avaricious; Indians have always occupied the higher position of givers; they had been teachers of the world and not looters of others' wealth. It was for this reason that he was proud of his ancestors.

In his Kolkata speech the Swami had said:

Each nation has its own peculiar method of work. Some work through politics, some through other lines, with us religion is the only ground along which we can move. The Englishman can understand even religion through politics. Perhaps the Americans understand even religion through social reforms. But the Hindu can understand even politics when it is given through religion; sociology must come through religion, everything must come through religion. For, that is the theme, the rest are the variations in the national life-music. And that was in danger.

It seems that we are going to change this theme in our national life, that we are going to exchange the backbone of our existence, as it were, that we were trying to replace a spiritual by a political backbone. And if we could have succeeded, the result would have been annihilation. But it was not to be. So this power became manifest. I do not care in what light you understand this great sage, Ramakrishna it matters not how much respect you pay to him, but I challenge you face to face with the fact that here is a manifestation of the most marvellous power that has been for several centuries in India, and it is our duty, as Hindus, to study this power, to find what has been done for the regeneration, for the good of India, and for the good of the whole human race through it. And long before ideas of universal religion and brotherly feeling between different sects were mooted and discussed in any country in the world, here, in sight of this city, had been living a man whose life was a parliament of religion as it should be.[6]

He went on to elucidate Ramakrishna Paramahansa's concept of world religion and universal brotherhood in these words:

As you have pointed out to me, we have to conquer the world. That we have to! India must conquer the world, and nothing more than that is my ideal. It may be very big, it may astonish many of you, but it is so. We must conquer the world or die. There is no other alternative. The sign of life is expansion; we must go out, expand, show life, or degrade, fester and die. Now, we all know about the petty jealousies and quarrels that we have in our country. Take my word, it is the same everywhere. The other nations with their political lines have foreign policies. When they find too much quarrelling at home, they look for somebody abroad to quarrel with and the quarrel at home stops. We have these quarrels without any foreign policy to stop them. This must be our eternal foreign policy, preaching the truths of our Shastras to the nations of the world. I ask you who are politically minded, do you require any other proof that this will unite us as a race? This very assembly is a sufficient witness.[7]

6. *Ibid.* Vol. III, p. 314.
7. *Ibid.* Vol. III, p. 316.

Capitalism, by its very nature, wants to expand. So our emerging bourgeois class declared the conquering of the world by their spiritual power as being their ideal. By so doing they tried to pitch blind bourgeois nationalism against blind imperialist nationalism and, thereby, they sought to protect their past and be proud of it. On the other hand, they adopted it as a standing foreign policy and tried to organise themselves as a united race.

When Western capitalism transformed itself into imperialism, it was already excelling itself in military power and industrial civilization. Yet they sought to intellectually disarm the vanquished races by establishing the superiority of their religion over the religion of these races and sent out missionaries to propagate Christianity as 'world religion.' In a way it was the imperialists who conceived the idea of world religion. The missionaries claimed that since Christianity was the religion of prosperity and the victorious, so it was the most superior religion. He demolished this claim in his Kumbhakonam speech in the following words:

I have become used to hear all sorts of wonderful claims put forward in favour of every religion under the sun. You have also heard, quite within recent times, the claims put forward by Dr. Burrows, a great friend of mine, that Christianity is the only universal religion. Let me consider this question awhile and lay before you my reasons why I think it is Vedanta, and Vedanta alone that can become the univeral religion of man, and that none other is fitted for the role.

Excepting our own, all the other great religions in the world are inevitably connected with the life, or lives of one or more of their founders. All their theories, their teachings, their doctrines and their ethics are built round the life of a personal founder, from whom they get their sanction, their authority, and their power, and strangely enough, upon the historicity of that life, as has been the case in modern times with the lives of almost all the so-called founders of religion—we know that half of the details of such lives is not seriously believed in and that the other half is seriously doubted— if this becomes the case, if that rock of historicity, as they pretend to call it, is shaken and shattered, the whole building tumbles down, broken absolutely, never to regain its lost status.

Everyone of the great religions of the world excepting our own, is built upon such historical characters, but ours rests upon principles. There is no man or woman who can claim to have created the Vedas. They are the embodiment of eternal principles; sages discovered them; and now and then the names of these sages are mentioned—just their names; we do not even know who or what they were. In many cases we do not know who their fathers were, and almost in every case we do not know when and where they were born. But what cared they, these sages, for their names? They were the preachers of principles, and they themselves, so far as they went, tried to become illustrations of the principles they preached.

At the same time, just as our God is an Impersonal and yet Personal God, so our religion is based upon principles—and yet with an infinite scope for the play of persons, for what religion gives us more incarnations, more prophets and seers and still waits for infinitely more? The Bhagwata says that incarnations are infinite, leaving ample scope for as many as you like to come. Therefore, if any one or more of our prophets are proved not to have been historical, it does not injure our religion at all; even then it remains firm as ever, because it is based upon principles, and not upon persons. It is in vain to try to gather all the peoples of the world around a single personality. It is difficult to make them gather together even round eternal and universal principles. If it ever becomes possible to bring the largest portion of humanity to one way of thinking in regard to religion, mark you, it must be always through principles and not through persons.

Yet as I have said, our religion has ample scope for the authority and influence of persons. There is that most wonderful theory of *Ishta* which gives you the fullest and the freest choice possible among these religious personalities. You may take up any one of the prophets or teachers as your guide and the object of your special adoration; you are even allowed to think that he whom you have chosen is the greatest of the prophets, greatest of all the *avatars*; there is no harm in that, but you must keep to a firm background of eternally true principles; the strange fact here is that the power of our incarnations has been holding good with us only so far as they are illustrations of the principles of the Vedas. The glory of Sri Krishna is that he has been the best preacher of our eternal religion of principles and the best commentator on the Vedanta that ever lived in India.

The second claim of Vedanta upon the attention of the world is that, of all the scriptures of the world, it is the one scripture the teaching of which is in entire harmony with the results that have been attained by the modern scientific investigations of external nature.[8]

The ideal of 'as many paths as sects' as propounded by Ramakrishna Paramahansa meant that all religions are true and good for their respective followers. This emphasises not harmony, but a compromise among religions which, in other words, is the principle of 'live and let live.' However, Vivekananda adopted an aggressive line and, rejecting the claim of any other religion being the world religion, put forward his own claim. This aggressive line was adopted

---

8. Complete Works of Vivekananda, Vol. III, p.182.

by him even at the Parliament of Religions. It was inevitably so because he had been thrown up by the wave of Renaissance and he was destined to fight the political battle there through the medium of religion. His own mind was clear on this point. He had himself admitted that he did not go to America merely with the objective of participating in the Parliament of Religions. It was of secondary importance. However, it did pave the way for him and make his task easier for which he was thankful to the members of the Parliament of Religions. But he was even more thankful to the people of America for their hospitality and for the feeling of brotherhood that they exhibited in a greater measure than any other race.

On 5th May, 1895 he wrote to Alasinga Perumal:

If you could send and maintain for a few years a dozen well-educated strong men to preach in Europe and America, you would do immense service to India, both morally and politically. Every man who morally sympathises with India becomes a political friend.

It was in the same letter that he had referred to his new discovery that Dvaitism, Vishishtadvaitism and Advaitism were the three stages of Vedantic philosophy which follow one another in that sequence. In this way, all religions were included in the Vedantic philosophy. This theory is based on the principle of harmony. He was thinking of writing a book to explain this theory but, perhaps, could not take it up. But, after his new discovery, he had become convinced that sooner or later. Vedanta would become the world religion and that on this depended the future of India and the entire human race and the realisation of the dream of universal brotherhood.

In his Chennai speech, to which we have already referred, he had expressed the hope that the Hindu race would conquer the world.

On his expressing similar views in London, prior to his return home, the correspondent of *India* asked him the

question: 'And is India finally to conquer her conquerors?'
To this he replied:

> Yes, in the world of ideas. England has the sword,
> the material world, as our Mohammedan conquerors
> had before her. Yet Akbar the Great practically became
> a Hindu; educated Mohammedans, the Sufis, are hardly
> to be distinguished from the Hindus....[9]

Vivekananda, who was imaginative by nature, had gone
abroad with a dream of securing financial aid for the poor
masses of India. This dream was broken soon after he
reached America. When he returned home, he came with
another dream—that of conquering the world in the spiritual
field. This was essentially the dream of the emerging
capitalist and bourgeois class which was trying to bring
about national unity in a country which was divided and
beset with social evils. Speaking in Chennai on the subject
'The Work Before Us,' he said:

> Therefore, young men of this city, I specially ask you
> to remember this. We must go out, we must conquer
> the world through our spirituality and philosophy. There
> is no other alternative, we must do it or die. The only
> condition of national life, of awakened and vigorous
> national life, is the conquest of the world by Indian
> thought.[10]

Kalidasa, in his ஐடிwork *Meghdoot*, in his poetic
fantasy, had made the cloud a messenger of Yaksha who
described to it the route it had to follow in its journey
from the South to the North. In so doing the poet presented
an attractive picture of the greatness, vastness and the beauty
of India—a country whose unity was being forged by the
mighty sword of the Gupta dynasty. It was to strengthen
such unity on emotional basis that, later on Shankaracharya

---

9. Complete Works of Vivekananda, Vol. V, p. 125.
10. Complete Works of Vivekananda, Vol. III, p. 277.

set out from the South and, fighting the evils of Buddhism, founded the four Dhams (abodes of God) in the four corners of the country. And now, when the country was bound by the shackles of slavery, the third attempt to bring about national unity on the basis of spirituality and philosophy (there being no other method available) was made by Vivekananda who, in his journeys from Rámnad to Almora, unfurled the flag on which was inscribed the Vedantic slogan of victory 'Yatra jeeva tatra shiva' (the Lord resides in every being). He explained the theory of this slogan that as long as man considered himself to be a body, he was no more than a spark of an eternal fire and that if he considered himself to be a soul then alone he was the personification of the universe.

Now that he was on his own soil, he spoke out frankly and said all that he considered not proper to say while he was in foreign lands. He boldly used the sword of self-criticism to demolish false beliefs and evil customs and practices without which it was impossible to remove the contradictions from which the masses suffered.

In his Dacca speech he confessed that, before he went round the country he was not aware of its natural beauty and was, likewise, ignorant about the greatness and the beauty of his country. He was, therefore, pained to see that the people of this great country, though they claimed to be greatly devoted to religion, were indifferent to religion as a result of the spread of European thinking. He, however, conceded that he was aware of the adverse physical and material circumstances in which his countrymen were forced to make a living.

These adverse material circumstances had created a number of thinking people of different levels; they were categorised into different classes[11] by Vivekananda. He

---

11. This classification was not in terms of classes as defined by Marx. It was based on ideology and it was possible for people belonging to different economic classes to belong to the same such class.

thought that the first category was of those reformers who wanted to reform, rather, recast the Hindu religion in order to regenerate it. No doubt, there were some good thinkers among them, but there were many who were trying to blindly follow others and were ignorant—about their own objective. Such reformers were very enthusiastic about injecting alien ideas in our religion. They thought that the Hindu religion was not a true religion, as it was based on idol worship. They did not bother to find out the significance of idol worship and dared to defame Hindu religion on that account on being prompted by others. There was another category who were engaged in the futile task of finding a scientific basis of Hindu customs and practices and talked in terms of electric and magnetic energy, etc. Vivekananda thought that it would not be surprising if such people defined God as concentration of electrical energy.

Our foreign rulers had attacked our religion not only with the help of Christian missionaries, but also on the basis of science. An attack on our religion was an attack on our culture and tradition. Vivekananda understood it well, and the so-called intellectuals, boastful of being Marxists, should also understand that, when religious ideology gets transformed physically into various institutions, as has happened in the thousands of years' history of the society having class divisions, then the culture and tradition of each country develops through and is preserved in these institutions. When there is stagnation in the development of culture and tradition due to material stagnation, it is harmful to try to demolish these institutions and to impose on them borrowed alien ideas even though they are progressive, excellent, logical and scientific. Such an attempt, made in the name of reforms and revolution, would result in the erasing, distortion or negation of history. After being cut off from his past and his traditions, man is reduced to a creature without backbone. He can neither be patriotic nor revolutionary. It was because of this that Vivekananda felt that the so-called reformers and patriots did not know what in reality were the ills of the society and were unnecessarily making much of secondary issues like idol worship, widow remarriage and child marriage.

Vivekananda was of the view that the reform movements of the past century were only a pretention. They were concerned only with the first two classes, not with the rest. So far as widow-remarriage was concerned, 70 per cent of the women of this country were not affected by that problem. He pointed out that all such reform movements were concerned only with upper classes who had become educated at the cost of the neglect of the common man. These upper classes had spared no efforts to keep their house clean and to show themselves to the British as being handsome. This could not be called reform. For bringing about reform it was necessary to go to the root. A united Indian nation could be built only by eradicating evil from the bottom to the top.

The most important task at that time was to organise a united Indian nation. He had made this task to be the mission of his life and wanted all the well-wishers of the nation to do likewise.

He exhorted the people not to forget this great mission. He felt that Indians, particularly the Bengalis, were being influenced by Western thinking, which was the reason for their backwardness. If people wanted to achieve national glory, then they would have to eschew alien thinking, although they could learn a lot from the West for bringing about development. It was necessary for our people to learn technology and the physical sciences from the West just as the Westerners needed to learn from us about religion and spiritualism. It was also necessary for Hindus to remember and believe that they were the teachers of the world.

Although there was no harm in asking for political rights and the like, yet rights and facilities could be claimed only through friendship. And friendship could be achieved only on the basis of equality. There could not be any friendship between two parties, when one of them continued to beg from the other. It was not possible for us to become strong without mutual cooperation with the British. He, therefore, exhorted Indians to go to England, not as beggars, but as teachers of religion for a mutual exchange according to their respective capacity. If the Indians wished to learn from them the means of acquiring material happiness why should they not, in return, teach them the means to achieve eternal happiness.

To those who were looking with hope towards Europe and praised the political system, i.e., the democracy prevailing there, Vivekananda said:

On the other hand, the political systems that we are struggling for in India have been in Europe for ages, and have been found wanting. One after the other, the institutions, systems and everything connected with political government have been condemned as useless; and Europe is restless, does not know where to turn. The material tyranny is tremendous. The wealth and power of a country are in the hands of a few men who do not ask, but manipulate the work of millions of human beings. By this power they can deluge the whole earth with blood. Religion and all things are under their feet; they rule and stand supreme. The Western world is governed by a handful of Shylocks. All those things that you hear about constitutional government, freedom, liberty and parliament—are but jokes![12]

However, Vivekananda did not lose sight of anything that was good in the West and learnt a lot during his stay there, as we have already stated. On the basis of his immense experience, comparative study, and with all the generosity of his heart, he had sincerely reached the conclusion that

_____

12. *Complete Works of Vivekananda*, Vol. III, p. 158.

the welfare of mankind depended on harmony between the spritualism of the East and the materialism of the West and on exchange of ideas and learning from each other. He continued saying:

> The West is groaning under the tyranny of the Shylocks, and the East is groaning under the tyranny of the priests; each must keep the other in check. Do not think that one alone is to help the world.[13]

His concept of harmony was based on unbiased knowledge. Therefore, on the one hand, he attacked the education system introduced by Macaulay, which sought to create misconceptions and make us hate our past and thus create a feeling of inferiority among us, on the other, he also did not spare the evil practices popularised by the priestly class to serve their selfish interests.

He warned the countrymen against the twin dangers of ridiculing all Hindu thinking under the evil influence of Western thinking and of justifying and rationalising all the evil religious practices on the authority of the Vedas. He said that he would prefer Indians to be agnostics to their foolishly following evil practices. He advised people to save themselves from these twin dangers. He wanted Indian people to be bold, full of blood and have nerves of steel. He exhorted them to get rid of useless ideas which were weakening.

Vivekananda had understood it well that it was only culture, and not merely the fund of knowledge, that could withstand the force of the changing age. This understanding had come to him as a result of a deep study of the history, philosophy and literature of not only his country, but of the entire world. He was a walking encyclopaedia of his times. His learning did not make him conceited. Rather,

---

13. Complete Works of Vivekananda, Vol. III, p. 158

it had filled him with humility, civility and generosity of heart. Although, at no place did he mention Marx, yet he had fully understood the truth expounded by Marx that a new society does not drop from above, but is born out of the womb of the old. Radical change and burning the roots does not mean destroying everything and beginning everything from scratch. If anything has to be destroyed, it is the evil beliefs and the evil practices.

To bring about national solidarity we needed men with a strong backbone, iron muscles and nerves of steel. For building men of such type it was necessary not only to destroy the evil beliefs and practices, but also to understand and imbibe all that was healthy and living in our ancient culture, and transform the same into physical force; while, on the other hand, the so-called reformers were only ridiculing religious practices and, intoxicated by their shallow Western knowledge, believed that this would reduce the contradictions between the various castes and sects and take the country towards progress. Vivekananda gave no importance to such reformers and to their childish prattle.

In his Jaffna speech Vivekananda defended the wisdom of old practices like caste system. Though, on the face of it, they appeared to be a part of religion, yet such practices were created and were necessary for the preservation and protection of our nation and would, probably, die out when they were no longer needed. He conceded that as he grew older, he felt hesitant to criticise such customs which were invented as a result of the experience of several centuries. He, therefore, did not feel inclined to change or destroy such customs merely on the advice of any greenhorn foreign reformer who himself belonged to a society which was not organised in a stable manner and did not have any social laws which had endured for a number of centuries.

He was firmly of the view that it was not possible for our people to be hammered into the mould of other nations. He said that he was not against the social customs of other races, yet what was good for them could not necessarily be good for us. What was food for them might turn out to be poison for us. While their present customs were developed on the basis of a different kind of science, a different kind of traditional experience, our own were developed as a result of our own tradition and experience of thousands of years. It was, thereafter, necessary for us to follow our own nature and customs.

It is for this reason that Vivekananda felt that, before trying to reform our religion it was necessary to propagate it first. Before inundating India with socialistic or political ideology it was necessary to flood it with religious ideas.

This was the main point in the speeches of Vivekananda made from Colombo to Almora. His younger brother Bhupendranath Dutta has written that all the secret revolutionary organisations that were formed in the first decade of the twentieth century were inspired by these thoughts. All the revolutionaries took inspiration from his speeches and in all the searches of the homes of these revolutionaries taken by the police till 1927, Vivekananda literature was inevitably found.[14]

The foreign rulers had sought to distort our history with a view to creating misconceptions and contradictions among the people. Swamiji demolished these in his speeches. For example, a misconception had been created that the fair complexioned Aryan race came from an alien land and, after defeating the dark skinned Indians, made them their slaves and gave birth to the caste system. Vivekananda rejected this theory as being concocted. He said:

> The only explanation is to be found in Mahabharata, which says that in the beginning of the Satya Yuga there was one caste, the Brahmins, and then by difference of occupation they went on dividing themselves into different castes, and that is the only true and rational explanation that has been given. And

---

14. *Swami Vivekananda : Patriotic Prophet*, p. 213.

in the coming Satya Yuga all the other castes will go back to the same condition.[15]

Even today, the effort to divide North from South on this basis continues. In his Chennai speech Vivekananda had said:

> There is a theory that there was a race of mankind called Dravidians entirely different from another race in northern India called the Aryans, and that the southern Indian Brahmins are the only Aryans that came from the north, the other men of southern India belong to an entirely different caste and race to those of southern Indian Brahmins. Now I beg your pardon Mr. Philologist, this is entirely unfounded. The only proof of this is that there is a difference of language between the north and the south. I do not see any other difference. We are so many northern men here, and I ask my European friends to pick out the northern and southern men from the assembly. Where is the difference?[16]

Thus, it is impossible to pick out Aryans and the dark-eyed tribes from an assemblage of Hindus, Sikhs, Muslims, Christians, Brahmins, Kshatriyas and those belonging to the lower castes. Later on, the Huns, Kushans, Tartars, Greeks and other races also came to India and got mingled here. It is not possible to distinguish between these races now. There-fore, it follows, that the intention behind this theory was to create a feeling of hatred for the past and the cultural tradition of this country. Since Aryans, as such, are not distinguishable, all the hatred is directed against Brahmins and the Sanskrit language. This feeling of hatred has been made so widespread that the law-giver Manu is held to be responsible for the present condition of the exploited

---

15. *Complete Works of Vivekananda,* Vol. III, p. 295.
16. *Ibid*, p. 392.

and the oppressed Shudra castes and, out of revenge, copies of *Manusmriti* are burnt. But has this burning of the copies of Manusmriti brought about any change in their condition? Is it not like fighting in the air and wasting our energy?

Foreign propaganda and our own ignorance are at the root of these misconceptions. The archaeologists have reached the conclusion that originally there were five nomadic races—the Mongols, the Aryans, the Negroes, the Slavs and the Semetic. They went and settled down wherever they found good grazing grounds and other natural facilities. Later on, these races got subdivided into Huns, Mughals, Tartars, Shakas, Kushans, Darads and Ravishas, etc. How can one single out Aryans from among them? How did the Dravidians come to exist as a separate race?

It is no doubt true that the higher castes monopolised all the power and erected the barriers of custom around the castes. Life from birth till death was bound by stringent rules and regulations. Untouchability became widespread and the Hindu religion was reduced to a religion of the kitchen. The higher caste people enslaved not only the castes belonging to the working class, but also women of their own castes by depriving them of the right to education and freedom.

Vivekananda considered this to be the main reason for the decay and fall of the country. He thought that it was for this reason that God in His greatness, made them suffer the vengeance. Those who had sucked the blood of the poor, who had been educated at the cost of the poor, who had made themselves strong at the cost of their poverty, were, in their own turn, taken as slaves and sold in thousands, their property was plundered for centuries and their women and daughters were disgraced. It was not without reason that all this happened.

The monopoly of the higher castes has now been broken. There is no sense in quarrelling over the past. Now the question before us is that of uplifting the downtrodden and providing them with education. It is only in this way that we can atone for the past and build the future of the country.

Vivekananda was of the view that people should be educated in the language they speak and they would learn a lot in this way. It was also necessary to make the people acquainted with culture. He thought that the only way to bring about equality among the castes was to inculcate among the people knowledge and education which are the strength and pride of the upper castes.

Mere change of religion does not bring about a change in nationality and culture. Only that person can be called a foreigner, who is economically and mentally linked with some other country. People belonging to all the castes and communities in our country form a common nation, have a common culture and are inspired by a common great past. The theory of a composite culture is a myth and baseless and has been advanced by foreign rulers to create divisions.

In his speech entitled 'Future of India,' Vivekananda has said:

Here we are the Aryan, the Dravidian, the Tartar, the Turk, the Mughal, the European—all the nations of the world, as it were, pouring their blood into this land. Of languages the most wonderful conglomeration is here; of manners and customs there is more difference between two Indian races than between the European and Indian races.

The common ground that we have is our sacred tradition, our religion. That is the only common ground, and upon that we shall have to build. In Europe, political ideas form the national unity. In Asia, religious ideals form the national unity. The unity in religion, therefore, is absolutely necessary as the first condition of future India. There must be the recognition of one religion throughout the length and breadth of this land.

What do I mean by one religion? Not in the sense of one religion as held among the Christians or the Mohammedans, or the Buddhists. We know that our religion has certain common grounds, common to all our sects however varying their conclusions may be, however different their claims may be. So there are certain common grounds; and within their limitation this religion of ours admits of a marvellous variation, an infinite amount of liberty to think and live our own lives. We all know that, at least those of us who have thought, and what we want is to bring out these life-giving common principles of our religion, and let every man, woman, and child, throughout the length and breadth of this country, understand them, know them, and try to bring them out in themselves. This is the first step and, therefore, it has to be taken.[17]

Religion—*dharma*—has been used here in a wider sense and it includes the entire society, its customs, culture and tradition. The Vedantic principle which has been referred to here, claims to state that 'man essentially is divine' and whatever we see around us becomes unique due to this consciousness of divinity. Therefore, there is no quarrel or confrontation of Vedanta with any other belief of the world.

Thus, according to Vivekananda, national feeling can be strengthened in our country by propagating this principle. It will also help in realising the dream of universal brotherhood.

In one of his incomplete articles about religion Vivekananda expressed the view that it was likely that the number of sects, instead of decreasing, would go on increasing till every person became a sect in himself. This

---

17. Complete Works of Vivekananda, Vol. III, p. 286.

Robert Ingersoll, agnostic philosopher and orator

would then prepare the ground for an over-all unity. Puranic stories and rituals would continue to divide the people. People would differ about the greatness of the ideal preceptor of the principle commonly acceptable to them.

We shall analyse this theory in the next chapter so as to be able to understand the class character of Vivekananda and the contradictions inherent in his thinking.

8

SPIRITUAL ADVAITISM VERSUS MATERIAL ADVAITISM

"Man is born to conquer nature and not to follow it."
-Vivekananda

While speaking on the Hindu religion in the Parliament of Religions, Vivekananda had said:

> Science is nothing, but the finding of unity. As soon as science would reach perfect unity, it would stop from further progress, because it would reach the goal. Thus chemistry could not progress further when it would discover one element out of which all other elements could be made. Physics would stop when it would be able to fulfil its services in discovering one energy of which all others are but manifestations, and the science of religion would become perfect when it would discover Him who is the one life in the universe of death, Him who is the constant basis of an ever-changing world, one who is the only soul of which all souls are but delusive manifestations. Thus is it through multiplicity and duality, that the ultimate unity is reached. Religion can go no further. This is the goal of all science.[1]

In this context we have to see how religion was born,

---

1. *Ibid.* Vol. V, pp. 12-13.

how it passed through its stages of development to reach the final stage of spiritual Advaitism. Is it possible to put a full stop to the development of thought after this stage?

Man is a rational animal. Among the other living beings, he is endowed with the most developed brain which gives him great power. While the other animals have adapted themselves to nature for the sake of their survival, man has rebelled against nature and adapted it to his needs. He is not the slave, but the conqueror of nature. Through his power of thinking he has discovered fire, water, electricity; has invented machines and conquered nature by discovering its laws.

Man has himself undergone a change in an effort to change nature. During this struggle, man has been transformed from a beast to a human being. Therefore, this transformation has not been brought about by a divine hand. It is through his own struggle that he has created the divine forces such as God and the devil. All thoughts were born out of material circumstances, man tested them through experiment, rejected all that was irrelevant and gave concrete shape to what was material and thereby formulated principles. In this way, gradually, literature, arts, culture and religion were developed. In one of his speeches on 'Maya and the Conception of God' Vivekananda has said:

> In all the religions of the world the one question they propose to discuss is this: Why is there disharmony in the universe? Why is there evil in the universe? We do not find the question in the very inception of primitive religious ideas, because the world did not appear incongruous to the primitive man. Circumstances were not inharmonious for him; there was no clash of opinions, to him there was not antagonism of goal and evil. There was merely a feeling in his own heart of something which said yea, and something which said nay. The primitive man was a man of impulse. He did what occurred to him, and tried to bring out

through his muscles whatever thought come into his mind, and he never stopped to judge, seldom tried to check his impulses. So with the gods, they were also creations of his impulse. Indra comes and shatters the forces of demons. Jehovah is pleased with one person and displeased with another, for what reason no one knows or asks. The habit of enquiry had not then arisen, and whatever he did was regarded as right. There was no idea of good or evil. The Devas did many wicked things in our sense of the world; again and again Indra and other gods committed many wicked deeds, but to the worshippers of Indra the ideas of wickedness and evil did not occur, so they did not question them.[2]

Evidently, the primitive man was more engaged in fighting the fearful powers of nature. He was not able to understand these forces, still he carried within himself the determination to control them. At that time his chief problem was that of survival and he subsisted on whatever he could get—game or fruit. He was trying to change nature through his acts and imagination. It was in his effort that he attributed divinity to fearful forces and started worshipping them wishing them to become blessings instead of being curses. Thereafter, through his imagination, he created gods who would help him to fight against those forces. For example, we can see the man of the Vedic age trying to woo *Varun*, Pavan and Agni through his worship and Indra comes to his help by breaking the mountains with his *Vajra* and destroying evil power.

The man of the Vedic age is basically materialistic. He and his gods both belong to the earth. He has no conception of any heaven or hell, soul or God beyond this earth. His prayers and worship are simple as he himself is. He prays: 'Let me live for hundred years, hear for hundred years,

---

2. Complete Works of Vivekananda, Vol. II, p. 107.

speak for hundred years and live for hundred years without misery.'

He looks up to the clouds gathered in the sky and prays: 'Let the rains come on time, let the earth be full of crops, let the country be without sorrow, let man be fearless.'

It took several centuries for the language and the verse, in which the Vedas are written, to develop. And the Vedas were composed thousands of years back. In the intervening period, man conquered nature. This development in the thinking of the Indian race traced by Vivekananda in the following words:

There was an inquisitiveness in the race to start with, which very soon developed into bold analysis, and though, in the first attempt, the work turned out, might be like the attempt with shaky hands of the future master—sculpture, it very soon gave way to strict science, bold attempts, and startling results.

Its boldness made these men search every brick of the sacrificial altars, scan, cement, and pulverise every word for the scriptures; arrange, re-arrange, doubt, deny, or explain the ceremonies. It turned their gods inside out, and assigned only a secondary place to their omnipotent, omniscient, omnipresent creator of the universe, their ancestral Father-in-heaven; or threw Him altogether overboard as useless, and started a world-religion without Him with even now the largest following of any religion. It evolved the science of geometry from the arrangement of bricks to build various altars, and startled the world with astronomical knowledge that arose from the attempts accurately to time the worship and oblations. It made their contributions to the science of mathematics the largest of any race, ancient or modern, and to their knowledge of chemistry, of metallic compounds in medicine, their musical notes, their invention of the bow—instruments

—all of great service in the building of modern European civilization. It led them to invent the science of building up the child-mind through shining fables, of which every child in every civilized country learns in a nursery or a school and carries an impress through life.[3]

After the Vedic age, when man was free of initial struggles and got the time to think and contemplate, only then he developed the concept of soul and God. What was the basis of this concept?

According to Vivekananda, there are contrary opinions about the question posed in the beginning of the poetical Kathopanishad whether man exists after death or not? Every school of philosophy in the world has answered the question in its own way. In many ways efforts have been made to know about the truth, the life hereafter and to find the solution for the restlessness of soul, and all efforts to avoid this question would fail as long as death remains a reality.

Vivekananda has cited all examples about soul and God from the Upanishads and the Gita; he includes the Upanishads among the Vedas. While analysing the philosophy of the Vedas he has divided religion into two parts—the theoretical and the ceremonial. In a letter written to a disciple from Almora on 1st June, 1897 he wrote:

The objections you show about the Vedas would be valid if the word Vedas meant Samhitas. The word Vedas includes three parts, the Samhitas, the Brahmanas, and the Upanishads, according to the universally received opinion in India. Of those, the first two portions, as being the ceremonial parts, have alone been taken up by all our philosophers and founders of sects.

The idea that the Samhitas are the only Vedas is very recent and has been started by the late Swami Dayananda. This opinion has not got any hold on the orthodox population.

---

3. *Ibid.* Vol. VI, pp. 157-58.

The reason of this opinion was that Swami Dayananda thought he could find a consistent theory of the whole, based on a new interpretation of the Samhitas, but the difficulties remained the same, only they fell back on the Brahmanas. And in spite of the theories of interpretation and interpolation a good deal still remains.[4]

We feel that the reason for treating the Samhitas as Vedas and distinguishing the Vedas from the Upanishads is that man's thinking basically is not spiritual but materialistic. Man lives under the open sky in direct contact with nature, struggles against nature and also worships it. This alone is the basis of the formulation of his thoughts. On reaching the age of the Upanishads man got the leisure to think of realities about death and the life after death and beyond the universe. The stories of Nachiketa, Satyakama, Jadabharata and Virochan, etc. relating to the same are very inapt and inconclusive. They only refer to the word 'Soul' and do not lay down any definite concept. This concept was laid down in the Gita and was later on developed by the Vedantists like Shankaracharya, Ramanuja, Ramakrishna Paramahansa and Vivekananda.

We have now to study this concept from the point of view of historical materialism. Let us take the example of the Gita. The central idea of this book is contained in the episode when Arjuna, when faced with the Kaurava army, puts down his arms and tells his charioteer Krishna that he would not fight with his own relatives, as it was a sin to kill them. Thereupon Krishna tells him,'Arjuna, you are under an illusion, the soul is immortal and cannot be killed by any one, nor does it ever die. Those of whom you think of slaying are already dead. Therefore, give up cowardice and fight, because it is your dharma as a Kshatriya. If you are victorious you will rule the world, if you die

---

4. *Ibid.* Vol. V, p. 99.

you will enjoy the fruits of heaven.' It was not, in fact, the question of cowardice. In the Vedic age, which is regarded as primeval communism, people used to live as tribes. There used to be wars between different tribes, but in the same tribe it was a sin even to abuse a fellow tribesman, not to speak of killing him. The Kauravas and Pandavas belonged to the same tribe. Arjuna was under the influence of old tribal customs and that is why he refused to fight. But when the battle of Mahabharata was fought, the concept of private property had been born. Krishna, being the son of King Nanda, was himself aligned to the concept of property and was its great spokesman. The new concept of the soul being immortal and not dying nor being killed by someone was born out of the need of being free from the regret of killing one's brethren for the sake of property.

The age of society based on the concept of personal property was definitely an age of progress from primeval communism and the new ideology sought to take man on the path of progress. Therefore, Krishna not only gave a new ideology in place of the old tribal concepts, but also offered to them the double benefit of fighting to be victorious to rule the world or to enjoy the fruits of heaven if killed in battle.

With the origin of private property, society was divided into two classes. One was that of workers, who performed labour, but were deprived of the luxuries and comforts of life. The other was the class of property-owners who ceased to be workers, who ruled over others through their power of thinking and enjoyed all the comforts and luxuries of life. With the division of society came the division of thinking—of 'doing' and 'not doing'—the division of the workers and the propertied. In this context Vivekananda says:

Here are two Sanskrit words : the one is *pravritti*, which means revolving towards, and other is *nivritti*, which means revolving away. The "revolving towards" is what we call the world, the "I and mine;" it includes all those things which are always enriching that "me" by wealth and money and power, and name and fame, and which are of a grasping nature, always tending to accumulate everything in one centre, the centre being "myself." That is the *pravritti*, the natural tendency of every human-being; taking everything from everywhere and heaping around one centre, that centre being man's own sweet self. When this tendency begins to break, when it is *nivritti* or "going away" from one's self, then begin morality and religion.[5]

The owners of property possessed all the facilities. They did not have to work with their hands; they had only to use their brain. Their idea of happiness developed in them the idea of sorrow in the same proportion. Therefore, they conceived of an unchanging world beyond the ever-changing world that existed. Vivekananda says:

Then there is the tremendous fact of death. The whole world is going towards death. Everything dies. All our progress, our vanities, our reforms, our luxuries, our wealth, our knowledge, have that one end—death. That is all which is certain. Cities come and go, empires rise and fall, planets break into pieces and crumble into dust, to be blown about by the atmospheres of other planets. Thus it has been going on from time without beginning. Death is the end of everything. Death is the end of life, of beauty, of wealth, of power, of virtue, too. Saints die and sinners die, kings die and beggars die. They are all going to die. And yet this tremendous clinging to life exists. Somehow, we do not know why we cling to life, we cannot give it up. And this is *maya*.[6]

This led to the concept of the unreality of the world

5. *Ibid.* Vol. I, pp. 83-84.
6. *Principles and Practices of Vedanta in the Words of Vivekananda.* Ed. by Christopher Isherwood, pp. 34-35.

and the reality of Brahman. We shall later on discuss the theory of maya.

Vivekananda says, 'When Gita was first preached, there was then going on a great controversy between two sects. One party considered the Vedic *yajnas* and animal sacrifices and such like *karmas* to constitute the whole of religion. The other preached that the killing of horses and cattle cannot be called religion. The people belonging to the latter party were mostly sanyasins and followers of *jnana*. They believed that the giving up of all work and the gaining of the knowledge of the self was the only path to *moksha*.' In fact, it was a debate between the materialists and the idealists. The abstract materialistic thinking prevailing from the Vedic times was sought to be replaced by gross ceremonial shape in the form of *yajnas* and animal sacrifice. The people who were living the life of luxury and comforts had only the ambition of knowing about the self and achieving moksha; they were becoming more and more inclined inwards and for them man had himself become a problem more complex than any other problem. The materialists stoutly opposed them. Among them was the school of Charvaka philosophy. This philosophy was so popular that it is known by the name of Lokayat (people's philosophy). To sum up, idealism is the theory of *nivritti*, of "not doing" and materialism is the philosophy of *pravritti*, of "doing." Vivekananda says:

Then, there were the Charvakas, who preached horrible things, the most rank, undisguised materialism, such as in the nineteenth century they dare not openly preach. These Charvakas were allowed to preach from temple to temple, and city to city, that religion was all nonsense, that it was priestcraft, that the Vedas were the words and writings of fools, rogues and demons, and that there was neither God nor any eternal soul. If there was a soul, why did it not come back after death drawn by the love of wife and child? Their idea was that if there was a soul it must still love after death, and want good things to eat and nice dress. Yet no one hurt these Charvakas.[7]

The Charvaka literature was, however, destroyed later. Vivekananda continues to say about the Charvakas:

Charvakas, a very ancient sect in India, were rank materialists. They have died out now and most of their books are lost. They claimed that the soul, being the product of the body and its forces, died with it; that there was no proof of its further existence. They denied inferential knowledge, accepting only the perception of the senses.[8]

The commentary written by Shankaracharya is nothing but a repudiation of the Charvaka philosophy. The materialists were condemned as immoral and Vamacharis (followers of the wrong path) and it was propagated that they preached eating, drinking and being merry even if one had to borrow from others. They were depicted as being possessed of beastial tendencies who limited themselves to the enjoyment of senses, although the enjoyment of senses also was the privilege of the propertied classes and the working classes were denied that privilege.

The spiritualists, while repudiating the Charvaka philosophy, found in it a back-door entry to the philosophy of Kapila. Therefore, they supported it and reaped benefits from the thoughts of this great thinker.

According to Vivekananda, the Sankhya philosophy of Kapila was the first school of thought in the world, which presented logical thinking about the universe and deserves the admiration of the thinkers about reality. It called Kapila the father of philosophy, who invited attention. Kapila has been mentioned in the earliest of the Shrutis. His direct

---

7. *Ibid.* Vol. II, p. 114.
8. *Ibid*, Vol. VIII, pp. 29-30.

knowledge was surprising and provided the yogis with the proof of direct knowledge. He had no telescope or microscope and yet his direct knowledge was of a high calibre and his analysis of things surprising and complete.

According to Kapila, there is no God as creator of the universe. The three attributes of *sattva*, *raja* and *tama* con-stitute the *brahmanda*. As *buddhi* (mind or intellect) is the creation of *prakriti* (nature), it is a part of it. Yet there is the entity of *purusha* which is separate from buddhi and *prakriti* and makes them active.

As Kapila considers both *prakriti* and *purusha* to be timeless and independent, he can be called a Dvaitist. His belief in the timeless and independent existence of prakriti makes him a materialist.

The spiritualists amended the concept of Kapila by calling purusha an *atman* (soul) and transformed it into Vedantic philosophy.

According to Vivekananda, the first objection of Vedantist to Sankhya concept is that it is not complete analysis. If prakriti and atman are both independent entities then we shall have two independent entities, and arguments which prove the omnipresence of atman will also apply to prakriti, making it an entity without space, time and causation. If *prakriti* be such, it would not reach completion or would not progress. Thus we have to accept independent entities which is not possible.

According to the philosophy of Vedanta, prakriti is bound by space, time and causation while atman, being beyond space, time and causation, is immutable and eternal and is a part of independent and eternal entity called *Ishwara* (God) who is the creator of the universe. To this concept were added the theories of *maya* and *karma*. The two are complementary to each other and complete the philosophy of protection of private property. In the Gita, which is the sacred book in favour of protecting private property, we listen to Krishna saying to Arjuna:

O Arjuna, many lives of Mine have passed, and so have yours. I know them all (but) you know not.

Similarly, he says about *maya*:

Since this divine maya of Mine which is constituted by the *gunas* (qualities) is difficult to cross over (therefore), those who take refuge in Me alone cross over this maya.'

We can say that the Vedantic philosophy is another name for the spiritual aspect of the Sankhya philosophy. All the sects of the Hindu religion like the Vaishnava, Shaiva, and those founded by Kabir, Nanak and Dadu are essentially Vedantic. They may be having differences about the existence of God and the form in which He exists, however, they are broadly divided among Dvaitists, Vishishtadvaitists and Advaitists. The most notable among those who developed the Vedantic philosophy are Shankaracharya, Ramanuja, Ramakrishna Paramahansa and Vivekananda. As we can not discuss this subject in greater detail, we shall only briefly refer to Dvaitism, Vishishtadvaitism and Advaitism.

Dvaitism is the first stage of religion. According to this theory there is the existence of an eternal God, an eternal nature and innumerable souls which are also eternal.

Vishishtadvaitism is the second stage. According to this theory, God Himself exists in the form of universe and man. We are all part of him, we are all one. Yet there is a rigid individuality among men and between man and God.

Advaitism is the third and the last stage of religion. According to this theory, there can be no end of what is eternal. If this eternal entity can be divided into parts then each of those parts will also be eternal. Even if this hypothesis of separating the parts is accepted, the parts will eventually come together. Hence the eternal entity is not many and the same eternal soul is being reflected in what appear to be innumerable different souls. It is this eternal soul which forms the mind of the man and is known as *jivatma*.

We have already stated how Vivekananda added the theory of evolution to the Vedantic philosophy while analysing the philosophy in England and America. He proudly revealed his discovery that Dvaita, Vishishtadvaita and Advaita are the three progressive stages of religion. *Dvaita* is the lowest and *advaita* is the highest among them.

In making this discovery, Vivekananda excelled his preceptor Ramakrishna Paramahansa. He had said to one of his disciples:

So I preach only the Upanishads. If you look, you will find that I have never quoted anything but the Upanishads. And of the Upanishads, it is only that one idea—strength. The quintessence of Vedas and Vedanta and all, lies in that one word ... strength and fearlessness. My own ideal is that giant of a saint whom they killed in the Mutiny, and who broke his silence, when stabbed to the heart, to say—"And thou also art He."

But you may ask, "What is the place of Ramakrishna in this scheme?"

He is the method, the wonderful unconscious method! He did not understand himself. He knew nothing of England or the English, save that they were queer folk from over the sea. But he lived a great life and I understand the meaning thereof.'

Vivekananda understood his Guru, his country and his own self. We have already stated that he was fighting a political battle through the medium of religion. That is why he laid great stress on the word 'strength.'

He berated his disciples by telling them that they had no blood flowing in their veins and they were paralysed. He therefore exhorted them to develop the quality of Raja, so that the people of the country could be made capable of facing the struggle of life. He said that he found no strength, no enthusiasm and no talent of mind in the country.

What could such inert beings achieve? He said that it was for this reason that he had taken a lifetime vow to awaken the people and that he was born only to accomplish this mission. He solicited the help of his followers in this task and exhorted them to go from village to village and—awakening all the people from a Chandala to a Brahmin—make them strong. He wanted his countrymen to be taught how to stand on their own feet, eat well and enjoy life. It was the quality of Rajas that had to be developed first among them; only later they could be taught how to achieve liberation after death and how to shake off the bonds of enjoyment.

The country was devoid of any sign of life, according to him. The people who considered themselves educated had only passed some examination by reading something in a foreign language. They were only fit to get jobs as clerks or magistrates. That education had not benefited the country. The country, which was once a granary, was ravaged by famines. The existing education offered no solution to these problems. He said he preached the development of the quality of Rajas so as to enable people to grow more. What was the use of the Shastras when the country was starving? It was better to throw them in the Ganges. It was essential first to teach the people how to grow more food and then only they could be given lessons about God. He felt that no one would be interested in listening to the religious stories so long as one's wordly needs were not fulfilled. Therefore, he exhorted the people to awaken their intrinsic power and mobilise the people of the country around that. There was no time to be lost. The first priority was to be given to the production of food grains and religion could come afterwards.

While saying all this to his disciples, Vivekananda was overwhelmed by emotions of sorrow and pity and his face glowed with a crimson glow. There was fire in his eyes. The disciples were so awstruck by his emotional eruption that they were left speechless. Vivekananda later on added that he could clearly see the future. There was no escape from what was coming and no alternative of what he had suggested. He said that those who were intelligent could foresee the future.

He felt that there was a new dawn on the horizon ever since the birth of Ramakrishna and soon there would be the brilliance of daylight.

This happened in 1898. Around that time some students came to him and requested him to give them lessons on the Gita. Swamiji told them, 'Go and play football in the field. You will achieve heaven sooner by playing football than by learning Gita. The country needs muscles of iron and nerves of steel.'

Such words could have been spoken not by a sanyasin preaching religion, but by a national leader. For him religion was secondary. His life-time mission was to awaken the people to a new dawn, to prepare them for a political fight. That is why his thinking became progressively scientific. In 1900 he again went abroad. On 20th March he spoke these words in San Francisco:

Gradually the word 'nature' and the idea of uniformity came to be applied to internal phenomena, the phenomena of life and mind. All that is differentiated is nature. Nature is the quality of plant, the quality of animal, and the quality of man. Man's life behaves according to definite methods; so does his mind. Thoughts do not just happen, there is a certain method in their rise, existence and fall. In other words, just as the external phenomena are bound by law, internal phenomena, that is to say the life and mind of man, are also bound by law.[9]

This was different from what he spoke in London during his first foreign visit:

These days there is a controversy as to whether this

9. *Ibid.* Vol. VIII, p. 244.

body made up of the five gross elements causes the development of the power of thinking or whether it is the power of thinking that creates the body. Decidedly, all the religions of the world say that the power of thinking illumines the body and do not subscribe to the contrary opinion.

On 24th January, 1894 he wrote to his Chennai disciples from Chicago:

My whole ambition in life is to set in motion a machinery which will bring noble ideas to the door of everybody, and then let men and women settle their own fate. Let them know what our forefathers as well as other nations have thought on the most momentous questions of life. Let them see specially what others are doing now, and then decide. We are to put the chemicals together, the crystallisation will be done by nature according to her laws. Work hard, be steady and have faith in the Lord. Set to work, I am coming sooner or later. Keep the motto before you,—'Elevation of the masses without injuring religion'.[10]

According to this concept of religion, thoughts have their own separate existence. All the knowledge reposes in the soul which is a part of independent God which is the truth. One who realises this truth by going beyond the senses knows about Brahman and he is liberated from ignorance and every other bond. That highest being does not act as there is no need for him to act. He rules the world only through his thought power. According to this idealistic theory, persons like Buddha and Christ are the makers of history.

He said in London on 23rd November, 1895:

"The greatest force is derived from the power of thought. The finer the element, the more powerful it is. The silent power of thought influences people even

---

10. *Ibid*, Vol. V, p. 25.

at a distance, because mind is one as well as many. The universe is a cobweb; minds are spiders.[11]

In other words, a man will become a tiger if he considers himself to be a tiger and a jackal if he considers himself to be a jackal, and if he realises his own self and considers himself to be Brahman he will become Brahman. The theory of Satyagraha, which said 'Swarajya is within you' was also the same. Gandhi used to say that a man becomes a complete Satyagrahi if he achieves the highest truth within himself by such non-violent acts as fasting, sacrifice, etc.; then no power on earth can defeat him. When such a complete Satyagrahi looks into the eyes of his adversary, the adversary would give up all enmity and would become a complete Satyagrahi under his influence. It is wrong to retaliate against evil and injustice, because it only leads to evil. The best way to make the world pure is by propagating good thoughts.

But capitalism in every country, in its political fight, has made science and not religion its tool. The first capitalist revolution took place in France in 1879. The group known as Encyclopaedists of France, led by Didars, prepared the ground for this revo-lution. These Encyclopaedists were materialists. From then onwards, materialism became the main thinking of Western intellectuals. But at the end of nineteenth century, when capitalism gave up its progressive role and transformed itself into reactionary imperialism, only those intellectuals remained aligned to this thinking who had come under them influence of Dialectical Materialism of Marx.

Vivekananda was the best spokesman of the emerging bourgeois class of our country. During his journeys abroad he benefited from knowledge of scientific reality. He hated imperialism and wanted to raise and awaken the oppressed and exploited people of the country. Therefore, it was natural for him to cross the stop line—the highest point of *advaitism*.

---

11. *Ibid.* Vol. VIII, p. 225.

That is why we find him speaking these words in San Francisco:

> The external and internal natures are not two different things. They are really one. Nature is the sum total of all the phenomena. "Nature" means all that is, all that moves. We make a tremendous distinction between matter and mind; we think that the mind is entirely different from matter. Actually, they are but one nature, half of which is continually acting on the other half. Matter is pressing upon mind in the form of various sensations. These sensations are nothing but force. The force from the outside evokes the force within. From the will to respond to or get away from the other force, the inner force becomes what we call thought.[12]

According to Dialectical Materialism, mind is the organised form of matter and all thoughts are born out of physical circumstances. Mao Tse-tung has this to say about the origin of right thoughts:

'Where do correct ideas come from? Do they drop from the skies? No. Are they innate in the mind? No. They come from social practice, and from it alone; they come from three kinds of social practice, the struggle for production, the class struggle and scientific experiment. It is man's social being that determines his thinking. Once the correct ideas characteristic of the advanced class are grasped by the masses, these ideas turn into a material force which changes society and changes the world. In their socal practice, men engage in various kinds of struggle and gain rich experience, both from their successes and from their failures. Countless phenomena of the objective external world are reflected in a man's brain through his five sense organs—the organs of sight, hearing, smell, taste and touch. At first, knowledge is perceptual. The leap to conceptual knowledge, i.e., to ideas, occurs when sufficient perceptual knowledge is accumulated. This is one process in cognition. It is the

---

12. *Ibid.* Vol. VIII, p. 245.

first stage in the whole process of cognition, the stage leading from objective matter to subjective consciousness, from existence to ideas. 'Whether or not one's consciousness or ideas (including theories, policies, plans or measures) do correctly reflect the laws of the objective external world is not yet proved at this stage, in which it is not yet possible to ascertain whether they are correct or not. Then comes the second stage in the process of cognition, the stage leading from consciousness back to matter, from ideas back to existence, in which the knowledge gained in the first stage is applied in social practice to ascertain whether the theories, policies, plans or measures meet with the anticipated success. Generally speaking, those that succeed are correct and those that fail are incorrect, and this is especially true of man's struggle with nature. In social struggle, the forces representing the advanced class sometimes suffer defeat, not because their ideas are incorrect, but because, in the balance of forces engaged in struggle, they are not as powerful for the time, being as the forces of reaction; they are, therefore, temporarily defeated, but they are bound to triumph sooner or later.

Man's knowledge makes another leap through the test of practice. This leap is more important than the previous one. For it is this leap alone that can prove the correctness or incorrectness of the first leap, *i.e.*, of the ideas, theories, policies, plans or measures formulated in the course of reflecting the objective external world. There is no other way of testing truth. Furthermore, the one and only purpose of the proletariat in knowing the world is to change it. Often, a correct idea can be arrived at only after many repetitions of the process leading from matter to consciousness and then back to matter, that is, leading from practice to knowledge and then back to practice. Such is the Marxist theory of knowledge, the dialectical materialist theory of knowledge.

Continuing his San Francisco speech, Vivekananda says:

Both matter and mind are really nothing but forces;

and if you analyse them far enough, you will find that at root they are one. The very fact that the external force can somehow evoke the internal forces shows that somewhere they join each other. They must be continuous and, therefore, basically the same force. When you get to the root of things, they become simple and general. Since the same force appears in one form as matter and in another form as mind, there is no reason to think that matter and mind are different. Mind is changed into matter, matter is changed into mind. Thought force becomes nerve force, muscular force. Nature is all this force whether exposed as matter or mind.[13]

Vivekananda tried to bring out the co-relation between Vedanta and materialism by expounding the dialectic principle that matter is constantly changing into consciousness and consciousness into matter:

The difference between the subtlest mind and the grossest matter is only one of degree. Therefore, the whole universe may be called either mind or matter, it does not matter which. All the troubles arising from the conflict between materialism and spirituality are due to wrong thinking. Actually, there is no difference between the two. I and the lowest pig differ only in degree. It is less manifested, I am more. Sometimes I am worse, the pig is better.[14]

In fact, what Swamiji wants to convey is that if every object like the body, the mind, the soul, the spiritualist and the materialist are all Brahman, then where is the difference? All are inclusive of one another. However, the example that he has quoted, comes as an antithesis to his proposition, which would not be acceptable even to the spiritualists, not to speak of the materialists.

---

13. *Ibid.* Vol. VIII, p. 245.
14. *Ibid*, Vol. VIII, p. 246.

The Vedantists, and even his fellow-disciples, did not accept this concept of harmony. One day, one of his brother-monks reproached him jestingly for having introduced into Ramakrishna's ecstatic teaching Western ideas of organisation, action and service, of which Ramakrishna had not approved... Then suddenly he declared:

You think you have understood Sri Ramakrishna better than myself! You think *jnana* is dry knowledge to be attained by a desert path, killing out the tenderest faculties of the heart! Your *bhakti* is sentimental nonsense, which makes one impotent. You want to preach Ramakrishna as you have understood him, which is mighty little! Hands off! Who cares for your Ramakrishna? Who cares for your bhakti and *mukti*? Who cares what your scriptures say? I will go into a thousand hells cheerfully, if I can rouse my countrymen, immersed in *tamas*, to stand on their own feet and be men inspired with the spirit of Karma Yoga .... I am not a servant of Ramakrishna, or anyone, but of him only who serves and helps others, without caring for his own bhakti or mukti.[15]

It was only Vivekananda who had understood the message of Ramakrishna to serve the living beings, for Lord Shiva resides in living beings. Ramakrishna possessed great knowledge, he was a *jnani* although outwardly he appeared to be a *bhakta*. Vivekananda carried the mantle of his Guru and developed his knowledge from out of that shell. His fellow-disciples were incapable of understanding the true message of Ramakrishna and looking into that shell. For them bhakti and mukti, foolish emotions, were enough. Therefore, it was natural for them to consider Vivekananda's life's mission of service as pursuit of Western ideals.

Such people who, consciously or unconsciously, served

15. *Life of Swami Vivekananda*, Vol. III, pp. 159-161.

the interest of the rulers-exploiters, paid homage and respect to the outer shell of Ramakrishna's and Vivekananda's ideas by burying them under foolish emotionalism and also entombed the knowledge of these two great men in some books and memorials. It was done, because Vivekananda had, by the end of the nineteenth century, brought national thinking to the threshold of materialism, which was a danger signal to the establishment, with the help of which the theory of bhakti and mukti survives. But if we want to take our country forward, we shall have to give concrete shape to Vivekananda's dream of new India and develop national thinking, from where he left it.

Therefore, we propose to take the kernel out of the shell with the help of the theory of historical materialism, locate the point to which Vivekananda had brought our national thinking to, and develop it further. For this we have to understand the inner contradictions in his thinking which, in fact, were the inner contradictions of the rising bourgeois class, of which he was the spokesman. For analysing his thinking, let us refer to his example of a pig. What is the meaning of his saying, 'A pig is less manifested and I am more manifested?'

According to the Vedantic philosophy,

From the highest to the lowest and most wicked man, in the greatest human beings and the lowest worms under our feet, is the soul, pure and perfect, infinite and ever-blessed. In the worm that soul is manifesting only an infinitesimal part of its power and purity, and in the greatest men it is manifesting most of it. The difference consists in the degree of manifestation, but not in the essence. Through all beings exists the same full and perfect soul.[16]

This would mean that the same pure and sacred soul

---

16. *Complete Works of Vivekananda*, Vol. VI, p. 24.

resides in an ant, pig and a man. The only difference being that it is less manifested in an ant, more in a pig and most in a man.

How is this possible?

As the mind changes, its character grows, as it were, more and more clear and gives a better reflection of the soul. Thus it goes on, until the mind has become so purified that it reflects fully the quality of the soul; then the soul becomes liberated.[17]

In this way the soul casts its reflection on the mind. The goal of the soul is to achieve liberation and to achieve liberation it has to be born in every form of a living being. The theory of transmigration has been explained thus:

The soul, as it were, taking up a lower body and trying to express itself through that. It finds that to be insufficient, is rejected, and a higher one comes; so on and on until a body is found through which the soul manifests its highest aspirations. Then the soul becomes free.[18]

According to Vivekananda, from the lowest stage of an amoeba, man is the highest stage of development. In other words, by the time the soul reaches the stage of a man it becomes so developed, that it realises its true character and struggles against nature to reach the highest and to realise its own self as Brahman, which is not possible for birds, animals or other beings. In this context he says:

'We are not born as helpers of nature, but competitors with nature. We are its bond masters, but we bind ourselves down. Why is this house here? Nature did not build it. Nature says, "go and live in the forest." Man says, "I will build a house and fight with nature."

---

17. *Ibid.* Vol. VI, p. 22.
18. *Ibid*, p. 23.

And he does so. The whole history of humanity is a continuous fight against the so-called laws of nature and man gains in the end. Coming to the internal world, there, too, the same fight is going on, this fight between the animal and the man, between light and darkness. And here too, man becomes victorious. He, as it were, cuts his way out of nature to freedom.[19]

In his struggle against nature man continuously excels himself, reaching to higher stages. His concept about worship and the worshipped also passes through a process of development and improvement. In this struggle, the concept of worship and the worshipped has ever been changing; Vivekananda says:

> There is no God separate from you, no God higher than you, the real 'You.' All the Gods are little beings to you, all the ideas of soul and Father in heaven are but your reflection. God himself is your image. 'God created man after his own image.' That is right. Throughout the universe we are creating gods after our own image.[20]

The German materialist thinker Feurbach also asserts that man has created God according to his own imagination.

The primitive man saw the fearful form of nature and created gods in that form. When the despotic ruler declared himself to be the representative or image of God upon the earth, God resided in the skies, the heaven. When democracy came and everyone got the right of vote, God not only descended on earth but started living in every home.

While speaking on Raja Yoga in New York, Vivekananda said:

> The Yogi proposes to himself no less a task than to master the whole universe, to control the whole of

---

19. *Ibid*. Vol. VI. p.39.
20. *Ibid*, Vol. III, p. 24.

the nature. He wants to arrive at the point where what we call "nature's laws" will have influence over him, where he will be able to get beyond them all. He will be the master of the whole of nature, internal and external. The progress and civilization of the human race simply means controlling this nature.[21]

Then, as he always did, he tried to harmonise religion with science:

The externalists and the internalists are destined to meet the same point, when both reach the extreme of their knowledge. Just as a physicist, when he pushes his knowledge to its limits, finds it melting away into metaphysics, so a metaphysician will find that what he calls mind and matter are but apparent distinctions, the reality being one.[22]

But the materialists ask this question; if man is becoming more and more refined in his struggle against nature, if, as we have seen, physical circumstances are also changing and nature is progressing towards greater upheavals and if man, accordingly, is also changing ever for the better, why is it necessary to equip him with mythical wings of soul and God?

What is the proof of the existence of an entity which is beyond space-time causation? How is it possible to perceive something which is beyond our senses?

If the only achievement of eternal knowledge and eternal happiness is the truth which is beyond sense perceptions, then what was the sense in learning, from England and other Western countries, the secrets of achieving worldly happiness and teaching them in return, to be eternally happy?

Again, when the Yogis are roaming the wilds in search

---

21. *Ibid*. Vol. I, p. 132.
22. *Ibid*, Vol. I. p. 133.

of truth—God, which is beyond sense perceptions, why do they go to the door of a householder to beg for food when they are hungry? Why don't they satisfy their hunger by chanting His name? By begging for food by saying 'Alakh Niranjan' (God is invisible) do they not concede their defeat that though they searched for Him everywhere, they have not been able to find and see Him?

No idealist has an answer to such questions. In the story which is considered to be the best among stories about the soul in the Upanishads, Yama is frightened by the question put to him by the boy Nachiketa asking whether soul exists after death or not. When Nachiketa insists on an answer from Yama, who is reluctant to give a reply, he says, 'The idea of soul and life hereafter, about which you inquired, cannot be understood by a child such as you who is ignorant due to worldly attachment...it is not proper to disturb your mind by useless arguments because the ultimate reality cannot be subjected to logic, it can only be directly perceived?' Swami Vivekananda takes upon himself the onus of explaining the reply given by Yama by saying, 'It has ever been said that every religion gives strength only on the basis of faith. We have been taught to believe things with our eyes closed. This blind faith is very bad, no doubt. But if we analyse blind faith we shall find a great truth hidden behind it.'

What is this great truth—this even Vivekananda does not tell. While trying to harmonise religion with science, he said in one of his speeches on 'Reason and Religion :

> We are absolutely one, we are physically one, we are mentally one, and as spirit, it goes without saying, that we are one, if we believe in spirit at all.[23]

Is that great truth nothing, but surrender of blind faith before logic?

---

23. *Ibid*. Vol. I, p. 133.

Does it not mean to convey that we should accept the blind faith and the mystery as propounded by Upanishads, believing it to be a great truth, even if we reject those of other religions.

Does it not give credence to the foolish concept of *bhakti-mukti*?

In fact, foolish emotionalism is an inseparable part of religion. But because Vivekananda had always based himself on logic and had developed to the highest possible stage of being the best spokesman of the rising bourgeois class and also because he applied the theory of evolution to Vedantic philosophy, he does not find it easy to digest this fact as his other fellow-disciples did.

In another speech about Vedanta in practical life he says, 'It is necessary to put the claims of religion to the test of logic. That religion claims to be exempted from the test of logic, no one can say. No real decision can be made about religion without subjecting it to the standard of logic. Religion may order us to do something grotesque.'

History bears testimony to the grotesque shape religion has taken time and again. The greatest disservice done by our religion is that it has made us self-centred. Vivekananda himself admitted:

> Hitherto the greatest fault of our Indian religion has been in its knowing only two words: renunciation and mukti. Nothing for the house-holder![24]

Moreover, materialism has itself, by now, developed to the stage of dialectical and historical materialism. It has also realised the fact that whatever we see in the universe is matter in different shapes and forms. It is only matter which is the omnipresent, omnipotent and eternal entity which the spiritualists call God. All the imaginary qualities that the spiritualists have attributed to God are present in matter.

---

24. *Ibid*. Vol. VIII, p. 267.

Matter cannot exist without motion. Matter gets into motion through time and space. Matter cannot exist without space and time and likewise, space and time cannot exist without matter. This is Einstein's theory of relativity.

According to Dialectical Materialism, everything gets divided into two parts after coming into existence. The unity of and the clash between these two opposite parts leads to continuous progress. This law of unity and natural clash of these two elements is an independent law which governs equally nature, society and human thinking.

Even the theory of Dialectical Materialism is no exception to this law. Hegel, by setting the highest limit of his thinking, tried to contradict the theory of evolution. Vivekananda also committed the same mistake. But the materialists set no limits to human thinking, nor bring it to a full stop. The theory of Dialectical Materialism was propounded by Marx and Engels. Mao Tse-tung developed it further and enriched it. Other Marxists are adding something to it and contributing to its development in a measure.

Moreover, at no stage of Dialectical Materialism does man transgress the laws of nature to rise above it. On the other hand, he makes use of these laws and benefits from them by understanding them.

Science cannot be reconciled with religion in any way. Marx says, 'The theory of a nation is real only to the extent where it can realise the needs of that nation?' Mao Tse-tung says the same thing in these words, 'The future of philosophy depends only on the needs of social classes.'

In the next chapter we shall discuss the practical aspect of the question as to how the philosophy of Vedanta fulfilled the social needs of the exploited classes. But we have already discussed its theoretical aspect and seen how it was that in the hearts of the exploiting classes the desire to achieve *moksha* or *nirvana* was first born. It were they who smuggled the concept of soul, being an entity beyond body and mind, into the Sankhya philosophy through the back door.

In this context, Vivekananda played the historical role

of adding the theory of development to the philosophy of Vedanta and used it as a weapon for fighting against the imperialists and the pseudo-reformers, thereby fulfilling the social needs of the emerging capitalist class.

We have also seen that in this attempt he transgressed the limits of religion. Such a transgression is inevitable, because it is not possible to reconcile science and religion. Therefore, in the face of assertion made by science that independence of soul is a mere illusion, Vivekananda finds himself in a dilemma, which is reflected in his speech on "Fundamentals of Religion' :

> Now, on the one hand, the denial of freedom as an illusion is no explanation, on the other hand, why not say that the idea of necessity or bondage or causation is an illusion of the ignorant? Any theory which can fit itself to facts which it wants to explain, by first cutting as many of them as prevent its fitting into them, is on the face of it wrong. Therefore, the only way left to us is to admit that there must be something beyond both the mind and the body which is free and...[25]

What does the phrase 'there must be' convey? It is his own inner conflict and dilemma which compels him to leave the sentence incomplete. He had nothing more to say. At a time when Vivekananda was in a dilemma, the reigning national poet Chakbast wrote the following lines: 'What is this life but the organised manifestation of five elements. The disintegration of these elements is called death.'

Lenin held the view, 'Man gets only one life to live. He should live it in such a way as to have no regrets at the time of his death of having wasted it uselessly.'

---

25. Complete Works of Vivekananda, Vol. IV, p.383.

9

FROM VEDANTA TO HISTORICAL MATERIALISM

"In many matters we overlook the crux and run after the shell."

-Vivekananda

Vivekananda has repeatedly stressed that religion is the back-bone of our nation. In fact, however, religion is not the back-bone of any country in the East or the West and we do not have monopoly of religion.

Marx has defined religion to be the wrong interpretation of facts. We have seen how in every country man has, in his struggle against nature, changed it by his actions. But he has also used his imagination and has wrongly interpreted facts due to his ignorance. As society developed, man faced the struggle of production, class struggle and conducted scientific research. Through such experiences, he understood facts better and, as his knowledge increased, false notions about religion disappeared in the same proportion; religion became more and more realistic and practical. This law of historical materialism was as much applicable to our country as to others. This is the pure truth. It, however, becomes qualified under the peculiar circumstances prevailing in a country. But no country, including ours, is exempt from this law. Therefore, religion is not the back bone of our country or any other country in the East or West. No country can claim the monopoly of religion. We should also not make such a claim, because it is foolish to make a claim which is based on what is unreal. It was due to our follies that our country became slave along with the religion, of which we are proud.

It would be wiser now to find out what the practical form of Vedanta was in our history of several thousand years and, from out of this legacy, we have to pick out the crux, develop it and reject all that is irrelevant. If we do this we shall be able to identify the real problems of our nation and set our goals and direction for future development. Unfortunately, we have been ignoring all that is crucial and concentrating on that which is irrelevant.

The importance of Vivekananda is not that he preached religion, but that he helped us to understand and adopt our national legacy and to solve our problems. We are obliged to him for the fact that a century back he took the kernel out of the shell and drew the nation's attention to it. It is the misfortune of our country that we have neglected what is crucial and concentrated on what is irrelevant. Anti-national elements distorted the real meaning of what he wanted to convey, when he said that religion was the backbone of our nation. On the other hand, they conspired to hide it from us with the result that we were lost.

However, it is better late than never. A century in the life of our nation is not a long duration. Let us now pick up the chain of thinking where Vivekananda left it, develop it further and come back to the path from which we had been lost.

We have already stated that Vedantic philosophy rests on the twin theories of *karma* and *maya*. Now we have to consider what is their practical form in the social life and what dialectic relation do they have with the physical and economic situation prevailing in the country?

Whatever be the explanation of the theories of rebirth and karma given in the Gita, Vedanta and other works, the physical basis of the origin thereof is that with the coming of private property, Indian society got divided not only into classes, but also into castes. The Brahmin and the

Kshatriya castes were considered superior and all the comforts of life were available to them. The rest of the prople were considered belonging to no caste; they were called Shudras and led a life of misery and poverty in spite of the fact that they produced everything. The theory of karma appeased both the exploiters and the exploited. The higher caste people presumed that they had performed good deeds in their previous birth, as a result of which they had been born in the higher caste and, thus, had the right to live on the labour of others. The exploited, or the Shudras were made to understand that all the troubles and sorrows that they were undergoing were the result of their evil deeds in the previous birth and, if they selflessly performed their duty assigned to them in the present caste, they would also be reborn in a higher caste and would be liberated from he bonds of hard labour.

The Caste system is peculiar only to our social organisation and, therefore, it is only in our country that the theories of karma and rebirth developed. Religious thinking in other countries developed according to the physical circumstances prevailing there. This is how Vivekananda brings out this point:

> 'We find a sort of soul idea—of a double—to be the most ancient. Inside the body, according to them, there is another body which is moving and working here; and when the outer body dies, the double gets out and lives on for a certain length of time. In Egypt the inner body also dies. That is why we find among the ancient Egyptians such solicitude to preserve the dead body of a person by embalming, building pyramids, etc.'

The Muslims and the Christians bury their dead, because they believe that the dead would rise from their graves on the Day of Judgement and would be sent to heaven or hell according to their virtuous or evil deeds. The concept of hell and heaven is prevalent among the Hindus also. Besides, places like the Chandralok have also been conceived, where the soul has to reside according to its *karma*. But this concept belongs to the Dvaitists. Vivekananda does not believe in any such concept. He says:

> There are also the ideas of heavens and other places, but these are thought to be second rate. The idea of heaven is thought to be a low idea. It arises from the desire for a place of enjoyment. We foolishly want to limit the whole universe with our present experience. Children think that the whole universe is full of children. Mad men think the whole universe a lunatic asylum, and so on. So those to whom this world is but sense-enjoyment, whose whole life is in eating and feasting, with very little difference between them and brute beasts—such persons are naturally found to conceive of places where they will have more enjoyments, because this life is short. Their desire for enjoyment is infinite, so they are bound to think of places where they will have unobstructed enjoyment of the senses; and we see, as we go on, that those who want to go to such places will have to go; they will dream, and when this dream is over, they will be in another dream where there is plenty of sense-enjoyment; and when that dream breaks, they will have to think of something else. This will be driving them from dream to dream.[1]

In other words, man's consciousness takes shape according to the social situation. It is only those, who enjoyed all the pleasures of life, who conceived of heaven in the life hereafter and others, who were deprived of such pleasures, were warned against the consequence of going to hell if they indulged in evil deeds (theft, dishonesty, harming private property).

The theory of rebirth is also the same kind of concept. Vivekananda does not reject this concept in an outright manner as it is based on Vedanta. But his faith in this concept

---

1. *Ibid*. Vol. VI, p. 25.

wavers, because of his scientific thinking. He has analysed the views for and against this concept:

The concept of rebirth is very important for us, because the controversy of rebirth and genetic inheritance of cells is, in fact, a controversy between spiritualism and materialism. If genetic inheritance is sufficient to solve the problem, then materialism cannot be rejected and the soul theory is not needed. But, if it is not sufficient, then the theory that the soul brings with it its past experiences, is wholly true. We have no alternative, but to choose one from the two—either rebirth or materialism. The question is, which one to choose?'

Does it not require courage for a sanyasin and a preacher of religion to pose even such a question?

Elsewhere, he says that there were two kinds of people—one who consider themselves divine and manifestation of soul and God; the other consider that they only possess a body. Earlier, Indian thinkers have stressed the point that the body is perishable. Just as a man casts off his worn out clothes and wears new ones, in the same way the soul casts off the old body and acquires a new one.

Vivekananda continues to say : 'So far as I am concerned, I have been led to hold a contrary belief because of the circumstances I was in and the education and training that I received. I remained more in contact with Christians and Muslims who are particularly attached to their body.' Vivekananda's father believed in enjoying life. For him religion was secondary. As such, he would not shake off what he had inherited from his father, even though he was reborn after accepting Ramakrishna Paramahansa as his Guru. He remained the same restless Narendra who was born in the Kayastha clan known for its intellect.

The story about Buddha says that he was born to serve and support the human race. But when he forgot the mission of his life amid the luxuries of the palace, an angel sang a song to him to awaken his real self which said, 'We are continuously flowing in a stream and changing, without any pause or stop.' When Buddha, as a prince, was smitten by the fear of death, he felt disturbed and left his home. He thought of achieving immortality, *nirvana*, through suppressing his desires in this ever-changing world.

Although Buddha did not believe in soul and God, he accepted rebirth as a fact of life. According to the Gita, the soul takes one birth after the other, while, according to Buddhism, the *samskaras* (training or refinement of mind) acquired in one birth are passed on to the next birth and rebirth occurs according to the deeds performed in the previous birth. This is, in fact, another way of accepting what Buddhism has rejected.

In the Vedic social system man's life was divided into four periods—Brahmacharya, Grihastha, Vanaprastha and Sanyasa which was the last. It was Buddha who started the practice of becoming a sanyasin at a young age. In this way, achieving moksha became the primary aim of life; everything else was now secondary. History bears testimony to the harm caused by this practice. Vivekananda says, 'Buddha brought us disaster as Christ did to Greece and Rome.'

Vivekananda had, in great humility, paid rich tributes to Buddha giving him the status of an incarnation of God. But, when his thinking became more scientific, we find him analysing in an objective manner the disaster brought to the country by Buddha.

According to him, the country was brought to ruination at just the time when there were as many as a lakh of monks in a monastery in the Buddhist state. The Buddhists, Muslims and Christians—all of them have the wrong notion that all people should be governed by the same law. This is palpably wrong because due to difference in nature the rules of conduct for different individuals are different. Nothing can be achieved by uniting them by force. Buddha says that nothing is worth achieving except moksha. Vivekananda advised householders not to adopt such a course, but to act according to the *dharma* as laid down by the Shastras. He said that moksha was, no doubt, greater than dharma but dharma came first in sequence and had to be performed first. According to him, it is in this respect that the Buddhists got misled and created troubles. *Ahimsa* was no doubt good; it was decidedly a great principle, but, according to the Shastras, if a householder did hot retaliate on being slapped, he was committing a sin.

Suffice it to say that Buddha, being afraid of revolution, was a supporter of rejection. His historical role was not progressive, but that of a reactionary.

The Jain religion has no faith in the existence of God as the creator of universe. But they believe that the soul achieves divinity through good deeds. Mahavira was reborn as a man from a lion. The Jains lay great stress on *aparigraha* (non-acquisition), in addition to ahimsa and karma. But in practice, they are foremost in acquisition of wealth. Although they feed the ants and drink filtered water, yet they unabashedly indulge in the hateful acts of profiteering and usury.

Vivekananda speaks about the olden days, of how the kings used to take away all the wealth of their people for their own enjoyment, for maintaning their families and appeasing the priest. Of course, the Vaishyas were their suppliers.

Buddha says, if there was no visible universe, to whom would we show our great mercy? But this great ideal of great mercy has reduced the people to a pitiable condition to which Vivekananda referred in his Kumbhakonam speech after his return from Europe:

My friends, I must tell you a few harsh truths. I read in the newspapers how, when one of our fellows is murdered or ill-treated by an Englishman, howls go up all over the country; I read and weep, and the next moment comes to my mind the question: Who is responsible for it all? As a Vedantist I cannot but put the question to myself? The Hindu is a man of introspection; he wants to see things in and through himself, through the subjective vision. I, therefore, ask myself: who is responsible? And the answer comes every time. Not the English; no, they are not responsible, it is we who are responsible for all our misery and all our degradation, and we alone are responsible. Our autocratic ancestors went on treading the common masses of our country, till under this torment the poor people nearly forgot that they were human beings. They have been compelled to be merely hewers of wood and drawers of water for centuries, so much so, that they are made to believe that they are born as slaves, hewers of wood and drawers of water. With all the boasted education of modern times, if anybody says a kind word for them, I often find our men shrink at once from the duty of lifting them up, these poor downtrodden people, not only so, but I also find that all sorts of most demoniacal and brutal arguments, culled from the crude ideas of hereditary transmission and other such gibberish from the Western world, are brought forward in order to brutalise and tyrannise over the poor all the more."[2]

In the Gita it has been stated, 'One should not unsettle the understanding of the ignorant, attached to action (by teaching them *jnana*); the wise man, himself steadily acting, should engage the ignorant in work.'

Vivekananda has referred to this shloka of Gita in his speech on 'Evils of Anthoriatarianism and said:

> With all my respects for the Rishis of yore I cannot but denounce their method in instructing the people. They care never to explain to them the reason why. This method was pernicious to the very core, and instead of enabling men to attain the end, laid upon their shoulders a mass of meaningless nonsense. Their excuse

2. *Ibid.* Vol. IV, p. 383.

for keeping the end hidden from view was that the people could not have understood their real meaning, even if they had presented to them, not being worthy recipients. The Adhikarivada is the outcome of pure selfishness. They knew that by this enlightenment of their special subject they would lose their superior position of instructors to the people. Hence their endeavour to support this theory. If you consider a man too weak to receive these lessons, you should try the more to teach and educate him; you should give him the advantage of more teaching, instead of less, to train up his intellect, so as to enable him to comprehend the more suitable problems. These advocates of Authoriatarianism ignored the tremendous fact of the infinite possibilities of human soul. Every man is capable of receiving knowledge, if it is imparted in his own language. A teacher who cannot convince others should weep on account of his own inability to teach the people in their own language, instead of cursing them and dooming them to live in ignorance and superstition, setting up the plea that the higher knowledge is not for them. Speak out the truth boldly, without any fear that it will puzzle the weak?[3]

The higher caste people never wanted the Shudras— and not only *bhangis* and *chamars*, but also other working class people like the barbers, washermen, ironsmiths and carpenters were counted as Shudras and were and still are untouchables—not allowed to learn the Shastras. It was only Ekalavya who learnt the art of archery through his own efforts and was asked by Dronacharya to cut off his right thumb in lieu of *Gurudakshina*. The higher caste people wanted them to continue to live in a maze of ignorance and continue to worship their primitive gods. Sri Krishna says again:

> If you are a *jnani*, do not disturb the childlike faith of the *ajnani* (ignorant).

---

3. *Ibid.* Vol. V, p.190.

Those who worship these other gods verily worship me.

The Shudras have been taught to go on working without thinking. Although the higher caste people had their objectives to achieve and to work for, and Sri Krishna offered them the twin benefit of fighting and winning to rule or dying in the battle and going to heaven, the Shudras were expected to work and that too without any desire.

It was said that an act, performed as duty and for the sake of duty, alone destroys the bonds of karma. Shudras are told : 'Action is your duty, reward is not your concern.' In fact it was never intended that Shudras should get rewarded for their actions. They were supposed to work without any desire. They were told to say: 'The world is full of sorrows no doubt but, for this reason, I cannot give up my love for God. I worship Him so that He may take away my sorrows. I love Him because He is the personification of love.'

Thus love was also made an abstract entity like God, beyond the reach of logic and reason. It was said that sorrows and troubles were the results of the karmas of previous births. In order to be free from bonds of attachment and maya and from sorrows, the Shudra was advised to work and worship God without attachment, without any desire. He had no need to acquire jnana, to understand his karma and its result.

On reaching America, Vivekananda wrote to Alasinga Perumal on 20th August, 1893:

No religion on earth preaches the dignity of humanity in such a lofty strain as Hinduism and no religion on earth treads upon the necks of the poor and the low in such a fashion as Hinduism. The Lord has shown me that religion is not at fault, but it is the Pharisees and Sadducees in Hinduism, hypocrites, who invent all sorts of engines of tyranny in the shape of doctrines of *paramarthika* and *vyavaharika*.[4]

They were not only inventing engines of tyranny, but were also sucking the blood of the working classes in collusion with the foreign rulers. During his journey across the country, Vivekananda had himself seen these exploited people living a miserable life. He continues:

Their sleep is never disturbed. Their nice little brown studies of life never rudely shocked by the wail of woe, of misery, of degradation and poverty, that has filled the Indian atmosphere—the result of centuries of oppression. They little dream of the ages of tyranny, mental, moral and physical, that has reduced the image of God to a mere beast of burden; the emblem of the Divine Mother, to a slave to bear children, and life itself a curse.[5]

The Vedanta philosophy was preached to the common people through the Upanishads and stories of Mahabharata and the Puranas. One such story was used for this purpose by Vivekananda in his discourse of Jnana Yoga which is as follows:

There was once a sanyasin, a holy man, who sat under a tree and taught the people. He drank milk, ate only fruit, and made endless *pranayams*, and felt himself to be very holy. In the same village lived an evil woman. Everyday the sanyasin went and warned her that her wickedness would lead her to hell. The poor woman, unable to change her method of life which was her only means of livelihood, was still much moved by the terrible future depicted by the sanyasin. She wept and prayed to the Lord, begging Him to forgive her because she could not help herself. By the by, the holy

4. *Ibid*. Vol. V, p. 13.
5. *Ibid*. Vol. V, p. 13.

man and the evil woman died. The angels came and bore her to heaven, while the demons claimed the soul of the sanyasin. "Why is this!' he exclaimed, 'have I not lived a most holy life, and preached holiness to everybody? Why should I be taken to hell while this wicked woman is taken to heaven?' 'Because', answered the demons, 'while she was forced to commit unholy acts, her mind was always fixed on the Lord and she sought deliverance, which has now come to her. But you, on the contrary, while you performed only holy acts, had your mind always fixed on the wickedness of others. You saw only sin, and thought of only sin, so now you have to go to that place where only sin is."[6]

Let us analyse this story.

First of all, why should a woman be compelled to commit the hateful act of selling her body in a society which boasts of being humanitarian? Secondly, prostitution is an integral part of the system of exploitation. Therefore, instead of making amends, the evil woman who was forced to sell her body was pacified—indeed all the exploited and oppressed working class people are thus pacified—to continue doing her work, howsoever hateful or painful the work might be, without expecting anything in return, keeping faith in God and that if she did so she could go to heaven.

Thirdly, see no evil, hear no evil and speak no evil. In other words, don't pay attention to the rudeness of big people. Otherwise, you would go to hell where there is nothing, but evil, like the sanyasin who ate only fruit and drank only milk.

Fourthly, Vivekananda believes that the concept of heaven-hell is invented by the wealthy class. This is with the intention of assuring the poor people, on the one hand, to be pure as to be freed from the bonds of rebirth and

---

6. *Ibid.* Vol. VIII, p.19.

go to heaven and, on the other, to threaten them with the dire consequence of going to hell, so as to prevent them from rebelling out of dissatisfaction.

The poor people are advised not to feel jealous about the wealth of others and to be satisfied with their lot. Thus the standards of morality for the higher and the lower classes were different.

The Ramayana and Mahabharata have both been greatly glorified. These two works, without doubt, made a great contribution in the development of language and literature as well as in the organisation of society. Both these epics are written in rich Sanskrit. But both of them are based on Vedantic philosophy and have propounded double standards of morality.

For the purpose of our analysis, let us take up Yudhishthira, a prominent character of the story. All his life he never spoke an untruth. He was rewarded for this by being allowed not only himself to enter heaven bodily, but also to take along his brothers and his dog with him. But in the battlefield of Kurukshetra, when the Pandavas were faced with a crisis and it was realised that it was impossible to kill Dronacharya without taking recourse to untruth, Krishna hatched a conspiracy and made Yudhishthira, the pious, to say these words to Dronacharya: 'Ashwathama is killed, man or elephant, I don't know.'

Yudhishthira knew that the elephant named Ashwathama had been killed, to make this conspiracy work, was he not guilty of collusion? Did he not allow himself to be used by Sri Krishna? In what way can it be called a moral act or an act of truthfulness?

Tulasidas has aptly said, no blame comes to the privileged.

Let us now take the example of Ramayana. It is said that king Dasharatha obtained the approval of the people for making Rama the king. If the people's verdict had any sanctity, why was it set at naught because of the obstinacy of Kaikeyi?

Secondly, Rama being the ideal character, made a great sacrifice. In order to keep the word of his father he gave up the throne. Bharat also made a great sacrifice and, instead of himself sitting on the throne, placed the wooden sandals of his elder brother on it. The question is, for whom, the sacrifice was made? The throne was not passed on to some washerman or carpenter. If the people, instead of approving the name of Rama, had proposed the name of some other able and wise man, could he have been made the king? Vivekananda says:

Neither under the Hindu kings, nor under the Buddhist rule, do we find the common subject—people taking any part in expressing their voice in the affairs of the state. True, Yudhishthira visits the house of Vaishyas and even Shudras when he is in Varanavata; true, the subjects are praying for the installation of Ramachandra to the legacy of Ayodhya; nay, they are even criticising the conduct of Sita and secretly making plans for bringing about her exile; but as a recognised rule of the state they have no direct voice in the supreme government. The power of the populace is struggling to express itself in indirect and disorderly ways without any method. The people have not yet the conscious knowledge of the existence of this power. There is neither the attempt on their part to organise it into a united action, nor have they got the will to do so; there is also a complete absence of that capacity, that skill, by means of which small and incoherent centres of force are united together, creating insuperable strength as their resultant.[7]

He continues:

There cannot be the least doubt about it that the germ of self-government was at least present in the shape

7. *Ibid.* Vol. IV, p. 439.

of village Panchayat, which is still to be found in existence in many places of India.

But the germ remained for ever the germ; the seed though put in the ground never grew into a tree. This idea of self-government never passed beyond the embryo state of the village Panchayat system and never spread into society at large.[8]

The quotations have been taken from the article entitled 'Modern India' written by Vivekananda in 1899 in Bengali. It is one of the finest specimens of Bengali literature. In the beginning, he was an idealist and considered Buddha and Christ to be the makers of history. But we find him totally transformed in this article. Let us take another example, to prove the point:

Whether the leadership of society be in the hands of those who monopolise learning or wield the power of riches or arms, the source of its power is always the subject masses. By so much as the class in power severes itself from the source, by so much is it sure to become weak. But such is the strange irony of fate, such is the queer working of maya, that they from whom this power is directly or indirectly drawn, by fair means or foul—by deceit, strategem, or by voluntary gift—they soon cease to be taken into account by the leading class. When in course of time, the priestly power totally estranged itself from the subject masses, the real dynamo of its power, it was overthrown by the then kingly power taking its stand on the strength of the subject people; again the kingly power, judging itself to be perfectly independent, created a gaping chasm between itself and the subject people, only to be itself destroyed or become a mere puppet in the hands of the Vaishyas, who now succeeded in securing a relatively

8. *Ibid*, p. 442.

greater cooperation of the masses of the people. The Vaishyas have now gained their end; so they no longer deign to count on help from the subject people and are trying their best to dissociate themselves from them; consequently, here is being sown the seed of the destruction of this power as well.[9]

According to historical materialism, the common masses are the makers of history. Theirs has been the main force behind all revolutions. But the benefits of such revolutions have been usurped by one exploiting class after the other. Vivekananda has given a historical perspective of how, after the age of primeval communism, came the ages of slavery and feudalism. He has divided the capitalist age into three parts—one based on the power of learning, the other based on the power of arms and the third based on the power of wealth. In his analysis he aptly comes to the conclusion that the Vaishya class has now alienated itself from the masses, consequently, here is being sown the seed of destruction of this power as well.

Capitalism had transformed itself into imperialism after having played its progressive role. Lenin, in his pamphlet on 'Imperialism—The Last Stage of Capitalism,' basing himself on the English book 'Imperialism' by J.A. Hobson, has described the last state of capitalism as of its decay. Did Vivekananda not make a correct prediction about imperialism in 1899, much before Hobson and Lenin? Is there any doubt about his being a first-rate thinker? Is it possible for a preacher of religion to make such a prediction? Vivekananda continues:

They themselves, the reservoir of all powers, the subject masses, creating an eternal difference between one another, have been deprived of all their legitimate rights,

---

9. *Ibid.* Vol. IV, pp. 470-71.

and they will remain so, as long as their sort of relation continues.

A common danger, or sometimes a common cause of hatred and love, is the bond that binds people together.

By the same law that herds of beasts of prey together, men also unite into a body and form a caste or a nation of their own.

Self-love is the first teacher of self-renunciation. For the preservation of the individual's interest only one looks first to the well-being of the whole. In the interest of one's own nation is one's own interest; in the well-being of one's nation is one's own well-being. Without the cooperation of the many, most works can by no means go on—even self-defence becomes an impossibility. The joining of friendly hands in mutual help for the protection of the self-interest is seen in every nation, and in every land of course, the circumference of this self-interest varies with different people....

The present government of India has certain evils attendant to it, and there are some very great and good parts in it as well. Of highest good is this, that after the fall of Pataliputra Empire till now, India was never under the guidance of such a powerful machinery of government, as the British wielding the sceptre throughout the length and breadth of the land. And under this Vaishya supremacy, thanks to the strenuous enterprise natural to the Vaishyas, as the objects of commerce are being brought from one end of the world to another, so at the same time, as its natural consequence, the ideas and thoughts of different countries are forcing their way into the very bone and marrow of India. Of these ideas and thoughts, some are really most beneficial to her, some are harmful, while others disclose the ignorance and inability of the foreigners to determine what is truly good for the inhabitants of this country.[10]

Such a correct and beautiful analysis of the benefits and evils of the foreign imperialist rule could only have been based on historical materialism and not on Vedantic philosophy. While Sri Ramakrishna saw the British rulers as merely white men, Vivekananda had stayed in England and very well understood their imperialist character and their role in India. He further says:

> But gradually the idea is being formed in the minds of the English public that the passing away of the Indian Empire from their sway will end in imminent peril to the English nation, and be their ruin. So, by any means whatsoever, the supremacy of England must be maintained in India. The way to effect this, they think, is by keeping uppermost in the heart of every Indian the mighty prestige and glory of the British nation. It gives rise to both laughter and tears simultaneously to observe how this ludicrous and pitiful sentiment is gaining ground among the English.[11]

Through Macaulay's system of education, the propaganda of Christian missionaries and writings of poets like Rudyard Kipling, every effort was made to impress the Indians with the glory of the British race, to cut them off from the tradition of Kalidasa and Kabir and bring them into the tradition of Milton and Shakespeare. Every effort was made to create the impression that the British had come over to India across the seven seas out of compassion to civilize the barbaric Indians braving the sun and heat of this land. To a great extent they were successful in this effort. Consequently, we are still in doldrums half a century

---

10. *Ibid.* Vol. IV, p. 471.
11. *Ibid*, pp. 474-75.

after they left and the un-Indianisation of the colonial system of education started by them is still continuing.

Vivekananda continues to say in this article on 'Modern India':

It has been said before that India is slowly awakening through her friction with the outside nations; and as the result of this little awakening, is the appearance, to a certain extent, of free and independent thought in modern India. On one side is modern Western science, dazzling the eyes with the brilliance of myriad suns and driving in the chariot of hard fast facts collected by the application of tangible powers direct in their incision; on the other are the hopeful and strengthening traditions of her ancient forefathers, in the days when she was at the zenith of her glory—traditions that have been brought out of the pages of her history by the great sages of her own land and outside, that run for numberless years and centuries through her every vein with the quickening of life drawn from universal love— traditions that reveal unsurpassed valour, superhuman genius, and supreme spirituality, which are the envy of gods—these inspire her with future hopes.[12]

Our past was not wholly bad, most of it was good. A man becomes great on the basis of both his good and bad qualities. So does a nation. We have to learn from our ancestors' good and bad qualities. The division of society into classes brought spiritual and cultural advancement through the creation of private property. Our mythology is the evidence of our extraordinary power of imagination. There was a wonderful development of architecture, painting, literature, music, dance and other fine arts. The Vedas, Upanishads, the Sankhya philosophy, the Nyaya philosophy of Gautam, the Mimamsa of Vyasa, *Ramayana, Mahabharata, Chanakya-Niti, Shukra-Niti, Manusmriti, Panchatantra,*

---

12. *Ibid*. Vol. IV, pp. 475-76.

Kathasaritsagar, Ajanta, Ellora and Konark, etc., are all legacies of our thousands of years old society based on class division. What great effort must have brought about these achievements!

In 'The Historical Evolution of India,' Vivekananda writes:

> This analytical power and boldness of poetic visions which urged it onward, are the two great internal causes in the make-up of the Hindu race. They together formed, as it were, the keynote to the national character This combination is what is always making the race press onwards beyond the senses—the secret of those speculations which are like the steel blades the artisans used to manufacture—cutting through bars of iron, yet pliable enough to be easily bent into a circle.

> They wrought poetry in silver and gold; the symphony of jewels, the maze of marble wonders, the music of colours, the fine fabrics which belong more to the fairyland of dreams than to the real—have at the back of them thousands of years of working of this national trait.

> Art and sciences, even the realities of domestic life, are covered with a mass of poetical conceptions, which are pressed forward till the sensuous touches the supersensuous and the real gets the rose hue of the unreal.[13]

Vivekananda also speaks about the British effort to break our links with our great cultural tradition and to un-Indianise us. In the 'Future of India' he says:

> The education that you are getting now... is merely and entirely a negative education. A negative education or any training that is based on negation, is worse than death. The child is taken to school, and the first thing he learns is that his father is a fool, the second

---

13. *Ibid*. Vol. VI, p. 158.

thing that his grandfather is a lunatic, the third thing that all his teachers are hypocrites, the fourth that all the sacred books are lies! By the time he is sixteen he is a mass of negation, lifeless and boneless.... Education is not the amount of information that is put into your brain and runs riot there, undigested all your life.[14]

He wrote a letter to Justice Subramanyam from Chicago on 3rd January, 1895. The letter is long but contains an analysis of the caste system in the light of Vedantic philosophy and was written in the context of his plan of work for India:

I fully agree with the educated classes in India that a thorough overhauling of society is necessary. But how to do it ? The destructive plans of reformers have failed. My plan is this. We have not done badly in the past, certainly not. Our society is not bad but good, only I want it to be better. Not from error to truth, nor from bad to good, but from truth to higher truth, from good to better and best. I tell my countrymen that so far they have done well—now is the time to do better.

Now take the case of caste—in Sanskrit, *jati*, i.e., species. Now, this is the first idea of creation. Variations *(vichitrata)*, that is to say *jati*, means creation. "I am One, I become many" (various Vedas). Unity is before creation, diversity comes in creation. Now if this diversity stops, creation will be destroyed. So long as my species is vigorous and active, it must throw out varieties. When it ceases or is stopped from breeding varieties, it does. Now the original idea of jati was this freedom of the individual to express his nature, his prakriti, his jati, his caste; and so it remained for thousands of years. Not even in the latest books is

14. *Ibid*, Vol. III, pp. 301-2.

inter-dining prohibited; nor in any of the older books is inter-marriage forbidden. Then what was the cause of India's downfall ? The giving up of this ideal of caste. As the Gita says, with the extinction of caste the world will be destroyed. Now does it seem true that with the stoppage of these variations the world will be destroyed? The present caste is not the real jati, but a hindrance to its progress. It really has prevented the free action of jati, i.e. caste or variation. Any crystallised custom or privilege or hereditary class in any shape really prevents caste (*jati*) from having its full sway; and whenever any nation ceases to produce this immense variety, it must die. Therefore, what I have to tell you, my countrymen, is this, that India fell because you prevented and abolished caste. Every frozen aristocracy or privileged class is a blow to caste and is not caste .... Everything is hideous because the building is unfinished. We had to stop building during centuries of oppression. Now finish the building and everything will look beautiful in its own place. This is all my plan. I am thoroughly convinced of this.[15]

Two years later, on 30th May, 1897, he wrote another letter to Prabhdadas Mitra from Almora in which also he threw some light on his plan of action and on Vedanta philosophy:

'In my views, besides, much perversion has supervened.' The word 'perversion' has been used satirically, for this is what Prabhdadas Mitra thought about Vivekananda while, in fact, his views had changed for the better.

'One attributeless absolute Brahman, I see, I fairly understand and I see in some particular individuals the special manifestations of that Brahman; if those individuals are called by the name of God, I can well follow—otherwise the mind does not feel inclined towards intellectural theorisings such as the postulated creator and the life.

---

15. *Ibid*. Vol. IV, pp. 371-73.

Such a God I have seen in my life, and his commands I live to follow.

Another great discrepancy: The conviction is daily gaining on my mind that the idea of caste is the greatest dividing factor and the root of maya; all caste either in the principle of birth or of merit is bondage: Some friends advise, "true, lay that all at heart, but outside, in the world of relative experience, distinctions like caste must be maintained."

Vivekananda was not given to compromises. So long as he considered merit to be the basis of caste he supported it. But on realising that caste based on merit is also a wrong concept and the cause of dividing men, he did not hesitate to cast aside even the Gita and the Upanishads. National unity was more dear to him than what the Shastras said.

The idea of oneness at heart (with craven importance of effort, that is to say), and outside, the hell-dance of demons—oppression and persecution—any, the dealer of death to the poor, but if the Pariah be wealthy enough, "Oh, he is the protector of religion."

Vivekananda had fully understood the hypocrisy of the apologists of religion and supporters of caste system. He had seen that behind the caste codes lay their desire to preserve their superiority and behind all talk about *bhakti-mukti* was their selfish interest of enjoying the fruits of heaven. These were the people who had criticised Vivekananda for adopting the food habits of the *rnlechchas*. Replying to this unfair criticism he says:

Over and above, I come to see from my studies that the disciplines of religion are not for the Shudra; if he exercises any discrimination about food or going out to foreign lands, it is useless in his case, only so much labour lost. I am Shudra, a mlechcha, so I have nothing to do with all that botheration. To me what would mlechcha's food matter or Pariah's? It is in the books written by priests not in books revealed by God.

From Vedanta to Historical Materialism ∗ 223

Let the priest enjoy the fruits of their ancestors' achievement, while I follow the word of God, for my good lies here.

"Another truth that I have realised is that the altruistic service only is religion, the rest, such as ceremonial observances, are madness—even it is wrong to hanker after one's own salvation. Liberation is only for him who gives up everything for others, whereas others who tax their brains day and night harping on 'my salvation,' 'my salvation,' wonder about their well-being ruined, both present and prospective; and this I have seen many a time with my own eyes. Reflecting on all these sundry matters, I had no heart of writing a letter to you. If not withstanding all these discrepancies, you find your attachment for me intact, I shall feel it to be a very happy issue indeed.[16]

In 1893 Vivekananda had addressed Prabhdadas Mitra as 'Revered Sir,' and had paid tributes to him for his learning. But the same gentleman was now, in 1897, addressed as 'Dear Sir' and his learning was referred to satirically. It was because Vivekananda now understood that people like him did nothing but repeat what had been stated in the Shastras and cared only for their own mukti; they had shut up all their learning inside a shell; they had closed all doors of development for themselves and were like a frog in the well. Vivekananda had taken the life-time vow of serving the living beings, particularly of awakening and uplifting the exploited and oppressed people of India. Jnana for him was not something dry and lifeless, but something to be used for solving the burning problems being faced by the nation at that time. He was concerned about the slavery of Mother India and had cried over the fall of the nation. He had aligned himself with it and its history; this brought about a rapid transformation in his thinking and personality.

---

16. *Ibid*. Vol. V, p. 393.

He analysed the social problems of the country in detail in a letter written to Shrimati Mrinalini Basu on 26th December, 1898:

What is education? Is it book-learning? Is it diverse knowledge? Not even that. The training by which the current and expression of will are brought under control and become fruitful, is called education. Now consider, is that education as a result of which the will, being continuously choked by force through generations, is well-nigh killed out; is that education under whose say even the old ideas, let alone the new ones, are disappearing one by one; is that education which is slowly making man a machine? It is more blessed, in my opinion, even to go wrong, impelled by one's free will and intelligence than to be good as an automation. Again, can that be called society which is formed by an aggregate of men who are like lumps of clay, like lifeless machines, like heaped up pebbles? How can such society fare well? Were good possible, then instead of being slaves for hundreds of years, we would have been the greatest nation on earth, and this soil of India, instead of being a mine of stupidity, would have been the eternal fountain-head of learning.

Is not self-sacrifice, then, a virtue? Is it not the most virtuous deed to sacrifice the happiness of one, the welfare of one, for the sake of the many? Exactly, but as the Bengali adage goes, 'Can beauty be manufactured by rubbing and scrubbing? Can love be generated by effort and compulsion?' What glory is there in the renunciation of an eternal beggar? What virtue is there in the sense-control of one devoid of sense power? What gain is the self-sacrifice of one devoid of idea, devoid of heart, devoid of high ambition, devoid of the conception of what constitutes society? What expression of devotedness to a husband is there by firing a widow to commit *sati*? Why make people do virtuous deeds by teaching superstitions? I say, liberate, undo the shackles of people as much as you can. Can dirt be washed by dirt? Can bondage be removed by bondage? Where is the instance?[17]

Then referring to Vedantic philosophy he said:

Worship with desire, with attachment, comes first. Commence with the worship of the little, then the greater will come itself.

Mother, be not anxious. It is the big tree that the great wind strikes. 'Raking a fire makes it burn better;' 'A snake struck on the head raises its hood.'—and so on. When there comes affliction in the heart, when the storm of sorrow blows all round, and it seems light will be seen no more, when hope and courage are almost gone, it is then, in the midst of this great spiritual tempest, that the light of Brahman gleams. Brought up in the lap of luxury, lying on a bed of roses and never shedding a tear, who has ever become great, who has ever unfolded the Brahman within? Why do you fear to weep? Weep! Weeping clears the eyes and brings intuition. Then the vision of diversity—man, animal, tree—slowly melting away, makes room for the infinite realisation of Brahman everywhere and in everything. Then—

—'Verily, seeing the same God equally existing everywhere, he does not injure the Self by the Self, and so goes to the Supreme Goal. (Gita, XIII, 28)'."[18]

Vivekananda literally shed tears looking at the fall of the nation and the slavery of the motherland which cleared his vision and made him far-sighted. When he again went abroad in 1900, he addressed the upper classes of India in his 'Memoirs of European Travel' in the following words:

---

17. *Ibid.* Vol. IV, pp. 490-91.
18. *Ibid.* Vol. IV, p. 492.

However much you may parade your descent from Aryan ancestors and sing the glories of ancient India day and night, and however much you may be strutting in the pride of your birth, you, the upper classes of India,—do you think you are divine? You are but mummies ten thousand years old! It is among those whom your ancestors despised as 'walking carrions' that the little of vitality there is still in India is to be found; and it is you who are the real 'waking corpses.' Your houses, your furniture look like museum specimens, so lifeless and antiquated they are; and even an eye-witness of your manners and modes of life, is inclined to think he is listening to a grandmother's tale! When, even after making a personal acquaintance with you, one returns home, one seems to think one had been to visit the paintings of an art gallery!

In this world of maya, you are the real illusions, the mystery, the real mirage in the desert, you, the upper classes of India! You are the void, the unsubstantial non-entities of the future. Denizens of the dreamland, why are you loitering any longer? Fleshless, and bloodless skeletons of the dead body of past India that you are—why do you not quickly reduce yourselves into dust and disappear in the air? ... You merge yourself in the void and disappear, and let new India arise in your place. Let her arise—out of the peasant's cottage, grasping the plough, out of the huts of fishermen, the cobbler and the sweeper. Let her spring from the grocer's shop, from beside the oven of the fritter-seller. Let her emanate from the factory, from the marts and from markets. Let her emerge from the groves and forests, from hills and mountains.

These common people have suffered oppression for thousands of years—suffered it without murmur, and as a result have got wonderful fortitude. They have suffered eternal misery, which has given them unflinching vitality. Living on a handful of grain they can convulse the world; give them only half a piece of bread, and the whole world would not be big enough to contain their energy; they are endowed with inexhaustible vitality of Raktabija. And, besides, they have got the wonderful strength that comes of a pure and moral life, which is not to be found elsewhere in the world. Such peacefulness, such contentment, such love, such power of silent and incessant work, and such manifestation of lion's strength in times of action— where else will you find these! Skeletons of the Past, these, before you, are your successors, the India that is to be. Throw these treasure-chests of yours and those jewelled rings among them—as soon as you can; and you—vanish into air, sooner will you disappear then you will hear the inaugural shout of Renascent India— ringing with the voice of a million thunders and reverberating through the universe —'Wahe Guru Ki Fateh'—Victory to the Guru![19]

Looking into the past centuries back he said:

Just weigh the matter in your mind. Those uncared for lower classes of India—the peasants and weavers and the rest, who have been conquered by the foreigners and, are looked down upon by their own people—it is they who from time immemorial have been working silently without even getting the remuneration of their labours! But what great changes are taking place slowly, all over the world, in pursuance of nature's laws! Countries, civilizations and supremacy are undergoing revolutions. Ye labouring classes of India, as a result of your silent, constant labours Babylon, Persia, Baghdad, Samarkand, Spain, Portugal, France, Denmark, Holland and England have successfully attained supremacy and eminence!

And you ?—well, who cares to think of you ! My dear Swami,[20] your ancestors wrote a few philosophical

---

19. *Ibid.* Vol. VIII, pp. 308-9.
20. Trigunananda, Editor of 'Udbodhan,' for whom the memoirs were written.

works, penned a dozen or so epics, or built a number of temples—that is all, and you rend the sky with triumphal shouts; while those whose heart's blood has contributed to all the progress made in the world— well, who cares to praise them? The world-conquering heroes of spirituality, war and poetry are in the eyes of all, and they have received the homage of mankind; but where nobody looks, no one gives a word of encouragement, where nobody hates—that living under such circumstances and displaying boundless patience, infinite love, and dauntless practicality, our proletariat are doing their duty in their homes day and night, without the slightest murmur—well, is there no heroism in this? Many turn out to be heroes, when they have some great task to perform. Even a coward easily gives up his life, and the most selfish man behaves disinterestedly, when there is a multitude to cheer them on; but blessed indeed is he who manifests the same unselfishness and devotion to duty in the smallest acts, unnoticed by all—and it is you who are actually doing this, Ye ever-trampled classes of India. I bow to you.[21]

The above sentiments are not based on Vedanta, but Dialectical Materialism. When did Vedanta consider workers to be the makers of history and venerable? Rather, they were branded low as Shudras. Vedanta never shed tears for those who do not get the return of their labours. It only taught them to bear the beastly burden patiently without caring for the result. On Vivekananda saluting the workers of India, he was ridiculed by the so-called reformists for unnecessarily flattering the lower caste people—the hateful Shudras.

He asked them back, what benefit could he get by flattering the people of this country? He berated them for trying to gobble up all the help that he had brought from

---

21. *Ibid.* Vol. VII, pp. 340-41.

abroad for the orphans and famine-stricken people of India. Such people were not the true friends of the people.

Vivekananda believed that if somebody showed real love to the unlucky, poor, oppressed, ignorant, starving, quarrelling and jealous people of India, then India will again become alive. He compared his belief to that of a Japanese girl who believes that if she loves her doll truly, it would come alive. He believed that India could reawaken only when hundreds of large-hearted men and women give up all their desire for luxury and happiness and work for the uplift of the thousands of Indians who are going down deep into the pit of poverty and ignorance.

Vivekananda had such great love for the country and his fellow countrymen that he crossed the limits of Vedantic theory and the barriers of religion. He openly declared himself to be a socialist. Although he did not talk about class con-sciousness and class struggle yet, because of his love for his countrymen, he developed an inner sight with the help of which he saw through the machinations of Western capitalism and very well understood that democracy was nothing but the dictatorship of moneybags for their selfish ends, who start wars in order to find markets and earn profits in which the poor people are made cannon-fodder. In 'The East and the West' he writes:

> Of course we do not get the education which the common people in the West do, by the system of vote and ballot, etc., but, on the other hand, we have also not amongst us that class of people who, in politics rob others and fatten themselves by sucking the very life blood of the masses in all the European countries. If you ever saw, my friend, that shocking sight behind the scene of acting of these politicians—that revelry of bribery, that robbery in broad daylight, that dance of the Devil in man, which are practised on such actions,- you would be hopeless about man! "Milk goes a begging from door to door, while the grog-shop is crowded;

the chaste woman seldom gets the wherewithal to hide her modesty, while the woman of the town flutters about in all her jewellery!" They that have money have kept the government of the land under their thumb, are robbing the people and sending them as soldiers to fight to be slain on foreign shores, as that, in case of victory, their coffers may be full of gold bought by the blood of the subject people on the field of battle. And the subject people? Well, theirs is only to shed their blood. This is politics! Don't be startled, my friend; don't be lost in its mazes.

First of all, try to understand this: Does man make laws, or do laws make man? Does man make name and fame, or name and fame make man?[22]

In the eighteenth century, when the survival of religion became difficult with the development of science, Hegel added the theory of dialectics to idealism and in this way adapted it to the fast changing society. With the development of thought it is shaking off that which is irrational. When thought is free from all that is irrational, then it would attain the highest point of development and be identified with eternal truth. Then society would also reach its highest point of development. Hegel also said that the then existing Prussian government of Germany had reached the highest and eternal point of development and no further improvement therein was possible.

German leftist thinkers branded Hegel as a pro-government thinker for his having paid this compliment to the Prussian government and rejected his entire philosophy. But Marx explained to them that it was not proper to throw away the kernel with the shell; adding dialectism to idealism was a great achievement of Hegel and that Hegel's theory was upside down and it needed to be put back on its feet. Marx was of the view that society does not reflect thought but it is thought which is the reflection of society—the

22. *Ibid.* Vol. V, pp. 364-65.

physical situation. Thought has been developing with the development of society. No social situation can remain static and development also has no limits.

In this way Marx transformed Hegel's Dialectical Idealism into Dialectical Materialism or made it stand on its feet and predicted that just as feudalism has given birth to capitalism, in the same way capitalism would give birth to socialism. This prediction of Marx proved true. Human behaviour is the only standard by which the correctness of thought can be judged.

Vivekananda's achievement lies in the fact that he added the theory of evolution to Vedantic thought. While speaking at the Brooklyn Ethical Society in U.S. he said:

> In my opinion the external world is certainly an entity and has an existence outside of our mental conceptions. All creation is moving onwards and upwards, obedient to the great law of spirit evolution, which is different from the evolution of matter. The latter is symbolical of, but does not explain, the process of the former. We are not individuals now, in our present earthly environment. We shall not have reached individuality until we shall have extended to the higher state, when the divine spirit within us will have a perfect medium for the expression of its attributes."[23]

This is also Dialectical Materialism but is upside down and needs to be put back on its feet as Marx did in the case of Hegel's theory. But nobody paid any attention to it and we are facing the consequences.

We have already seen that from theoretical point of view, Vivekananda is ahead of Hegel and Feurbach. It was because Hegel and Feurbach kept themselves away from politics, whereas Vivekananda fought a political battle through the medium of religion. Secondly, by the end of the nineteenth century Marxism had become the most powerful ideology of Europe. Although Vivekananda has not referred to Marx and Engels by name, but it is impossible that a thinker like him did not read and imbibe their ideology. He has

---

23. *Ibid.* Vol. V, p. 236.

given a historical, materialistic analysis of society and has not only not lost sight of the subtlest changes, but has also made predictions. This is how he has predicted the establishment of the power of labour.

'Yet, a time will come when there will be a rising of the Shudra class, with their Shudra-hood; that is to say, not like that at present when Shudras are becoming great by acquiring the characteristic qualities of the Vaishya or the Kshatriya, but a time will come when the Shudras of every country, with their inborn Shudra nature and habits—not becoming in essence Vaishya or Kshatriya, but remaining as Shudras—will gain absolute supremacy in every society. The first glow of the dawn of this new power has already begun to break upon the Western world, and the thoughtful are at their wit's end to reflect upon the final issue of this fresh phenomenon. Socialism, Anarchism, Nihilism, and other such sects are the vanguards of the social revolution that is to follow. As the result of the grinding pressure and tyranny, from time out of mind, the Shudras, as a rule, are either meanly servile, licking doglike the feet of the higher class, or otherwise are as inhuman as brute beasts. Again at all times their hopes and aspirations are baffled, hence firmness of purpose and perseverance in action they have none:

"I shall make one fight against one lakh and a quarter Only when shall I be called Guru Gobind Singh."

"When Guru Gobind gives the Name, i.e. the invitation, a single man becomes strong enough to triumph over a lakh and a quarter of his foes.[24]

The workers acquire firmness and industriousness only after they align themselves with and adopt the concept of Dialectical Materialism.

---

24. *Ibid.* Vol. IV, pp. 468-69.

10

THE STORY OF
INDIAN RENAISSANCE

"Our eyes are in the front, not at the back."
                                        -Vivekananda

After returning home Vivekananda had said in his Kolkata
address:

> Along with it you have to understand one thing more.
> Such a thing is before us today. Before one of these
> tidal waves of spirituality comes, there are whirlpools
> of lesser manifestation all over society. One of these
> comes up, at first unknown, unperceived, and unthought
> of, assuming proportion, swallowing, as it were, and
> assimilating all the other whirlpools, becoming immense,
> becoming a tidal wave, and falling upon society with
> a power which none can resist. Such is happening before
> us. If you have eyes, you will see it. If you are truth-
> seekers, you will find it. Blind, blind indeed is the
> man who does not see the sign of the day! Ay, this
> boy born of poor Brahmin parents in out of the way
> village of which very few, if you have even heard,
> is literally being worshipped in lands which have been
> fulminating against heathen worship for centuries.
> Whose power is it? Is it mine or yours? It is none
> else than the power manifested here as Ramakrishna

Paramahansa. For, you and I, and sages and prophets, nay, even Incarnations, the whole universe, are but manifestations of power, more or less individualised, more or less concentrated. Here has been a manifestation of immense power, just the very beginning of whose workings we are seeing, and before this generation passes away, you will see more wonderful workings of that power. It has come just in time for the regeneration of India, for we forget from time to time the vital power that must always work in India.[1]

Group photo taken at Belur Math, 1899

Maxim Gorky called the nineteenth century as 'the century of light.' The capitalist revolution, which reached its culmination by the end of the eighteenth century, not only shattered feudalism and its economic base but also its religious beliefs. Human consciousness had broken the bounds of orthodoxy and superstition and taken a leap

---

1. *Ibid*. Vol. III, p. 313.

forward. New scientific inventions had led to a feeling of self-confidence and pride. In short, the development of science and intellectual thinking was illumining the entire world. The first spokesman of the renaissance brought by it in our country was Raja Rammohun Roy.

Romain Rolland considered Rammohun Roy to be an extraordinary man who started a new age in the spiritual history of this ancient land and was the first world citizen of India. In less than sixty years of his life he had not only imbibed the ancient Puranic epics of ancient Asia but also the modern scientific thinking of Europe.

Rammohun Roy was born in a rich Brahmin family in 1772. Despite being a Brahmin he studied Persian and Arabic in a Madarasa in Patna and at the age of 14 he read Aristotle and Euclid apart from the Koran. Between the age of 14 to 16 years he learnt Sanskrit at Benares and studied Vedanta and the Shastras. Before this he knew nothing about Hindu religion and philosophy. In this way, it was his second birth. He had already come under the influence of Sufi thought and after studying Vedanta he became a believer in the concept of one God and wrote a book entitled 'Fuhutul-Muhudrdin' in Persian which was critical of idol-worship. This displeased his orthodox father who turned him out of the home. For four years he travelled across India and Tibet. In Tibet he narrowly escaped being killed by followers of a Lama for criticising the orthodoxy and obscurantism of Buddhist religion.

When he was 20, he was called back home by his father and married off. But, when he started the movement against the sati practice, he was again tuned out by his father under the influence of orthodox Brahmins.

At the age of 24 he started learning English, Hebrew and Latin and read the Bible. Rammohun Roy was the first Indian to undertake a comparative study of all the religions. Such a study had not been undertaken at that time by any one even in Europe. In 1803, after the death of his father, his family accepted him back. From 1805 to 1815 he worked at many places under the collector. In the meanwhile, he translated the *Shankara Bhashya* and the five Upanishads into Bengali. In 1815 he sought retirement from service, had started living in Kolkata permanently. Now he devoted all his time to social reform and the reform of religion.

It was but natural that after the establishment of British rule, hordes of Christian missionaries started coming to India. They set up a big press at Srirampore and printed a lot of literature in Bengali to bring out the 'heathens' from 'darkness to light.' Their propaganda contained a attacks on Hindu religion, Hindu society and the thinking and practices of Hindus as being condemnable, cruel and beastly. It was made out that it was for this reason that they were deprived of happiness in this life and would have to go to hell in the life hereafter. It was said that, if they wanted happiness in this life and wanted to enter the Christian kingdom of heaven, they should seek the shelter of Christ and Mary and adopt the Christian religion. This was the only door of liberation open to them.

It was a difficult job for the missionaries to first learn the Bengali language and, thereafter, to carry on religious propaganda in that language. This method was not found to be useful. Finding so many obstacles in their propaganda work they thought of a plan to set up schools through which it would be easier to carry on propaganda work. This method really proved more successful.

Vivekananda commented about this new system of education that these schools inculcated among the students the Western traditions from the very childhood which led to doubts in their minds about the old traditions. Instead of being freed from evil traditions and seeking truth, they started judging truth by Western standards and started thinking that the Gurus of religion should be banished and the Vedas should be burnt because the West had said so. This led to a kind of wave which is called the wave of so-called reforms.

The role played by Rammohun Roy was entirely

different from the one played by the so-called reformers. He adopted the course of research and put up a stout defence against the evil propaganda of the missionaries. In 1820 he wrote a book entitled *The Precepts of Jesus: Guide to Peace and Happiness* based on the Bible. In this book he posed a question to the Christians that if God could be born as a pigeon why could He not have been born as Garuda? He told the missionaries that their interpretation of the Hindu religion was false and misleading and that, according to the Vedantic philosophy, there was only one soul residing in all living beings.

After coming to Kolkata in 1815 he set up an organisation called Atmiya Sabha with the help of some well-wishers. Through this organisation he wrote and published books and pamphlets whereby he carried on propaganda against the evil practices of Hindu religion and idol-worship and also against the baseless theories being propagated by the missionaries. He held the view that the real Hindu religion was based on the concepts of one God and universal brotherhood. The effect of his propaganda was that a famous missionary named William Andam rejected the Christian theory of triple entities and accepted the monotheism of Rammohun Roy. This came as a shock to the missionaries and they now came to know that the Hindu religion was not mere idolatry and ceremonials but was based on Vedantic philosophy. Now the missionaries like Marsman and Kerry of Srirampore started attacking Vedanta. However, their knowledge of Vedanta was shallow and they foolishly wrote all that was irrelevant. But Raja Rammohun Roy had made a deep study of the Bible, Vedanta and other religions. He, therefore, very coolly and logically demolished the propaganda of the missionaries. This Vedantic war became a well-known historical event.

Rammohun Roy's propaganda against idol-worship, superstition and evil practices also disturbed the orthodox Hindus. They set up a Dharma Sabha under the leadership of Raja Sir Radhakant Deb. These people supported idol-worship and burning of the widows and were of the view that the reforms proposed by Raja Rammohun Roy were against the Shastras and would lead to the destruction of Hindu religion. Therefore, the party of Sir Radhakant started severely criticising the Vedantic movement. But this debate led to a wave of awakening all over Bengal. People again started studying the Shastras which had, of late, been forgotten. Although his opponents were greater in number, yet Rammohun Roy got the support of some zealous young men and some liberal Englishmen like Edward Hyde and David Hare. The movement against the practice of sati was carried on for twelve years and was, ultimately, successful. The Governor-General, Lord William Bentinck, banned the practice of sati by a law promulgated on 4th December, 1822. On the advice of Rammohun Roy, the Governor-General also prohibited the practice of throwing the offspring into the Ganges.

A description of the society in Bengal during the period when Raja Rammohun Roy started his propaganda work is given by Satyendranath Mazumdar. According to this description, at the time of the beginning of British rule, the rich and middle class Bengalis had become corrupt in many ways. If they were rich, they used to have mistresses along with their wife or wives. They took pleasure in the poetry of Vidyasunder and such ribaldry. The middle class people of Kolkata wasted their time in watching bird-fights, flying kites; and enjoyed promenading in the gardens in the company of prostitutes wearing gaudy dresses. As the movement of Raja Rammohun Roy made headway, he became a common topic of discussion everywhere from the city to the village gatherings and even the inner precincts of the households.

Raja Rammohun Roy knew that people would get organised to fight for their political rights only after they are awakened and it would be only then that society in Bengal would become free from evil practices. Therefore, with this objective, he made all efforts to spread modern education. With the help of his British friends of liberal views, he established in 1817 the Hindoo College in which modern subjects like literature, history, mathematics, geography and science were taught.

Under the auspices of Ekata Sabha, Rammohun Roy established the Anglo-Hindu School. In this school Eastern and Western knowledge was imparted simultaneously. All the expenses of the school were borne by Rammohun Roy himself.

He also started publishing a Bengali weekly, *Samvad Kaumudi* to give publicity to his views. During 1821-24 scientific articles such as 'Qualities of Magnet,' 'The Behaviour of Fishes' and 'Story of the Baloon' were written by him and published therein. He also wrote textbooks on subjects like grammar of Bengali language, geography, astronomy, algebra. He started the use of full stop and semi-colon and in this way modernised it. He also wrote a number of pamphlets in Bengali and thereby made his contribution in making the language simple and easy as well as rich.

Through his weekly journal, he appealed to the British Government to open schools on the pattern of the Anglo-Hindu School to provide free education to children. But the East India Company Government decided to open only Sanskrit schools of the old type, and Raja Rammohun Roy strongly opposed it. The orthodox people raised a hue and cry at this and accused him of trying to destroy their religious institutions.

It has to be understood that the foreign Government was not at all interested in providing modern education to the Indians. Their only purpose of opening Sanskrit schools was to see that the people of our country remained ignorant and superstitious. Their intention was not to make people educated, but to appease the orthodox among them. The orthodox people were in great numbers and they raised a storm against Rammohun Roy. Even the intellectuals rejected him and wanted to continue the old practices as they were. But Raja Rammohun Roy and a handful of his

Indian and foreign supporters resolutely faced this opposition. The clash between the old and the modern views became sharper day by day.

Raja Rammohun Roy knew it very well that for eradicating injustice, orthodoxy and superstition, modern education was a necessity and he wanted to spread it wide as far as possible. But this did not at all mean that he was a supporter of Macaulay's system of education. The present system of education was introduced after his death and Macaulay had revealed the intention behind this policy in clear words—'the young men living on the banks of the Ganges would read Milton and Shakespeare and will be proud of our literature.' The real intention, however, was to un-Indianise us and to make us mental slaves. Macaulay's education served this purpose well and continues to do so even today.

On the contrary, Raja Rammohun Roy never let Indian culture and tradition to be lost sight of. This was the reason for his establishing the Vedanta College in 1825 wherein all facilities for teaching the ancient Shastras were provided. His concept of modern education was to bring about a harmony between ancient and modern thinking and between Eastern philosophy and Western science. It is wrong to accuse him of supporting Macaulay's system of education. Evidently, he is a victim of false propaganda.

The Moghul Emperor sent him to England in 1830 as his ambassador. He was to take part in the debate in the House of Commons about giving a new charter to the East India Company. He went to England in April 1831. He was accorded warm welcome in Liverpool, Manchester, London and in the Royal Court. There he cultivated the friendship of people like Bantham. From there he proceeded to France for some days and died at Bristol on 27th September 1833 from brain fever. His *samadhi* was built there on which it was inscribed:

'A true and determined man who believed in the oneness of God—he devoted all his life to human unity.'

The Story of Indian Renaissance * 241

In England, on the request of an English friend, Rammohun Roy had written his brief autobiography in which he said, 'I wrote a book against idol-worship at the age of sixteen years. At this I had to leave home due to differences with relatives and then I visited several provinces of India.' Ultimately, I was forced to visit other countries out of great hatred for the British rulers.' He felt very sorry for the fact that in India, one province after another was passing into the hands of the East India Company. He had seen with his own eyes the open loot of India by the British rulers which created great hatred for them in his heart. But his patriotism had no element of narrow-mindedness. This was the reason why he cultivated the friendship of Englishmen with liberal views and inspired his countrymen to reap the fullest benefit of their contact with Europe brought about by the British rule. He left no stone unturned in trying to bring about political consciousness among his compatriots through Bengali and Persian papers.

While going to England he travelled by a French ship simply for the reason that he was greatly impressed by the French Revolution of 1789 and had himself adopted the French ideal of 'liberty, equality and fraternity.' He had full sympathy for the French Revolution of 1830 also. At the Natal Port, he ran in his zeal to salute the tricolour flag of France and broke his ankle.

He always kept an eye on political developments taking place in the world and took deep interest in the freedom movements of other countries. When a Republican government came into office in Spain in 1821, he expressed his joy by holding a public reception in the town hall. It may be mentioned in this context that it was the time when the feudal system of Western Europe was crumbling and a world capitalist revolution was spreading fast in Europe and the American countries. At the time the feudal state of Spain tried its best to stem this tide and the barbaric Government of Spain resorted to inhuman atrocities on the people. They adopted primitive methods of carrying on their loot in the American countries, traded in slaves and impeded economic progress of those countries for quite long. In order to survive, the barbaric feudal imperialistic system of Spain created all possible obstacles in the path of the transition from feudalism to capitalism. But it is never possible to turn the wheel of history backwards. The result was that the foundations of this empire were shaken by the revolutionary onslaughts of the people of Holland. The feudal empire and its glory was brought to dust by the liberation wars of American colonies and the revolution of its own people. Thus the Spanish revolution had a special historical importance and was celebrated by Rammohun Roy for this reason.

He had full sympathy for the freedom-fighters of Ireland. When he received the news of the failure of the revolutionaries of Naples, he was so disturbed that he refused to meet an English friend. Later on, he wrote that from this unlucky news he had come to the conclusion that his dream of seeing the European and Asian nations free would not be fulfilled; especially the colonies of European nations would not be able to get the right of self-government. Under these circumstances he considered the struggle of Naples as his struggle and its enemies his enemies and that enemies of freedom and friends of authoritarianism had never succeeded and would never succeed.

The famous poet Mir Taqi 'Mir' wrote the following couplet in praise of the patriotism and universal humanism of Rammohun Roy:

'I feel hurt when someone is struck with a dagger. I have the pain of the whole world in my heart.'

Rammohun Roy was a reformer of many talents. He simultaneously worked in the fields of religion and politics, but he never compromised with untruth and evil practices. Every step that he took was taken with firmness and without fear. At that time it was a matter of great courage for him to go abroad when journey across the seas was considered to be a sin. Rammohun Roy was an able predecessor of Vivekananda. It would be no exaggeration to call him the builder of Modern India. Vivekananda had adopted three of his basic principles from him—acceptance of Vedanta, patriotism and equal love for Hindus and Muslims.

Rammohun Roy is called the founder of Brahmo Samaj, but this is a misconception, there being no truth in it. The Atmiya Sabha that he had established, was changed into Brahmo Sabha and continued to be based on Vedantic philosophy. After his death, his close friends and supporters Dwarkanath Tagore and Ramchandra Vidyavagish tried to keep it alive. But it was given a new lease of life by Debendranath Tagore (1817-1905) who was the son of Dwarkanath Tagore and father of Rabindranath Tagore. In 1843, he along with his twenty friends got initiated into the Brahmo Dharma. Romain Rolland has corroborated the fact that Debendranath Tagore organised the Brahmo Samaj and was its leader. It was he who formulated the beliefs, ideals and rituals of the Brahmo Samaj. He organised a regular worship for it and opened a seminary for priests. He himself used to teach and give speeches in that seminary and, in 1848, he published a book, *Brahmo Dharma* for the education of the followers of that faith. He believed that he had written that book by divine inspiration.

This Brahmo Dharma of Debendranath Tagore was not according to the ideals of Raja Rammohun Roy. Although Tagore also had faith in the Upanishads, yet he had based his religion on the rationalism of the West. The literary luminary Akshayakumar Dutta and Rajanarain Basu were among his associates. These people gave up idol worship and other ceremonials. However, they had no interest in social reform. On the contrary, Debendranath was propagating his new religion with expression of amity towards the Hindu religion. The result of this propaganda was that those students of the Hindoo College who were becoming sceptics or atheists now turned to this new religion.

In 1850 Debendranath Tagore banished the theory of

the infallibility of the Vedas and the concept of elitism from the Brahmo Samaj and brought about its final parting from Hindu religion. But young men with modern education took to the new religion and it very soon spread all over Bengal.

In 1858 Keshabchandra Sen became a member of the Brahmo Samaj. Debendranath's son Satyendranath was a class fellow of Keshab. It was he who brought him into the Brahmo Samaj. After completing his studies, Keshab had joined service in a bank, but soon became a leader of the Brahmos due to his talents and oratorial skill. There was no other orator of English and Bengali as great as Keshab. He greatly impressed the youth.

Debendranath Tagore was the head Acharya of Brahmo Samaj. Influenced by the brilliance of Keshab, he appointed him Acharya. But his appointment led to a storm as he belonged to a lower caste. Tagore had no guts to face the storm. In order to appease the opponents he removed Keshab from the post of Acharya.

This led to another storm raised by the young men with the result that Brahmo Samaj split into two parts. The first part, that remained under the leadership of Debendranath Tagore, came to be known as Adi Brahmo Samaj and the other, under the leadership of Keshab, came to be known as Nikhil Bharatiya Brahmo Samaj.

The removal of Keshab from the post of Acharya was, no doubt, the immediate cause of the division of Brahmo Samaj. But there were differences already growing which can be traced back to the past.

David Hare and Derozio were two enthusiastic collaborators in the field of reforms. David Hare was a Scot and had come to India as a trader. But after coming to India he gave away all his wealth for the spread of education and dedicated his life to social reforms. Derozio was an Anglo-Indian. He was appointed as a teacher in the Hindoo College at the age of 18. He was a talented writer and poet and was influenced by the Encyclopaediacs of France. He did not believe in any religion. He was wholly a materialist. Influenced by his poetic talent and attractive personality, most of the students of the college became free thinkers and rebels. They not only opposed idol worship and evil practices, but started hating the Hindu religion and the Hindu society itself.

When these young men, influenced by the Western system and the concept of individual freedom, joined the Brahmo Samaj, they inevitably clashed with Debendranath, the follower of the middle path, and his followers. This internal clash finally led to the division of Brahmo Samaj.

Keshab, who became the leader of the Nikhil Bharatiya Brahmo Samaj in 1866, had lost his mother in his childhood. He was brought up in an English school. He had not read Sanskrit at all. He was a devotee of Christ and considered Bible to be the best religious book. With the result that he brought into the new Samaj all the elements of Christianity. He got a tower in the shape of a cross built in the temple of worship with the result that the place came to be known as 'Keshab's Church.'

Like the proverbial new broom which sweeps cleaner, Keshab was so full of zeal that he insisted on his friends calling him the messenger of Christ or the servant of Christ. He used to celebrate Christmas by observing a fast on that day. He opened the gates of his temple of worship to people of all religions and castes and included portions of Bible, Koran and Zoroastrian text in his book of worship. However, Keshab and his followers were more inclined towards Christianity; therefore, in the Brahmo Samaj the method of worship, consciousness and fear of sin, repentance and crying in a fit of emotion were considered helpful in spiritual progress.

The field of activity of Brahmo Samaj was social reform. Keshab and his followers opened night schools, stressed on women's education and their freedom, violated the old restrictions on inter-dining and started the practice of inter-marriages which was made valid by the British Government by enacting a law in 1872. But the propagandists of the Brahmo Samaj were so enamoured of the Christian religion and its concept that they started making vitriolic attacks on Hindu society, Hindu customs and the ancient Shastras in their speeches. They became wholly devoid of liberalism, of tolerance and became narrow-minded and orthodox in their views. Saratchandra Chattopadhyaya has, in his novels, criticised the Hindu society but he has also drawn a vivid picture of the narrow-mindedness and orthodoxy of the Brahmo Samajists.

To every action there is a reaction. Consequently, the traditionalists among the Hindus organised the Hari Sabha to protect themselves from the attacks of Brahmo Samaj. Pandit Sasadhar Tarakchudamani and Swami Krishnanand of the Garibdas sect were their spokesmen. They gave a spiritual explanation of the concept of wearing the sacred thread, growing a tail of hair on the head and giving of alms. Brahmo Samaj was a movement of the middle class influenced by Western thoughts while Hari Sabha was one of well-to-do people who had no zest for life. Therefore, the hollowness of the latter was bound to be reflected in their propaganda. Even the children of twelve years gave speeches from the platform of Hari Sabha and spoke about the greatness of devotion to God. The audience would encourage them by clapping. On the one hand, the Acharyas and preachers of Brahmo Samaj were emitting fire against Hindu religion and Hindu society and, on the other, groups of obscurantists exposed the sham sainthood of the Brahmo Samajists in vulgar language and through ribald verses and stories. This controversy resulted in the creation of literature which was in bad taste and condemnable and brought an indelible blot on the Bengali language.

At such time, when Kolkata was in anguish due to the mutual recrimination of these two movements, the fame of Ramakrishna of Dakshineshwar started spreading gradually. We have seen that his was a talent of an illiterate and in the opinion of Vivekananda, he was a true jnani though outwardly he only appeared to be a mere Bhakta. He had heard the ancient Shastras by word of mouth and had very well imbibed all the important elements thereof. The speeches given in the meetings of Brahmo Samaj and Hari Sabha stood nowhere in comparison to his simple and easily understandable talks full of metaphors. Not only common men, but saints and sages of every sect, and professors and intellectuals felt drawn towards him. Ramakrishna stemmed the tide of Western influence and opened a middle path between Brahmo Samaj and Hari Sabha which brought back the zealous young men, eager to acquire knowledge, to the past traditions and protected the faithful from frivolity and orthodoxy.

Although Ramakrishna believed in idol worship and polytheism, he became the most popular religious teacher of his time. Keshab Chandra was greatly influenced when he came in his contact in 1875. He wrote in his *Sunday Mirror* that idol worship was nothing but the personification of godly qualities. If the idol was eliminated, all that would remain would be a beautiful symbol. He said that he had learnt that every idol that the Hindus worshipped represented a particular attribute of God and that every such attribute had been given a name. He suggested that the followers of the new religion worship only one God, who deserved to be the sole possessor of all those attributes which were worshipped by the Hindus in the shape of 33 crore gods.

Keshab visited England in 1870 and gave speeches there in his simple English before 40,000 people. He was welcomed as a collaborator of the West and a messenger of Christianity in the East. He was at the height of his fame when he returned. His Brahmo Samaj had profited much from the goodwill of the Government. He opened the branches of Brahmo Samaj in cities like Allahabad, Monghyr, Lucknow, Bombay, Simla and Lahore. In 1873 Keshab toured around the country to forge unity among the followers of the new religion. During the journey he had the idea to give a more popular base to Brahmo Samaj. With this intention he introduced the mysticism of Chaitanya and the practice of *sankirtan* (collective singing of devotional songs) in the worship of Brahmo Samaj. From morning till evening prayers were offered accompanied by the playing of Vaishnava musical instruments. Stories were recited and functions in honour of God were held. During the proceedings, Keshab who had never wept in his life, used to conduct the ceremonies as a priest with tears in his eyes.

This led to internal differences in the Nikhil Bharatiya Brahmo Samaj. When Keshab Chandra married off his minor daughter to the Raja of Cooch Behar, he was accused of giving up his ideals. A great number of members parted company and formed the Sadharan Brahmo Samaj.

The leader of Sadharan Brahmo Samaj was Nagendra-nath Chattopadhyay. Pandit Sasadhar of the Hari Sabha had a debate with him in which he claimed that it was not possible to worship God without giving Him some concrete shape. This was an old controversy between different sects of the Hindus which had been continuing since long. Christians had also joined this controversy. However, the most logical and philosophical stand was taken by the Buddhists. Buddha did not accept the existence of either soul or God. But, after a lapse of time, the Buddhist religion got divided into four sects—Mahayana, Hinayana, Sahajyana etc. It was through Mahayana that Buddhism spread in Tibet, China and Japan. The Tantric worship of Shakti was also introduced in Mahayana. Idols of Buddha, huge in many cases, started being worshipped in temples. The practice of idol worship and holding of big religious festivals in the temples started among the Hindus in the fourth century under the influence of Buddhism. Mahayana had great influence in West Bengal. The practice of making images in various forms and performing Shakti worship also started under the influence of this sect. It is said that the Goddess Ekjata, whose worship was started by Nagarjuna in Bhutan, was none other than Goddess Kali.

In other words, a religion, even if it does not believe in the existence of God but believes in rebirth, will have to provide its followers some concept of highest power ultimately.

Even though the founders and protagonists of a religion may continue to assert that God is without attributes and formless, its ordinary illiterate followers would certainly start attributing certain qualities to Him and giving Him some form. As religion is nothing but an interpretation of facts, the beliefs of religion, to whichever age and country it might pertain, are bound to be based on blind devotion and superstition. So long as religion exists, obscurantism, in some form or the other, will also continue to exist. In a society divided into classes, the exploiting and the ruling classes administer and will continue to administer opium to the exploited and subject classes. Idol worship is one of the many forms in which obscurantism exists. Even before the Christian missionaries, Muslims claimed to be destroyers of idol worship and began a Jehad against idol worship; Brahmo Samaj and Arya Samaj also tried their best to remove the blot of idol worship. But we find that the Muslims, Christians, Brahmo Samajists and Arya Samajists themselves are exhibiting the some kind of obscurantism and idol worship continues as before. Not only the common illiterate people but even educated people, graduates and engineers, visit the Hanuman Mandir and Vaishno Devi and offer worship to Kali.

Some of our educated friends, particularly those who claim to be intellectuals and progressive, do not even try to understand the historical role of Vivekananda. They call him reactionary simply because he supported idol worship. But the question is, when people like Raja Rammohun Roy and Keshab Chandra could not stop idol worship, how could Vivekananda have done it? He had no intention of posing as an intellectual and a great thinker by opposing idol worship. On the other hand, he had to protect the common illiterate people of India from the cultural attack of the imperialists which he did by supporting idol worship.

In his letter to Miss Hale of America, written on 30th

October, 1899, he expressed the view that movements like Brahmo Samaj were an expression of gratitude for the British rulers and they supported a truth that suited the masters. However, there was no clash between the forces of progress and the Brahmo Samaj as the latter was almost without life. The struggle for progress, along with new ideas, which was the demand of the nation, was going to be more serious and more difficult.

The Brahmo Samajists and other educated people like them had given up their national pride and adopted the British pride as their own. They were breaking away from their past history and traditions and becoming 'purely modern.' They considered everything praised by the British to be excellent and true. Ramakrishna, who was an idol worshipper, stemmed this tide of blindly following the West.

Vivekananda once narrated an incident how Ramakrishna ridiculed the blind followers of the West. Someone once told Ramakrishna that a boy, who always criticised the Shastras and was of low mental calibre, was praising the Gita. Thereupon, Ramakrishna said, 'He is praising the Gita because some English scholar must have praised it.'

The question of idol worship was not as material as that of protecting the national pride, national culture and tradition. Those who only talk of idol worship fail to understand this basic fact. Their knowledge of their history is based only on what the British have taught them. They do not know that foreign Muslim rulers, claiming to free the Kafir idolators from superstition, attacked our national pride, culture and tradition. The Bhakti movement of the medieval age was only a reaction to this attack. Kabir, Dadu, Nanak, Chaitanya and Tukaram protected the common masses from this attack and provided them with personal deities. Tulsidas, who called Lord Rama to be the incarnation of God, is branded as a reactionary without giving thought to the fact that Tulsidas organised a joint forum of Shaivas and Vaishnavas, including even the Shudras, to fight against the foreign cultural onslaught and thus played a very important role.

According to Vivekananda, the above reformist ideology came to India at a time when it appeared that the wave of materialism, which had attacked India, would wash away the culture and the teachings of the ancient Aryan sages. In the past also the nation had successfully faced thousands of such waves, while this new wave was comparatively weaker. Wave after wave had been attacking India. Swords were brandished and the skies of India had reverberated with the cries of 'Allah-o-Akbar.' But gradually, these waves subsided and the national ideals sustained as before.

It is, no doubt, true that every society is based mainly on its economic system. Yet disregarding culture, which is the outer shell, amounts to disregarding the dialectic relationship that exists between matter and consciousness. Culture and traditions cement national unity. That is why, every conquering nation tries to destroy the culture and tradition of the conquered nation, because of the continuing danger to its victory which can never be politically stable. There is no need to dilate on the efforts made by the Muslim conquerors to destroy the Indian society from within. But it is better to understand the resultant problems, otherwise it is not possible to solve them. The Muslim rulers introduced Persian and Arabic in place of Sanskrit. It was an attempt to impose a foreign culture and tradition on our country. The result was that the intellectual class, which ruled the country, consisted of foreigners. Apart from this, the Muslim rulers did not repose much confidence in Indians, resulting in the continuing recruitment of forces from foreign countries. Therefore, the intellectuals and the army officers, who came from other lands, considered themselves superior to Indian Hindus and Muslims in the matter of language and culture. The word 'Vilayati' was used only for such people. These 'Vilayati' elements could never become part of our national life and ever remained foreigners.

In our country also there were elements who were professional courtiers. Among them the Kayasthas and Kashmiri Brahmins were notable. Education for them was only a means to earn their bread. Before the coming of the Muslims, they had been learning Sanskrit and were courtiers of the Indian princes. When the Muslims came they learnt Persian and became their courtiers and after the coming of the British, they immediately turned to learning English and became their courtiers. They made the language of their rulers their own language and broke off their links with past history and traditions of India. The guiding principle of their life was to flatter the ruling classes and be collaborators of the suppression and exploitation of the masses.

The Bhakti movement, which had started for the protection of culture, ultimately took the form of an armed struggle in Maharashtra and Punjab, resulting in the formation of the Sikh and Maratha states. However, according to Vivekananda, this period was one of intellectual decadence in India unlike that of the Moghul Court. These two empires had a short life and lost all their power after disintegrating the hateful Muslim rule, because they had nothing but hatred for culture and represented obscurantism.

This was followed by a period of turmoil, clashes between friends and foes, between the Moghul empire and its destroyers. The British and the French, who were till now peaceful, also joined the fray. For more than fifty years there was nothing but wars and looting. And, when the dust settled, the British emerged as victors over the rest.

The British traders were very cunning as rulers. They sharpened the differences prevailing among the people and created three classes as their brokers—the capitalists through their trade, the feudals through the permanent settlement of Cornwalis, and the intellectuals through Macaulay's system of education. These three classes were joined by similar elements, both native and foreign, of the Muslim period. Due to their class character they were anti-people and opposed to tradition. They surrendered themselves completely before the British and, in order to present a good image of themselves before the white masters, these very people became social reformers. It was only Vivekananda who took up the cause of the common masses and chided both the British rulers and their blind followers. He was a Kayastha who presented himself as a Kshatriya. (Netaji Subhash was also a Kayastha, whose Kshatriya behaviour was most amazing.)

Vivekananda told the Englishmen, who were boasting of civilizing us, that our great nation had two great qualities—the curiosity to acquire knowledge and a poetic insight; that this brave race started in its quest for learning and contributed more than any ancient or modern race in the development of the knowledge of mathematics, chemistry, medicine, music and archery and even the development of modern European civilization.

The other quality that this race possessed was a poetic symphony in the shape of its religion, its philosophy, its history, its ethics and its statecraft. Such a miracle was not possible except through the language which we call Sanskrit. Even for expressing the dry and difficult mathematical terms this language provided us with musical numbers.

It is only on the basis of these two qualities that our race is still alive. According to Vivekananda, if our practices and policies had been so bad, why were we not destroyed all through this period? There was no let up in the foreigners' efforts to destroy us. Why were the Hindus not destroyed as had happened in the case of other uncivilized countries? Why did the Indian territories not become so deserted as to let people of those countries come here and start cultivation as they did in places like Australia, America and Africa? Those foreigners, who considered themselves strong, were asked by him to understand that we had survived because we still had enough to contribute to the civilization of the world. The muslims and Turks destroyed ancient cultures like persia and ravaged entire central Asia but could not influence the sturdy. It in On culture beyond a point.

Vivekananda chided the blind followers of the British for going round saying that we were beasts, that the Europeans should civilize us and that Christ had come to India. He said that neither Christ nor Jehova had or would ever come to India. They were looking after their own homes and had no time to come here. The old Lord Shiva was still present in India, Goddess Kali still accepted sacrifice and the flute player still played on his flute here. The great Himalayas had the mount Kailas to its north where the good old Lord Shiva was presiding. Even Ravana with ten heads and twenty hands could not move Kailas. How could a poor Christian priest shake it? In this country the old Lord Shiva would ever continue to play on his *damaroo*. Goddess Kali would continue to accept sacrifice and Sri Krishna would continue to play on his flute. If they did not like it, they had better removed themselves from the scene. The country could not be ruined for a handful of people like them. The world was so big. Why did such people not go to some other place? They were eating the grain given by the old Lord Shiva and showing him disloyalty by singing the praises of Christ. It was a matter of shame for people who went and crawled before the Europeans, called themselves low and bad in every way. This might be true so far as they were concerned, but why did they include the whole country among them?

Distancing himself from such broker elements; Vivekananda said in March 1901 in his speech at Dacca:

> In contradiction to these, there is that ancient class who say, 'I do not know, I do not care to know or understand all these hair-splitting ratiocinations; I want God, I want the Atma, I want to go to that Beyond, where there is no universe, where there is no pleasure or pain, where dwells the Bliss Supreme;' who say, 'I believe in the salvation by bathing in the holy Ganga with faith;' who say, 'whomsoever you may worship with singleness of faith and devotion as the one God of the universe, in whatsoever form as Shiva, Rama, Vishnu, etc., you will get Moksha;' to that sturdy ancient class I am proud to belong.[2]

Even before this, in his Ramnad speech he had elaborated this point by saying:

I am sorry to say that most of the examples one meets nowadays of men who are imbibed with Western ideas are more or less failures.

"These are two great obstacles in our path in India, the Scylla of old orthodoxy and the Charybdis of modern European civilization. Of these two I vote for the old orthodoxy, and not for the Europeanised system, for the old orthodoxy man may be ignorant, he may be crude, but he is a man, he has a faith, he has strength, he stands on his own feet; while the Europeanised man has no backbone, he is a mass of heterogenous source— and these ideas are unassimilated, undigested, unharmonised. He does not stand on his own feet, and his head is turning round and round. Where is the motive power of this work?—in a few patronising pats from the English people. His scheme of reforms, his vehement vituperations against the evils of certain social customs, have, as the mainspring, some European patronage. Why are some of our customs called evils? Because the Europeans say so. That is about the reason that he gives. I would not submit to that. Stand and die in your own strength; if there is any sin in the world, it is weakness; avoid all weakness, for weakness is sin, weakness is death. These unbalanced creatures are not yet formed into distinct personalities; what are we to call them—men, women or animals While those orthodox people were staunch but were men. There are still some excellent examples.[3]

The examples of such ideal persons were Ramakrishna Paramahansa, his father Pandit Khudiram who refused to give false evidence despite feudal pressure, and Pavhari Baba. On the other hand, people like Debendranath Tagore, Keshabchandra and Justice Ranade lacked firmness although

2. *Ibid*. Vol. III, p. 450.
3. *Ibid*. Vol. V, p. 151.

they were of modern views. Infact, they only gave the appearance of greatness but were not really great. That is why Sri Ramakrishna Paramahansa had already warned his worthy disciple Narendra against such people. He advised him not to entertain a feeling of inferiority to them as they were destined to live only for a hundred years while Narendra would be remembered for a thousand years. He had correctly guessed about the firmness of Vivekananda's character.

The Rajas of Ramnad, Mysore and Khetri, who had helped Vivekananda to go to Chicago and had also joined in his welcome on his return by drawing his carriage and who were proud of their past and their lineage, were also more firm of character than the other so-called reformers.

But the main question was not that of reformers but of liberating the country from foreign slavery. Workers, peasants and the students were rising against exploitation and suppression. The class struggle between the emerging national capitalism and imperialism was becoming sharper. Anand Mohan Basu organised the student movement after returning from Cambridge and was later joined by Surendranath Banerjee. The latter had been expelled from the Indian Civil Service without rhyme or reason. According to Bipinchandra Pal, the impassioned patriotic speeches of Surendranath infused the student movement with a new life.

The national consciousness that was becoming stronger day by day in the latter part of the nineteenth century, was reflected in contemporary literature. Novels like *Anand Math*, written by Bankimchandra, were historical novels full of patriotism. They reminded the readers of the struggles carried on by their forefathers against slavery. In 1873-74, Bankimchandra also started the publication of a literary magazine called *Banga Darshan*. According to Bipinchandra Pal, this magazine played the same role as was played by the French Encyclopaedists in European thinking and French literature. Hemchandra and Madhusudan Dutta were powerful poets of the new consciousness. Dinbandhu Mitra wrote a play named *Neel Darpan* which gave a vivid account of the atrocities and the plunder of the peasants of Champaran by the white zamindars. The British government proscribed this play and deported the missionary who translated it into English.

The literary awakening did not remain confined to Bengal, but spread all over India. In north India, this new wave was represented by Bhartendu Harishchandra, Altaf Hussain Hali and Bhai Pooran Singh.

In his reminiscences, Bipinchandra Pal has said that more and more English-educated Bengalis began to be appointed on responsible posts in the administration. They were also competing with others in the fields of law and medicine. In their behaviour, these English-educated Bengalis exhibited independence of character and a self-confidence which were the gift of the new consciousness. All of them felt proud of their race which generated a feeling of patriotism and national pride. Hemchandra was a powerful exponent of such feelings.

The great revolution and national unity of Italy continued to inspire the youth for fifty years. Yogendranath Vidyasagar translated the biographies of Garibaldi and Mazzini into Bengali and Lala Lajpat Rai wrote their biographies in Punjabi which continued to be widely read upto 1930-32.

The growing national consciousness was bound to influence the reformist movements also. Under this influence Keshabchandra was forced to replace the modern outlook of Brahmo Samaj by a medieval outlook. These circumstances also led to starting of the Theosophist movement in 1876, as imperialist propaganda in a new form. The Theosophists were adopting the tactics of merging themselves in the orthodox native religion of the country in which they worked. They adopted the same tactics in our country and started propagating the concept of incarnation, mysticism and the miracles of Yogis hundreds of years in age living in the Himalayas. Needless to say that Vivekananda had seen through their anti-national and reactionary role.

In 1875 Swami Dayananda founded the Arya Samaj at Lahore. Earlier, he had come to Bengal and had talked to Keshabchandra. But he could not be reconciled to Brahmo Samaj because the followers of Keshabchandra had neither read Sanskrit nor had any faith in the Shastras. Dayananda himself was a great scholar of Sanskrit and considered the Vedas to be infallible and source of all knowledge. Moreover, Dayananda wanted to return to the past instead of being a modernist. Yet Arya Samaj played a very significant role in creating national consciousness in the North. The rising capitalist class of every country looks towards its past with pride and uses history as its arsenal in its national movement. It was natural for the emerging capitalist class of our country also to follow this practice.

These currents and cross-currents led to the emergence of a tidal wave to which Vivekananda had referred in his Kolkata address on his return from abroad. This tidal wave swallowed all the lesser waves all over the country.

Vivekananda was the symbol of this wave of new consciousness. He was also a true successor of Raja Rammohun Roy. He fully imbibed the three teachings of Raja Rammohun Roy's Vedanta, patriotism and equal love for the Hindus and Muslims and developed them further till the end of the nineteenth century in accordance with the circumstances prevailing at that time.

Vivekananda, with his extraordinary foresight, saw a new dawn rising in the East and laid the foundation of a new India in anticipation of greater events destined to take place in the future.

11

THE LAST PHASE

"Life is a battle. Let me die fighting."
—*Vivekananda*

On 1st December, 1900, Vivekananda reached Kolkata after his second visit abroad lasting one and a half years. As is evident from his memoirs of European travels, his political feelings were now stronger than before. The importance of his second journey lay in the fact that during this journey he came to understand very well that Western capitalism had now acquired the hateful form of imperialism. The disturbed state of his mind was reflected in a letter that he wrote to Mary Hale on 30th October, 1899:

> The British rule in India has one redeeming aspect which is that it has once again brought back India on the world stage. If it was done for the welfare of the people then, just as circumstances helped Japan, the result for India would have been even more surprising. But when the main aim is to suck the blood, there can be no welfare. Broadly, the old rule was better for the people because it did not deprive people of everything, there was some justice, some freedom in it.

> Only a few hundred modernised, half-educated men devoid of national consciousness are the show-pieces of modern British India—nothing else.

> The population of India has been growing rapidly in spite of centuries of anarchy during the period when the British struggled for victory over India, in spite

At Shillong, 1901 after illness

of the dreadful genocide committed by the British in 1857-58, in spite of the even more dreadful famines, which are the inevitable result of British rule (there is never any famine in the native states). Still, the population is not as much as it was when the country was completely independent—that is, before the Muslim rule. Indian labour and Indian production can easily provide for the subsistence of a population five times more than its present population so long as all that the Indians have is not snatched away from them.

This is the position today—now education would also not be allowed to spread any more. The freedom of the press has already been strangulated. We were disarmed already and now the little opportunity of self-government that was given to us earlier, is being taken away soon.[1] We are waiting to see what would happen next! People are punished with banishment across the seas for writing a few words of harmless criticism, other people are being sent to jails without trial, and no one knows when one would be beheaded.

For some years India has had an intimidating rule. English soldiers are slaying our countrymen, dishonouring our sisters for being sent back home after being given a pension and travelling at our cost! We are in darkness—where is God? Mary, you can afford to be an optimist, but is it possible for me to be one? Suppose you only publish this letter—then under the pretext of the law that has recently been enacted in India, the British government would forcibly take me away from here to India and would kill me without any legal proceedings. And I know that all your Christian governments would feel happy at this, because we are non-Christians. Can I also go to sleep and be an optimist? Nero was the most optimistic man. They do not want to publish all these fearful things in the form of news and if it is found necessary to publish something in the form of news then the Reuter correspondents concoct some false news. Even the murder of a non-Christian by a Christian is only legal entertainment. Your missionaries go to convey the message of God, but do not dare to speak a word of truth due to the fear of the British because the British would shoo them away the next day.

The property and land granted by the previous governments has been swallowed and the present government is spending on education less than even what Russia does. And what kind of education is it?

A little expression of originality is suppressed. Mary, if there is really no God who is the father of all, who

---

1. In 1882 Lord Ripon had given some rights of self-government which were later withdrawn.

is not afraid of protecting the weak from the powerful and if he can be bribed then there is nothing hopeful for us. Is there any God of some kind? Only time will tell.

"Well. I am thinking of coming to Chicago next week and would talk to you in detail about these matters. Do not give publicity to the source of this news.[2]

On his second journey to the West, Vivekananda was accompanied by Sister Nivedita and Swami Turiyananda. When Turiyananda suggested taking some Sanskrit books along, he said, 'Last time they saw a warrior, this time I want to show them a Brahmin.'

Vivekananda was born in a Kayastha family—though he regarded him as a Kshatriya—and he took another birth after accepting Ramakrishna Paramahansa as his Guru. In this way there was an amalgam of the qualities of a Kshatriya and a Brahmin in his personality. When he visited Chicago for the first time he presented his self as a Kshatriya warrior endowed with qualities of Rajas. But now he was starting on his second journey to the West. Asia had by that time awoken and the cultural attack of imperialism on India had been defeated. He did not have to enter into a debate this time but only to make the Europeans realise this fact in a calm and serene manner of a *satvik* Brahmin.

The change that had been brought about in the national goal in the historical context was disclosed by him in detail to a disciple during the course of a discourse. He expressed the views that people could not be united until they had a common goal. Till then it was futile to hold meetings, form associations and give speeches. Guru Gobind Singh achieved this by making both the Hindus and Muslims realise that they were living under a rule of tyranny. He did not himself set some new goal for them, but only drew the attention of the masses to the goal that was already before them. That is why he commanded the confidence of both Hindus and Muslims. He was a rare personality in the history of India.

---

2. Translated from the Hindi version.

Just as the Bhakti movement assumed the form of an armed resistance, in the same way the situation was developing now, too. Swami Vivekananda was clearly visualising the coming storm. He had, till now, talked of *bhakti-mukti* and the Shastras as being primary. He had great influence and was venerated by the fellow-disciples who obeyed him. However, he was sad because he found that they did not foresee all that, of which he had a foreboding. They were giving primary importance to what was secondary.

On 27th December he left Kolkata for the Mayavati Ashram in Almora. The founder of the Ashram, Mr. Sevier, had died during his absence. He wanted to console Mrs, Sevier and look into the management of the Ashram. While he was on his way, there was a heavy hailstorm which made his condition worse as his health was already in bad shape. He told Mrs. Sevier that his health was broken and that his mind was yet strong and active as before.

He found that the sanyasins had installed the image of Ramakrishna Paramahansa in one of the rooms of the Ashram where regular worship was held and devotional songs were sung. In the evening, when all had gathered near the altar, he told them in strong terms that outer (ceremonial) worship was contradictory to the *advaita* way of devotion. They were not supposed to concentrate on the physical features of their Guru, but to follow and publicise his ideals.

Ramakrishna's image was removed from the room the very next day.

In the Mayavati Ashram, Vivekananda kept himself busy in spite of his health being shattered. Every day he would write a great number of letters. He stayed at the Ashram for about a month during the course of which there were discussions about the Shastras. He also wrote three articles for the journal, *Prabuddha Bharat*. These articles were a part of his struggle. He never lost sight of misconceptions that were being spread by distorting history. The article about the social conference speech was written in this context. At this conference held in Lahore, Mahadev Govind Ranade, the leader of the Prarthana Sabha, had criticised the moralistic traditions and quoted the Vedas and the Shastras in support of his contention.

Vivekananda's article on this speech ended with the words:

> Vive Ranade and the social reformers!—Vive but, O India! Anglicised India! Do not forget, child, that there are in this society problems; neither you nor your Western Guru can yet grasp the meaning of, much less solve ![3]

When the cultural attack of the missionaries failed and the magic of the money of the Christian religion did not work, the Theosophical Society was created. The mission of this Trojan Horse was to spread hypocrisy and defeat the rising national awakening.

In his 'Stray Remarks on Theosophy' Vivekananda started by saying:

> The Theosophists claim to possess the original divine knowledge of the universe. We are glad to learn of it, and gladder still that they mean to keep it rigorously a secret. Woe unto us, poor mortals, and Hindus at that, if all this is at once let out on us! Modern Theosophy is Mrs. Besant. Blavatskism and Olcottism seem to have taken a back seat. Mrs. Besant means well at least—and nobody can deny her perseverance and zeal.[4]

Although weak in body, Vivekananda was still strong mentally. In a beautiful and sharp satirical style he writes:

> We cannot attribute a knowledge of all this to the writer of the articles in the *Advocate*, but he must not confound himself and his Theosophists with the great Hindu nation, the majority of whom have clearly seen through the Theosophical phenomena from the start and, following the great Swami Dayananda Saraswati who took away his patronage from Blavatskism the moment he found it out, have held themselves aloof.[5]

---

3. *Ibid.* Vol. IV, p. 307.
4. *Ibid.* Vol. IV. p. 317.
5. *Ibid,* p. 318

Madame Blavatsky and Olcott were the original leaders of Theosophy. In the beginning these people made Swami Dayananda their leader and started their work by exploiting his name. But in spite of being a revivalist, Swami Dayananda was a patriot. Very soon he found out the real intent of the Theosophists and distanced himself from them. Vivekananda continues:

> The only help the religion of the Hindus got from the Theosophists in the West was not a ready field but years of uphill work, necessitated by Theosophical sleight-of-hand methods. The writer ought to have known that the Theosophists wanted to crawl into the heart of Western society, catching on to the skirts of scholars like Max Muller and poets like Edwin Arnold, all the same denouncing these very men and posing as the only receptacles of universal wisdom. And one heaves a sigh of relief that this wonderful wisdom is kept a secret. Indian thought, charlatanry and mango-growing fakirism had all identified in the minds of the educated people in the West and this was all the help rendered to Hindu religion by the Theoeophists.[6]

The last para ends with even more biting sarcasm:

> The great immediate good effect of Theosophy in every country so far as we can see is to separate, like Prof. Koch's injections into the lungs of the consumptives, the healthy, spiritual, active, and patriotic from the charlatans, the morbids, and the degenerates posing as spiritual beings.[7]

But, in spite of this warning of Vivekananda, the people of Annie Besant continued their activities of encouraging the hyprocrites and the backward-looking people and were successful in their efforts to a great extent to blunt the sharpness of national consciousness.

Vivekananda returned to the Belur monastery on 24th

---

6. *Ibid.* Vol. IV, pp. 318-319.
7. *Ibid*, p. 319.

January, 1901 after traversing across the snow-covered track from Almora.

From there he set out with his mother on a pilgrimage to the holy places of East Bengal and Assam which proved to be the last journey undertaken by him. From Dacca he went for *darshan* to Kamakhyapeeth and Chandranath. On the way he rested for a few days at Goalpara and Guawahati. But during the rigours of the journey his asthma got aggravated. His disciples took him to Shillong in the hope that the climate of that place would suit him. But the stay there brought him no relief. His asthma became so acute that it appeared that he was approaching his end. However, he remained calm and was heard saying, 'What does it matter if I die? I have given to the world enough to think about.'

When he returned to the monastery after the journey, his diabates had also got aggravated. Swelling in parts of his body was visible. He was put under the treatment of a Vaidya. All were worried about his condition, but he always tried to cheer them up by his humorous talk. He never stopped talking to the visitors. He was especially pleased to meet the university students and the youth. For hours he would discuss with them about the bad days into which the country had fallen and the ways to remedy the ills thereof. In a forceful and cheerful voice he would preach to them to be strong. The disciples considered these discussions to be harmful for his health and would request him to desist from talking. But he would tell them to forget about such restrictions and that he would consider his labours to be successful even if one of them became an ideal man; that he was not worried about his death if it came about for the welfare of others; that he could not disappoint people who came to listen to him from far off places; that he would not keep quiet whatever they might do.

Bhupendranath Dutta has related an incident in his book.[8] The patriots of Kolkata decided to hold a celebration in honour of Shivaji so as to popularise patriotic leaders like him. But no one agreed to preside over the celebrations

---

8. Swami Vivekananda : *Patriot Proohet*, p. 224.

due to the fear of the government. At last they went to the Belur monastery and placed their problem before Vivekananda. His eyes were filled with tears on hearing them and he asked them to go to Narendranath Sen, the editor of *Indian Mirror*, and mention his name and that if Sen did not agree he would himself preside over the function.

Apart from talking to visitors, Vivekananda kept himself busy reading books. He kept up studying till the end of his life. Saratchandra Chakravarti has related in his memoirs of Vivekananda:

> Swamiji had lost his appetite and sleep as a result of following the strict regulation of his treatment prescribed by the Vaidya. Most of the time he went without sleep. Even then he gave himself no rest. Some time back a new set of *Encyclopaedia Britannica* was purchased for the monastery. Looking at the shining new books, one of the disciples said that it was difficult to read all those books in a lifetime. The disciple did not know that by that time Swamiji had already read first ten of the volumes and was going through the eleventh. Swamiji told him this and challenged him to ask him to quote from any part of the first ten volumes. The disciple was struck with wonder when Swamiji started quoting whole passages from the first ten volumes and replied to all the questions about what was contained in those volumes. He could only exclaim, 'it is beyond human power'.

Every year some Santhal men and women used to come to clean the monastery. They would meet him and talk to him. Once when he was talking in a humorous mood to them, some gentlemen came to the monastery to meet him. He sent back a message that he would not meet anyone, because he was enjoying his conversation with the Santhals.

One day Swamiji invited the Santhals for a meal in the monastery. He directed a rich fare of *puris*, sweets and curd to be prepared for them and himself fed them. While eating, one of the Santhals who had become more intimate with Swamiji, asked, 'Swamiji, we never get such good food—where do you get it from?' He then said,

'You are Narayanas; today I have entertained Narayana himself.;..'

Afterwards, turning towards his disciples, he said to them,

See how simple-hearted these poor illiterate people are! Will you be able to relieve their miseries to some extent at least? Otherwise of what use is our wearing the *gerua* (the ochre robe of the sanyasin)?.... Sometimes I think within myself, 'What is the good of building monasteries and so forth? Why not sell them and distribute the money among the poor, indigent Narayanas? What homes should we care for, we who have made the tree our shelter? Alas! How can we have a heart to put a morsel into our mouths, when our countrymen have not enough wherewithall to feed or clothe themselves?'.. .. Mother, shall there be no redress for them? One of the purposes of my going out to preach religion to the West, as you know, was to see if I could find any means of providing for the people of my country. 'Seeing their poverty and distress,' I think sometimes, 'let us throw away all this paraphernalia of worship—blowing the conch and ringing the bell, and waving the lights before the Image.... Let us throw away all the pride of earning and study of the Shastras and all sadhanas for the attainment of personal mukti—and going from village to village devote our lives to the service of the poor, and by convincing the rich men about their duties to the masses, through the force of our character and spirituality and our austere living, get money and the means wherewith to serve the poor and distressed .... 'Alas! Nobody in our country thinks for the low, the poor and the miserable! Those that are the backbone of the nation, whose labour produces food, those whose one day's strike from work raises a cry of general interest in the city—where is the man in our country who sympathises with them, who shares in their joys and sorrows? Look, how for want of sympathy on the part of the Hindus, thousands of Pariahs are becoming Christians in the Madras Presidency! Don't think that it is merely the pinch of hunger that drives them to embrace Christianity. It is simply because they do not get your sympathy. You are continually telling them, 'Don't touch me!' 'Don't touch this or that!' 'Is there any fellow-feeling or sense of *dharma* left in the country? There is only 'Don't-touchism' now! Kick out all such degrading usages! How I wish to demolish the barriers of 'Don't touchism' and go out and bring them together one and all, crying: 'Come, all ye that are poor and destitute, fallen and downtrodden ! we are one in the name of Ramakrishna!' Unless they are elevated, the Great Mother (India) will never awake![9]

A session of the All India Congress Committee was held at Kolkata in December 1901 which was attended by delegates from different parts of the country. Many of them came to the Belur monastery for a *darshan* of Swamiji. He talked to these leaders in Hindi and not in English. He expressed his desire for the establishment of a school of Vedic studies at Kolkata. The leaders gave him vague assurances of making all possible efforts to fulfil his desire.

The Congress at that time was an organisation of elements who were agents of the British. The delegates attending the conference were given a concession in the railway fare for attending the conference in the first and the second classes. Vivekananda had no hopes from these Anglicised patriots wearing neckties. He was thinking of recruiting sanyasins as preachers by establishing a school of Vedic studies and providing therein facilities for teaching Sanskrit, literature, philosophy, the Vedas and the Shastras. He also wanted to establish a monastery, like the one at Belur, for women under the guidance of Ramakrishna's widow.

In January, 1902 Vivekananda went for a short visit to Bodh Gaya, and on the way back, he rested at Kashi for a few days. When he returned to the Belur monastery in March, his health deteriorated. It was now difficult for

---

9. Romain Rolland, *Vivekananda*, pp. 180-81.

him to leave the bed. On Ramakrishna's birthday, about 30,000 people visited the monastery. Many of them wanted to meet him and talk to him. But they went back disappointed.

Whenever Vivekananda felt better, he would start doing some work. He felt restless if he had to sit doing nothing. He continued to work for four months from March to July in spite of his sickness. He had planned to write a number of books and had prepared some notes also. But he could not complete any of the books.

With the beginning of June he gave up taking interest in matters relating to the monastery and the Ramakrishna Mission. Whenever a fellow-disciple or his own disciple sought his advice, he would say, 'Do whatever you think best.'

On the 4th of July in 1902 he felt much better. He rose early that day and sat talking to people about the past in a cheerful mood. He talked to a few people who had come to meet him about general matters and had tea with them. Thereafter, he suddenly got up and went into the chapel and shut the windows and bolted the doors. Everyone was surprised at this strange behaviour. For three hours he remained in the chapel. When he came out into the court he was transformed. He was humming a song, 'My heart, let us go home' and continued to walk about the courtyard. All eyes were glued to him.

It is reported that Swami Premananda was standing close to him at that time. He was heard muttering to himself, 'Had there been another Vivekananda, he would have understood what Vivekananda has done. But many Vivekanandas will be born when the time comes?'

As the day passed, he returned to his room and lay down. At 9 he breathed his last. He was only 39 years of age at that time.

The shell had been broken and the flame was now scattered. Who carried forward this flame after him?

12

SUMMING-UP

"Truth is as easy to understand as it is great—simple in its own existence."

— *Vivekananda*

Three years after Vivekananda's death, events that he had foreseen and in preparation of which he had started his titanic struggle, started happening.

Dr. Pattabhi Sitaramayya has recorded in his *History of the Congress* that the first five years of the twentieth century were the years of the repressive rule of Lord Curzon. The powers of the Kolkata Corporation were reduced, a law against secret societies which were becoming quite active at that time was enacted by the government, universities were brought under government control which made education costlier, Indians were charged with having an untruthful character, a budget for twelve reforms was passed, Tibet was attacked (which was later called the Tibet Commission), and last of all, Bengal was divided—all these acts were performed by Curzon. These acts broke the back of the loyalists and led to the creation of a new spirit.

There was already a growing anger against the repression, loot and exploitation being carried on by foreign rule. Lord Curzon's plan for the partition of Bengal added fuel to this smouldering fire. Under the plan, the Bengali speaking province was divided into two parts. This led to a conflagration in which the people of other provinces also joined to fight for their problems. According to Dr. Sitaramayya, the whole country made the partition of Bengal a national issue. The agitation was made stronger by raising

Swami Vivekananda Temple, Belur Math

he problems of other states also along with the issue of partition. The Canal Colonisation Bill led to the creation of a storm among me militant people of Punjab. As a result of the agitation there, Lala Lajpat Rai and Ajit Singh were expelled from the country.

The repressive policy adopted by the government proved to be counter-productive. The agitation gained momentum as repression increased. In 1908 the situation reached a climax. Prosecution of newspapers became a common happening. *Yugantar, Sandhya* and *Bande Mataram*, which were the newspapers spreading the message of a new awakening, were closed down. Brahmobandhab, the patriotic editor of *Sandhya* died in the hospital. Lokmanya Tilak was arrested in Maharashtra on 13th July, 1908. He was awarded a sentence of six years in jail after a trial lasting five days. Later on six more months were added to the sentence. Harisaruttam Rao of Andhra was sentenced to nine months in jail. On an appeal by the government, the High Court enhanced the punishment to three years imprisonment. It became a general practice to award a sentence of five years in jail for sedition. However, soon the seditious activities went underground and reappeared in the form of bombs and pistols. Political assassinations also started taking place occasionally and among them, the most daring act was the assassination of Sir Curzon Wiley in London in 1907. It was executed by Madan Lal Dhingra who was later sentenced to death. The Parsee gentleman Dr. Lalkaka, who tried to save him, was also hanged afterwards.

A secret revolutionary organisation called Anusheelan Samiti was formed in 1908. Sister Nivedita, the Irish disciple of Vivekananda and Aurobindo Ghose were among its founder members. In the same year Khudiram Bose became a martyr after being hanged. He had thrown two bombs to kill Kingsford, the district judge of Muzaffarpur. His pictures adorned the homes of people all over India. Vivekananda's younger brother, Bhupendranath, was the editor of *Yugantar* which was the journal of the revolutionaries. When he was sentenced to a long term of jail sentence for spreading the cult of violence, his old mother expressed her happiness and 500 women went to congratulate her for her son's patriotism. Bhupendranath himself courageously declared in the court that he was leaving behind him 30 crore people who would keep his journal going.

The Gorkha Regiment was deployed in East Bengal and repressive laws such as the one prohibiting seditious meetings, the Press Act and the Criminal Law Amendment

Act were passed. But despite all this, the open as well as the secret struggle continued to gather strength. Although the struggle started on the issue of partition of Bengal, it soon became a countrywide movement which was based on a four point programme of boycott of foreign goods, Swadeshi (use of national goods), Swarajya (self-government) and national education. The Belur monastery of Kolkata became the centre of revolutionary activities and the government started thinking of closing it down. Romain Rolland has given the credit for this movement to Vivekananda and has said:

> If the generation that followed saw, three years after Vivekananda's death, the revolt of Bengal, the prelude to the great movement of Tilak and Gandhi, if India today has definitely taken part in collective action of organised masses, it is due to the initial shock, to the mighty message from Madras :
>
> 'Lazarus, come forth !'
>
> This message had a double meaning: a national and a universal. Although, for the great monk of the Advaita, it was the universal meaning that predominated, it was the other that remained the sinews of India. For she replied to the urge of the fever which has taken possession of the world at this moment of history—the fatal urge of nationalism, whose monstrous effects we see today. It was, therefore, at its very inception fraught with danger.[1]

There is no doubt that the message of Vivekananda spread all over the country and the events that he had predicted not only started happening but assumed the form of a strong movement in the face of which the British Government had to bend and the partition of Bengal was annulled. This was the first struggle, after the war of independence in 1857, that became successful which brought glory to the whole nation. Of course, there was a danger inherent in the message of Vivekananda of its developing

---

1. Romain Rolland, *Vivekananda*, p. 125.

in the form of narrow nationalism—Vivekananda had woken up a sleeping lion, as it were, and created a feeling of self-confidence in the nation about its being still alive, in spite of continuous foreign invasions, while those of Greece, Rome and Egypt had been wiped out. It was because there was a perennial current of culture which formed the nation's backbone and kept it strong and alive. No foreign nation could destroy it and enslave it for eternity. It was Vivekananda's message which had inspired the poet Iqbal to write the following lines:

'Saare jahan se achcha hindostan hamara
Hum bulbulain hain iski yeh gulistan hamara
Yunan-Missr-Roma sub mit gaye jahan se
Baaki magar hai ab tuk namo-nishan hamara.

(Our Hindustan is the best of all in the world. We are the birds for whom it is a garden (our nest), Greece, Egypt, Rome have all been wiped out but our identity still survives.)

It is only proper to praise the greatness, vastness and beauty of India because it strengthens national feeling. But by calling our country to be the best in the world this feeling gets changed into chauvinistic nationalism which is what actually happened. Thus our national song, throughout our freedom movement, has been describing our tricolour national flag as the flag of victory over the world. Nobody paused to think that achieving victory over the world has never been our goal; we only wanted to liberate ourselves from foreign slavery and also wished for similar freedom for other countries wherever they were. In the absence of this balanced thinking, our national feeling turned into foolishness which encouraged reactionary thinking.

In the beginning of the twentieth century, Western thinkers like Romain Rolland and H.G. Wells opposed the mutual bickering among nations, war and the cult of violence and placed before the world the ideal of universal brotherhood, love for humanity and world peace. Ramakrishna Paramahansa and Vivekananda naturally drew the attention of Romain Rolland because Advaitism is also based on the same ideals. He wrote the biographies of these two great Indians and thereby propagated the ideal of universal brotherhood. He was of the view that just as obscurantism divides people and induces the communities to fight with one another, in the same way, nationalism is a fatal tendency which divides human beings along geographical lines leading one nation to dominate over another and creates hatred and violence in place of mutual love. Romain Rolland has pointed out this danger which was inherent in the message of Vivekananda:

> We know the danger, we who have seen too many of such ideals—however pure they may have been—employed in the service of the most dirty passions! But how else was it possible to bring about within the disorganised Indian masses a sense of human unity, without making them first feel such unity within the bounds of their own nation? The one is the way to the other. All the same I should have preferred another way, a more arduous way, but a more direct, for I know too well that the great majority of those who pass through the national stage remain there. They have spent all their powers of faith and love on the way... But such was not the intention of Vivekananda, who like Gandhi in this, only thought of the awakening of India in relation to its service for humanity.[2]

Human unity is essentially a sacred ideal and appears to be a good ideal. But its weakness lies in the fact that it is based on an abstract concept. No human being exists as an abstract entity. In the present order of things, man is divided into nations; nations are further divided into classes. In such a situation, bringing about human unity leads, in reality, to the suppression of the nationalist feeling of the oppressed and the class-consciousness of the exploiters. This indirectly serves the interest of imperialists and the reactionary elements. So long as oppression and exploitation are not ended through the liberation of enslaved nations and a socialist revolution and so long as the class-based society is not replaced by a classless society, human unity

---

2. Romain Rolland, *Vivekananda*, pp. 125-26.

cannot take concrete shape. When H.G. Wells, in an interview with Stalin, analysed this ideal enthusiastically, Stalin called him a 'frog in the well.'

Because of this contradiction in the concept of nationalism, Romain Rolland confused between Vivekananda and Gandhi. He failed to understand both Gandhi and Vivekananda. He, therefore, continued his analysis in these words:

> Yet a Vivekananda, more cautious than Gandhi, would have disavowed the desperate effort of the latter to make the religious spirit dominate political action: for on every occasion—as we have already seen in his letters from America—he placed a naked sword between himself and politics... 'Noli me tengere!' 'I will have nothing to do with the nonsense of politics'.[3]

This means that Romain Rolland saw Vivekananda merely as a Swami and his religious aspect. He failed to see the fact that Vivekananda consciously fought our political battle through the medium of religion. It is, no doubt, true that Vivekananda's thinking suffered from the same contradictions, to a certain extent, from which the thinking of Romain Rolland suffered. But we have already said that Vivekananda was a spokesman of the emerging capitalist class of our country and, because of his class character, his thinking could not cross the limits of religious *advaitism* and stopped short of materialism. He did advise people to put aside all the gods for the next fifty years and to worship only the poor in the form of God (*daridranarayana*). It is one thing to serve the poor and the oppressed, but quite another to organise them for and recognise them as the motive force of revolution. But it was not possible for him to think along those lines because of his class character. What was needed was to put this concept back on its feet as Marx did with that of Hegel. It was only possible if he had been succeeded by another Vivekananda.

But his fellow disciples and his own disciples all

3. Romain Rolland, *Vivekananda*, p. 126.

belonged to the middle class. Like Romain Rolland, they only saw the religious aspect of Vivekananda and disregarded and are still disregarding his political concepts. The result is that the same obscurantism is being propagated in his name against which he struggled throughout his life. Because of his idealistic thinking, Romain Rolland failed to see the history of our national struggle in its proper context. The movement against the partition of Bengal, against which the British Government had to accept defeat, was led by Bal Gangadhara Tilak, Bipinchandra Pal and Lala Lajpat Rai—their names as Lal, Bal and Pal became popular in every household from Himalayas to Kanyakumari. Romain Rolland has unnecessarily bracketed Gandhi with Tilak. At that time Gandhi was in South Africa and the British imperialists were training him according to a set plan to make him a leader and induct him into the political arena of India.

Only reactionary interests are served by creating confusion between the progressive and reactionary elements. This has been happening in our country since the days of Mahabharata. This is what happened in the history of our freedom movement also. Unless these two elements are distinguished from each other, it is not possible to understand the roles of Vivekananda and Gandhi or Tilak. Unless we understand this difference, our national consciousness and class consciousness would remain suppressed and distorted.

The Congress, when it was established in 1885, was an organisation of the agents of British imperialism. These elements broke their links with the past and surrendered before the English. In their view everything of the West was good and that of our country hateful. They believed that the British had come across the seas only to civilize our people who were barbarous and uncivilized. The only way to save ourselves and achieve progress was to cooperate with them. Hence the Congress sessions were only a show of loyalty accompanied by some demands for a few posts and some rights of self-government.

But later, patriots also entered the Congress party and became so influential and powerful within the party that, in the Congress session held during the movement against the partition of Bengal, they turned out of the party the loyalist elements whose leaders were Ferozeshah Mehta and Gopal Krishna Gokhale. It was only then that the movement progressed further. This was a natural process, because it was impossible for the struggle against foreign rule to succeed unless patriots parted company with the loyalists.

Now it so happened that the patriotic elements who took the movement forward under the leadership of Tilak came to be known as extremists and the elements loyal to the British and expelled from the Congress became known as moderates or liberals. The intention was to confuse the progressive with the reactionary elements by identifying both of them as patriots with the result that those who deserved to be hated earned respectability and veneration.

When our freedom movement was progressing openly as well as secretly and the war situation was sharpening our national and class consciousness, the British rulers brought Gandhi from South Africa in January 1915 and let him loose in the Indian political arena. By now the age of singing the glory of the Western way of life and of the English race had passed. Gandhi was made to understand that the illiterate masses of India, according to their ancient tradition, easily and naturally accept an incarnation or a person of royal lineage as their leader. Therefore, he started dressing himself in a lion cloth and assumed the character of a mahatma and made a pretext of aligning himself with Indian culture. As a result, those loyalists who had been expelled at the Surat session of the Congress, again assumed control of the Congress party under the leadership of Gandhi.

In order to sabotage the achievements of Vivekananda from within, people like Annie Besant and C.F. Andrews were made the collaborators of Gandhi. The result was that Gandhi took the country fifty years back from the point to which it had been brought by Vivekananda.

Tilak, like Vivekananda, was also a mass leader who understood Indian culture and was proud of it. He wrote, 'Gita Rahasya' to inspire the youth for revolution. As against this Gandhi interpreted Gita in a reactionary sense describing struggle as an inner conflict. Manmathnath Gupta has analysed the role of Gandhi in this context in the following words in the Introduction to his book entitled 'Ve Amar

Krantikari.'

"Surprisingly, when Gandhiji wanted to turn the direction of the revolutionary national movement, he wrote a commentary of Gita entitled 'Anasaktiyoga.' In this commentary he propounded the concept of Ahimsa through the Gita by contending that the war fought at Kurukshetra was no war but a conflict between mind and the senses."[4]

Gandhi described the Congress and the Khilafat movement as examples of great national unity. In fact it was an unprincipled opportunistic alliance between Hindu revivalism and Muslim revivalism. The intention was to take away the leadership of Congress from the hands of Tilak. When Gandhi called off the movement on the pretext of the Chauri-Chaura incident, this unity crumbled like a castle of cards. National unity is possible only by properly resolving the contradictions. We have seen the result of avoiding such problems in the form of partition of the country.

By giving a non-violent interpretation of Gita and the philosophy of the Upanishads, Gandhi disarmed, mentally, the masses who were engaged in a struggle. After an attempt made to blow up the train of the Viceroy by a bomb in 1929, Gandhi wrote an article in Young India entitled, 'Cult of the Bomb.' From this article, and from the letter he wrote to the Viceroy before starting the salt satyagraha, it is clear that his fight was not against the organised reactionary violence of British imperialism but against the violent acts of our revolutionaries. Bhagat Singh and his comrades had very well understood this anti-revolutionary and anti-national role of Gandhi. In reply to the 'Cult of the Bomb,' they published a pamphlet entitled 'Philosophy of the Bomb' which was distributed all over the country clandestinely in 1930. It began with these words:

'From some of the recent events, among which the Congress resolution on the attempt to blow off the Viceroy's train and the article of Gandhiji published later in 'Young India' are notable, it is evident that the Indian National

4. Manmathnath Gupta, Ve Amar Krantikari, p. 6.

Congress has started a war against the revolutionaries in collaboration with Gandhiji.'

The pamphlet went on to explain that use of force for oppressing people and perpetrating injustice is violence but use of force for securing our rights is no violence and outlined the objective of the revolutionaries in the following words:

'The revolutionaries believe that a revolution is the only way of securing the freedom of the country. The revolution for which they are working day and night would not appear in the form of an armed struggle between the foreign gov-ernment and its supporters and the people, but would lead to the promotion of a new society. Such a revolution would bury the capitalistic system, inequality and all privileges. It would bring a message of happiness for you and for crores of people who are subjected to exploitation by foreign imperialists and Indian capitalists, it would bring a message of prosperity. This would bring out the real character of the country before the world and it would create a new state and a new society and the control of the country would be in the hands of the working classes. The dictatorship of the proletariat would be established, the classes who suck the people's blood would be deprived of political power. The revolutionaries foresee the signs of the coming revolution in the growing restlessness of the youth. They are impatient to destroy religious orthodoxy and mental slavery which are impeding revolution. As they continue to imbibe the revolutionary ideology they would grow more conscious of their slavery and this consciousness would create in them a thirst for freedom which would not be quenched till the shackles of slavery are broken. This thirst would go on increasing constantly and their blood would boil with the desire for freedom and they would come out in the battlefield to kill the tyrants. This movement is a necessary and inevitable stage of revolution. Though terrorism does not constitute total revolution, yet revolution cannot be achieved without terrorism. Our point of view is confirmed by all the revolutions that have taken place so far. Terrorism inspires fear in the hearts of tyrants. It proves that the masses are not satisfied with their present condition and are anxious to change it. In other countries also this movement would lead to revolution, a revolution which would usher in those countries social, political and economic equality.

'The objective of the revolutionaries has been explained above from which it is clear as to what they want to do for the country. They take their inspiration from the struggle that is going on all over the world between workers-peasants and the ruling classes. They believe that the method that they have adopted for the achievement of their goal has not failed till today.'

If the agents of the government in the garb of khadi-wearing Congressmen had not helped British imperialism, all governmental oppression to suppress this movement would have been definitely defeated.

This means that the dream of India which Vivekananda had dreamed and for the realisation of which the revolutionaries had shed their blood, was shattered soon after it was conceived as a result of the mean conspiracy that was called Gandhian philosophy. How can it be called *ahimsa* or non-violence? It was a cold-blooded violence committed by the native and foreign vested interests. The dangerous consequences of aborting or postponing revolution are now before us. Cheating, plunder and corruption, in the name of truth and non-violence, are rampant. In every state there have appeared dozens of hypocrites parading themselves as incarnations. Towards the end of every year numerous conferences on universal brotherhood and humanism are held. Big processions are taken out and meetings held and those so-called incarnations easily procure the support of big leaders and high officials. The vested interests of our country and outside spend their black money generously for such meetings and rallies. But when the poor masses of the country ask for bread, they are fired upon.

When Bhagat Singh and Chandra Shekhar Azad organised their party, called the Hindustan Socialist Republican Army, terrorism was entering the stage of collective revolution and this party was following the revolutionary ideology of Marx. Following the ideology of Marx was a natural sequence in the development of the national movement. It was because, after the Russian revolution of 1917, no people's revolution could have been successful without the Marxist ideology and the leadership of the Communist Party.

But it is our country's misfortune that after 1930, in the fourth decade, when Marxist ideology became popular and the people's movement appeared in the form of labour unions and Kisan Sabhas, the leadership of this movement was taken over by elements who were loyalists and agents of the British. Jawaharlal Nehru appeared in the garb of a socialist and the deceit that he along with Gandhi played on the people should have been unmasked by the Communist Party. But the Communist Party failed to play its role in such a situation, because its leaders also belonged to the higher and middle classes and had been trained under Macaulay's system of education. They were no more than opportunistic agents. Most of them had been educated in England. In fact, they were not Marxists but revisionists. Revisionism is the ideology of the exploiting classes, not of the working classes. Therefore, far from exposing the deceit of Gandhi and Nehru, they collaborated with them in defeating the revolution by becoming camp followers of the Congress High Command. The opportunism of these so called Marxist leaders stands exposed today.

What is to be understood is the fact that, as a result of the reins of leadership going into the hands of Gandhi, the process of the capitalist renaissance remained incomplete and the process of a socialist renaissance could not start. Subhas opposed Gandhi; and that is why he is the most respected leader after Tilak in the Congress party. But Subhas was not a Marxist and he could not fully evaluate the international situation. He did move a resolution for organising workers, peasants and the youth and for establishing a parallel gov-ernment, after a resolution for complete independence had been passed at the Lahore session of the Congress in 1929. But the resolution was rejected and he did not follow up his suggestions by himself doing what he had suggested. The tradition of armed resistance started by the Hindustan Republican Army was not carried forward by either the Forward Bloc or the Communist Party or any other party. The result was that when, after the war in 1946, the revolutionary urge reached its peak, no party was capable of giving it a lead. The result also was that the broker elements in the Congress and the Muslim League sabotaged the revolution and entered into a compromise with British imperialism.

Revolution is always a constructive historical force in which the best elements of the nation emerge and those that are worthless recede in the background and there is a healthy development of thought. In our country, however, revolution has been checked and derailed with the result that there is a break in the development of thought. This has led to decadence in literature and culture which has been misunderstood as progress and development in the absence of right direction. We would give the example of poet Iqbal in this context, who had first called India to be the best of all in the world and had become popular after writing these lines. Later, he became very popular among the leftists by writing 'Arise and wake up the poor people of my world.' But the same Iqbal was now talking about the world and Islamism. He considered it a sin to talk about his country. In his poem entitled "Vataneeyat' (nationalism) he has written:

'In taaza khudaon main bada sabse vatan hai
jo pairahan uska hai vah mazhab ka kafan hai.'

(Among the gods created by the present (capitalist) age, the greatest is the country which is wrapped in the shroud of religion).

This is abstract thinking based on the 'most sacred thinking' of 'idealists' like Romain Rolland and H.G. Wells. We have now to see where did this abstract thinking lead Iqbal to?

Iqbal, who was once influenced by the stirring call of Vivekananda and had written—'still our identity survives' was now seen standing in the Isle of Sicily and awakening the sleeping lion of Islam by saying:

'Main tera tohfa sal-e Hindustan lay jaoounga
Khuda yahan rota hai, auron ko vahan rulaoonga'

(I shall take your gift to India—
God weeps here, and I shall make others weep there.)

The result was that our history, tradition and heroes got divided. We started fighting amongst ourselves and still continue to do so and far away from the establishment of human unity, even national unity was shattered.

Communism is an international movement and Marx and Engels have given the call, 'workers of the world unite.' We have already stated that Marxism is nothing but material Advaitism. Our leftist leaders and progressive writers, moulded in the tradition of Macaulay's system of education and ignorant of our history and culture, have misinterpreted this call of Marx and Engels and have encouraged thinking by negating nationalism. I had the occasion to go through a book entitled *Present Indian Society* written by Ram Pyare Saraf, a leftist of Kashmir. In the Introduction it has been stated that the purpose of writing the book was to strengthen the forces of revolution. The writer claims that the cause of the formation of Pakistan was that Gandhi swore by the Vedas and Upanishads, that 95 per cent of the members of Parliament wanted Sanskrit to be the national language of India, and that the reactionary leaders of the Congress gave to 'Vande Mataram' the status of the national song.

The colonial system of education has created a great number of such strange creatures who are not rooted to their country, who do not consider this country to be their own and who do not identify themselves with the people of India. These so-called leftists are devoid of thinking and are incapable of communicating their thoughts. The result is that our philosophy and history have found no place in the history of the past 50 years and more.

Marxism is a scientific theory. It is of no use if we merely read it and quote it. It has to be adapted to the concrete situation prevailing in the country by knowing about the present and the past (including the ancient past) of India. Only by understanding the past is it possible to build the future? For this, it is necessary to acquire the knowledge of our history and philosophy and to believe that the Vedas, Upanishads, Ramayana, Mahabharata, Kapil, Kanad, Gautam,

Ramakrishna Paramahansa and Vivekananda are all our heritage. We have to interpret them from the point of view of historical materialism. Such an interpretation alone would be Marxism in a concrete form which would be easily acceptable to our people. It would then transform it into revolutionary material force. This is how Lenin achieved success, and Mao Tse-tung and Ho chi Minh also achieved success by adopting this method. Peopte become revolutionary only by following the cultural traditions. Mao Tse-tung went to the extent of saying that an army without a cultural background was an army without a mind and could not defeat the enemy.

The Ganga has been flowing on this land perennially through the ages. It cannot be differentiated from other currents flowing in other places. Because of its particular source, and because of flowing across a particular course, the special quality that the waters of this river possess cannot be said to exist in the waters of other rivers like Volga and Yangtze. Similarly, the special quality of the waters of Volga and Yangtze cannot be found in the waters of the Ganga. It is not possible to negate the special qualities of the waters of each one of them and to equate them as simple water. Only by knowing about the special qualities of each one of them can we acquire proper knowledge about the land in which they flow.

The stream of thought has been flowing in our country perennially just like the waters of the Ganga. It is not possible to block or cut off this flow at any stage. The process of development of our thought is conditioned by geographical, historical and social circumstances. We shall have to understand the special features of this process of development, ink our thinking with this current and develop it further rom where Vivekananda left it. Nothing can be achieved by merely quoting Marx. It is also essential to be aligned o their own thoughts. But it is even more essential to understand the cultural tradition and to become identified vith it. Those Anglicised reformers who branded Vivekananda as a reactionary not only remained cut off rom the national struggle, many of them played an anti-ational and anti-people role. The role of the communist and progressive leaders and writers after 1930 is well known. These so-called leftists, posing as internationalists, considered everything from the past to be hateful and only encouraged a tendency which was anti-tradition and anti-society.

Today the situation for a revolution is more ripe than before. The masses are ready for a revolution. But there is no revolutionary party to lead them, and the main reason for this is rejection of nationalism by these parties. Our illiterate and poor people cherish the heritage of past experience. Although their hands are rough and sore, because they have been working hard and have been subjected to atrocities, yet they have clung to this heritage with all their might. It is not possible to become revolutionaries of the future by gifting away the past to the reactionaries. The people do not lack revolutionary strength. The call of Kathopanishad—Awake, arise and stop not till the goal is achieved—has ever been giving them strength.

The workers, peasants, students and the working classes of India have now woken up and the experience of the past years has convinced them that the dream of a new India would not be realised without revolution. And those who assume their leadership will also have to understand that the party is not greater than the people : it is the people who are greater than the party.

□□